W9-BZO-698

How to find what you need in
The Little Penguin Handbook

If you want a quick overview of what's in this book, then you can look at the **Brief Contents** to the left.

If you see a chapter that interests you in this Brief Contents, then you can go to the page number listed or turn to the appropriate **Part opening page** for a detailed list of the contents of that part of the book.

If you want to know more about what's in a particular chapter or part, then you can also find a **detailed table of contents** inside the back cover.

If you want to know where to find help for a very specific issue or if you need to look up a particular term, then you can refer to the **Index** on page 327.

If you need help starting your research paper, refer to **"Research Map: Conducting Research"** at the beginning of Part 3.

If you need help with the documentation process for MLA style refer to **"MLA Documentation Map"** at the beginning of Chapter 17.

If you want information about APA, CMS, or CSE **documentation styles** for research writing, turn to the appropriate chapter in Part 4. You will find a complete index of sample citations for each documentation style.

You will also find **more help** at the back of this book:

- A list of **Common Errors** of grammar, punctuation, and mechanics that many writers make
- A **Revision Guide** of editing and proofreading symbols
- A **Glossary** with basic grammatical and usage terms, on page 317.

PEARSON   ALWAYS LEARNING

The Little Penguin Handbook

Second Custom Edition for College of DuPage

Taken from:
The Little Penguin Handbook, Third Edition
by Lester Faigley

The Penguin Handbook, Fourth Edition
by Lester Faigley

*Writing and Reading Across the Curriculum:
Brief Edition,* Fourth Edition
by Laurence Behrens and Leonard J. Rosen

Cover Images: Photographs courtesy of College of DuPage.

Taken from:

The Little Penguin Handbook, Third Edition
by Lester Faigley
Copyright © 2012, 2009, 2007 by Pearson Education, Inc.
Upper Saddle River, New Jersey 07458

The Penguin Handbook, Fourth Edition
by Lester Faigley
Copyright © 2012, 2009, 2006, 2003 by Pearson Education, Inc.
Published by Longman
New York, New York 10036

Writing and Reading Across the Curriculum: Brief Edition, Fourth Edition
by Laurence Behrens and Leonard J. Rosen
Copyright © 2011, 2009, 2007 by Laurence Behrens and Leonard J. Rosen
Published by Longman

Copyright © 2012 by Pearson Learning Solutions
All rights reserved.

Permission in writing must be obtained from the publisher before any part of
this work may be reproduced or transmitted in any form or by any means,
electronic or mechanical, including photocopying and recording, or by any
information storage or retrieval system.

All trademarks, service marks, registered trademarks, and registered service
marks are the property of their respective owners and are used herein for
identification purposes only.

Pearson Learning Solutions, 501 Boylston Street, Suite 900, Boston, MA
02116
A Pearson Education Company
www.pearsoned.com

Printed in the United States of America

3 4 5 6 7 8 9 10 V354 17 16 15 14 13 12

000200010271679476

MC

ISBN 10: 1-256-78864-3
ISBN 13: 978-1-256-78864-5

Brief Contents

PART 1
Composing

PART 2
Analyzing, Reflecting, Informing, Arguing

PART 3
Planning Research and Finding Sources

PART 4
Incorporating and Documenting Sources

PART 5
Effective Style and Language

PART 6
Understanding Grammar

PART 7
Understanding Punctuation and Mechanics

Chapters 1, 2, 10 through 39 taken from *The Little Penguin Handbook,* Third Edition by Lester Faigley

Chapters 3, 4, 5, 6, 7, 8, 9, and Chapter 11 pages 96–98 Create an Annotated Bibliography taken from *The Penguin Handbook,* Fourth Edition by Lester Faigley.

Appendix A and B taken from *Writing and Reading Aross the Curriculum: Brief Edition,* Fourth Edition by Laurence Behrens and Leonard J. Rosen.

Dear Students

Welcome to the Composition Program at College of DuPage! Your English 1101 and 1102 courses will be your introduction to writing in college, and we look forward to meeting you in these classes!

This special edition of *The Little Penguin Handbook* for the College of DuPage Composition Program will serve as a resource for college-level writing in your first-year composition classes. This guide will also serve you well both in other college-level classes and beyond college as you continue your academic studies and/or begin your career. It is our hope that you will keep this guide as a reference well beyond your time in English 1101 and 1102.

This edition was carefully chosen because it is compact, economical, and well written. However, what makes this edition special is that we have added several sections introducing you to information that the College of DuPage Composition Program faculty believes is important to your success.

Frequently Asked Questions

In our FAQ section, we responded to questions former students wished they had asked when they first came to COD. Whether or not your instructor assigns this section, we urge you to read it; you never know what questions you'll find that you didn't think to ask!

WPA Outcomes

We've also included the Outcomes Statement for first-year composition students from the Council of Writing Program Administrators (WPA). This council, a national organization of college writing programs, has agreed that these outcomes are skills that every successful student who has completed a college writing course sequence should have mastered. Here at COD, we use these outcomes as touchstones for our own writing program outcomes.

Sample Papers

Several of our students agreed to let us reprint their English essays with grades and comments for you to read. These papers were chosen to give you an idea of the variety of writing you may be expected to produce at COD, and as a way to understand what writing faculty expect from our students and how we respond to them.

Best wishes and good luck in your first year at COD!

The COD English Faculty

Frequently Asked Questions

What will I write in English 1101 and 1102?

You may not believe this just yet, but writing is the skill most valued inside and outside the academic world. Integral to this skill is the ability to think about ideas and information and effectively communicate these in writing. Why? The public and private world communicates through ideas and information. You already experience this in your life every day. You are confronted with this fact when you surf the web, where you view the vastness of ideas and information meant for innumerable audiences, including you. You are also part of this vast web of communication when you write to specific audiences on social network sites, blogs, email—as well as text messages. The writing assignments in English 1101 and 1102 will provide you with multiple opportunities to practice effective ways to write and think in writing so that you can confidently meet the needs of the many audiences you are certain to encounter as a citizen, professional, and individual. Some examples of assignments include learning how to:

- invent, draft, revise, and polish
- write narrative, analytical, persuasive, and research essays
- write summaries and responses
- write reports, proposals, letters, memos, and exams
- gather, assess, and integrate credible information

How many papers will I write in English 1101 and 1102?

Each instructor determines the number and lengths of writing assignments, which will include

- pieces meant strictly to help you explore your thinking
- drafts that focus, organize, and develop your thinking
- revisions that refine your thinking

Some or all of these pieces will be graded. In any case, the assignments will stretch your current writing practices from delivering a product to working a process, and you will be encouraged to think less about numbers and lengths of papers and more about writing something meaningful. That's as it should be so that you can learn to challenge and expand your thinking on topics you may not have previously considered. However, if you're still looking for specific numbers:

- In English 1101, you may write up to six graded assignments, each 500 or more words
- In English 1102, you may write a series of short assignments that lead to either a single, ten-page (2500-word) research-based essay or two five-page research-based essays.

What do instructors expect?

This is the number one question students ask, whether the course is English, Computer Science, Nursing, or Physical Education. It's a fair and important question that anyone would ask and want answered when they enter any new environment, including the college classroom. Guidelines are necessary to provide students comfort, structure, and some confidence that their efforts can result in a successful outcome. In the classroom, these guidelines are presented in the form of a syllabus, which is a detailed document that outlines the course objectives, rules of classroom engagement, assignments, grading standards, and such. On the first day of class, every instructor distributes to students a syllabus that details the specific guidelines and policies individual instructors have determined. Listed below, however, are the typical policies you will find on your syllabus.

- attendance, evaluation, and grading
- plagiarism and academic honesty
- submission of late work
- when graded assignments will be returned

- how much time outside of class you should devote to assignments, usually approximately six to twelve hours per week
- use of cell phones, laptops, headphones, and the Internet in class
- exceptions to the policies

You can know what English and any other instructors expect by reading their syllabus carefully on the first day and reading it periodically throughout the term. If you are unclear about anything in the syllabus, please ask your instructor. They will be more than happy to explain a class policy, clarify an assignment, or answer any other questions that you may have.

Can I get a good grade without being a good writer?

The idea of "a writer" carries eons of history that includes people whose gift with words, whose vision of a story, or whose unique voice makes them stand out across time and place. Examples are Shakespeare, Faulkner, Hemingway, Atwood, Morrison, and libraries of others too numerous to list. On a more practical level, however, the idea of "a writer" is simply one who writes. We may be accustomed to thinking of writers as those who have published articles, essays, nonfiction, fiction, poetry, and drama. These are the lucky people.

The rest of us are everyday writers who need to compose email messages; letters to thank, request, apologize, protest, and defend; and other texts to achieve a specific purpose and for a specific audience. In the workplace, writers need to compose memos, reports, plans, and marketing copy. Good writers are able to complete these types of everyday writing tasks to communicate their ideas more effectively and more permanently than can be communicated through the spoken word. If you desire to become a good writer, English composition will help you develop these skills. A good grade will be an indicator of your writing competence. However, in "real life" the rewards for being able to write well are far more lasting and valuable than a good grade.

Can I revise my essays to get a better grade?

As you work on your assignments, you are strongly encouraged to practice an extended process of generating ideas, drafting, and revising. At the end of this extended process, your instructor will grade your writing. If you want to further revise a final version of something your instructor has already graded, you will need to ask what the instructor's policy is. Keep in mind that earning a better grade usually involves substantial revision, not just surface corrections.

I'm not an English major. Why do I have to take writing courses?

As you now understand from the answers to previous frequently asked questions, English composition teaches more than the act of inattentively throwing words on paper in a socially acceptable form. Instead, English composition teaches:

- critical thinking
- clear communication with a purpose
- effective practices to recognize, identify, and match audience needs to a variety of written communication situations

As a matter of rule, if you plan to earn a BA or a BS degree, you must take the two-semester composition sequence, either here or at your transfer school.

As a matter of practicality, you might as well take your composition courses here at COD since it is cost effective.

What writing skills will instructors expect me to develop in English 1101 and 1102?

College-level English composition is not a repetition of English courses taken in high school, which may, primarily, have focused on reading, interpreting, and writing about literary works. In college-level writing courses, you are expected to apply, yet go beyond, high school writing and research skills to develop and use more advanced reading, thinking, writing, and research skills. Instructors evaluate the development of your skills to think and write at these more advanced levels and to effectively use standard American, college-level English.

English 1101 introduces you to college-level writing as a process of developing and supporting a thesis in an organized essay of 500 or more words. You will continue to develop your skills to:

- invent, develop, organize, revise, edit, and proofread
- plan, construct, analyze, and evaluate the effectiveness of your prose
- read a variety of texts that focus more on factual and informational ideas and less on fictional and literary ideas
- analyze and respond critically and creatively to the ideas and strategies in the texts of others
- use an appropriate style and voice
- use methods of research and citation at an introductory level

In English 1101, you will practice the above skills so that you are prepared to apply these skills and concepts in English 1102, or so that you are prepared to read, think, and write effectively and critically in any first- or second-year course as well as in the workplace.

English 1102 develops your ability to extend the writing process so that you can:

- independently apply appropriate research and selection methods
- evaluate a variety of sources
- integrate your own and source ideas into an organized, thesis-driven research essay
- further practice and apply the conventions of citation and documentation
- use diction and language appropriate to a researched essay
- observe the conventions of standard American, college-level English and acceptable prose, including spelling, punctuation, and grammar

What are the differences between English 1101 and 1102?

In both English 1101 and 1102 you will practice:

- focusing ideas toward a clear, insightful thesis
- developing ideas using relevant, credible evidence
- organizing ideas effectively
- editing for clarity

In English 1101, you will likely be assigned:

- personal essays that help you reflect on meaningful life experiences
- analytical pieces to build your skills to read about issues, take them apart to see how they function, and respond to them thoughtfully and intellectually
- library research and field observations to help you gather information that you will integrate into a project

In English 1102, you will focus on research-based assignments to learn how to:

- find, assess, and integrate multiple sources of information
- question and critique others' assumptions as well as your own
- develop your point of view in a sophisticated, well-supported, and documented piece of writing

Why do different English 1101 and 1102 classes have different readings and assignments?

Both English 1101 and 1102 are "articulated." This means that when you complete these two courses with a "C" or better, they will transfer to most Illinois colleges, including UIC, SIU, ISU, NIU, and most other community and city colleges. This is true even if you do not complete all of your General Education courses or two-year degree at COD. Articulation also means that the course objectives of COD's English 1101 and 1102 are equivalent to the course objectives in first-year writing courses at most Illinois colleges. Within the limits of these course objectives, instructors have the flexibility to teach their classes using readings, writing assignments, strategies, and materials that enhance both the teacher's skills and students' learning styles. Just keep in mind that while the readings and assignments may be different from instructor to instructor, the primary objective of English 1101 and 1102 is to give students instruction and practice in critical reading and writing.

Can I take English 1101 and 1102 in a format other than the traditional classroom?

Yes. Both courses are offered online. Many students have unrealistic expectations about online instruction. However, this alternative format will demand more than you might imagine. Students must keep in step with the course throughout the term to meet the requirements of:

- structured time frames
- assignment deadlines
- specific online class hours

To be successful in courses taught online, you must be prepared to:

- manage your time effectively to meet deadlines without the structure, support, and interaction that the classroom provides
- learn independently from the textbook and other materials with less guidance from an instructor

How can I find information about different instructors' backgrounds and/or teaching styles?

Every year at COD, more than one hundred instructors teach English 1101 and 1102. The best ways to become knowledgeable about instructors you are interested in taking a course with are to:

- contact them by phone or email
- ask other students who have taken a course with the instructor to share their experiences
- ask counselors and advisors who sometimes know certain instructors

Are the textbooks for English 1101 and 1102 expensive?

Although textbook prices continue to increase, students' ability to pay for textbooks continues to decrease. Many instructors try to choose textbooks that can be more affordable for students. However, textbooks can be expensive no matter how careful instructors are in their selections. Don't be surprised if your English textbooks cost $200 each semester. Count your lucky stars if you spend less.

How do I get placed in English 1101? 1102?

Students are often placed in English 1101 by ACT scores. Just provide proof that you earned an ACT composite score of 20 or higher, and you can automatically enroll in English 1101.

We don't test to place students in English 1102. You must earn the English 1101 credits to take English 1102. Most colleges offer and will transfer to COD your credits for an equivalent English 1101 course.

If you don't have an ACT composite score, or your score is below 20, you will take the Reading and Writing Placement Tests to determine your eligibility to enroll in English 1101. These tests are given at several sites:

- on the main campus in the Testing Center of Berg Instructional Center (BIC 2405)
- at the regional centers: Addison, Bloomingdale, Carol Stream, Naperville, and Westmont

Staff in these centers will help you choose the right tests. Before you go to the testing centers, call to get their hours of operation or visit the Testing Center web site http://www.cod.edu/admission/testing/placement.aspx

Depending on your reading *and* writing placement tests scores, you may be placed in a developmental course. Developmental Reading and Writing courses are designed to give you the skills and practice to improve your chances for success not only in English 1101 and 1102 but also in your other college-level courses.

The placement tests are important because your performance on them will dictate which English composition course you can enroll in. So that you minimize obstacles that can keep you from doing your best, use the same strategies for effective test taking that you used when you took the ACT or other standardized tests:

- get plenty of rest
- eat a good breakfast or lunch
- take your time
- allow plenty of time to complete your tests
- don't take too many tests in a single day

Do Developmental Writing and Reading courses "count"?

They count in your class schedule of how many hours you are enrolled—so they "count" for financial aid and health insurance. Developmental courses do not transfer, and they do not count toward a degree.

What if I'm not a native speaker of English?

COD offers placement tests designed for English Language Learners (ELL) or speakers of English as a Second Language (ESL).

If you did not attend high school in the United States, or if you have been in the United States only a few years, *especially* if the language you are most comfortable reading and writing in is not English, please let the staff know in the testing center. You should take the ESL Reading and Writing tests.

COD also has writing and grammar courses to help ELL/ESL students prepare for college-level academic writing. Sometimes ELL/ESL students who are generally prepared for English 1101, but who still need help with

English grammar and vocabulary, are asked to enroll in the English Language Community. If this option is recommended for you, we strongly encourage you to take it.

Can I "test out" of either English 1101 or 1102?

COD offers Credit by Demonstrated Competence for English 1101. As the name implies, you must *demonstrate* that you are already *competent* in the kinds of assignments we teach in English 1101. Credit for English 1101 is awarded if you pass a two-part test. The first part is a computerized, multiple-choice test. If you pass this first part, you will take the second part, which asks you to read an article and write a college-level essay in which you integrate your ideas with relevant ideas from the article.

Students may present a score of 3, 4, or 5 on the Advanced Placement English Language and Composition Examination to earn full credit for both English 1101 and 1102.

What role does technology play in writing classes?

Instructing

Almost all writing classes are scheduled in computer labs for at least one-third of the meeting time so that students can complete various writing assignments and activities during class and with the instructor's help and feedback.

Composing

Students are required to compose assignments on a computer using word processing software. Presenting handwritten work will not be a part of your professional future, so you need to use the college experience to gain keyboarding and word processing skills. If you are not adept at these skills, the College offers Office Technology Information courses that can help you become adept. In addition to gaining skills that will be professionally and personally valuable to you, the technology will enable you to more easily format, develop, revise, and edit what you compose.

Creating

Some English 1101 and 1102 assignments will develop your facility to:

- navigate a wide variety of online library resources and databases
- create web sitess, wikis, or PowerPoint presentations
- format your documents

All these skills are transferable to other classes as well as to most professions. Technology is an empowering tool; knowing how to use it is critical for everyone.

What kinds of resources are available to help me with my writing and/or reading skills?

Main Campus Writing and Reading Assistance

Writing and Reading Assistance in the Learning Commons provides students, staff, and community members free assistance to further develop their writing and reading skills. Writing and Reading Assistance offers one-on-one sessions with trained writing and reading coaches who are COD students and faculty members. Writing assistance includes talking through ideas and discovering topics, developing strategies for organizing and generating drafts, revising several drafts, and polishing the final draft. Reading assistance includes developing individualized strategies to help with speed, ease, and overall comprehension of both academic and non-academic materials.

Regional Centers Writing and Reading Assistance

Writing and Reading Assistance is also available at COD's Addison, Bloomingdale, Carol Stream, Naperville, and Westmont regional centers. These centers offer the same kinds of writing and reading assistance available on the main campus, although the hours of operation at the regional centers may be limited.

Tutoring Services

College of DuPage offers tutoring and a variety of other academic support services within the Learning Commons. Some tutoring services are free to eligible students, while other tutoring is available for a fee. Staff members will help you determine which services best suit your needs. For more information, visit http://www.cod.edu/academics/resources/academic_support/tutoring/index.aspx

OWL—Online Writing Lab at Purdue University

The Online Writing Lab (OWL) at Purdue University is a free online service that offers support through online reference materials and services to help students and members of the online community develop their writing skills. For more information, visit http://owl.english.purdue.edu/

What other assistance is available at the College?

Speech Assistance

Also located within the Learning Commons, the Speech Assistance Area helps students, faculty, staff, and community members improve their speaking skills. Trained professional coaches provide personal and group coaching to build and refine:

- delivery skills such as vocal quality, gestures, posture, eye contact, pronunciation, articulation, anxiety control
- speech writing techniques such as selecting topics, organizing, outlining, using visual aids, researching, and source crediting

For more information, visit http://www.cod.edu/academics/resources/academic_support/speech.aspx

Library

The Library provides onsite and remote access to resources, instruction, and services that support the academic program and the general information needs of the College community. Reference librarians are located in the center of the main floor of the Library. They can provide assistance on:

- research questions
- research materials
- documenting sources

You can also contact a reference librarian by using the "Ask a Librarian" feature on the COD Library web site, http://www.cod.edu/library/.

Counseling and Advising

Counselors can help you with:

- Career exploration and decision-making
- Personal concerns that interfere with educational or career goals
- Educational planning if you are undecided about your major
- Development of success strategies if you are on academic probation

Using a student-centered approach, advising specialists play an integral role at College of DuPage to link students and community members to essential academic information and support services to meet their diverse needs and promote their success. For more information, visit http://www.cod.edu/counseling/advising/index.aspx

The Center for Access and Accommodations

The Center for Access and Accommodations staff is available to meet with students who have disabilities. To request services, contact the office before classes begin, schedule an appointment, and bring documentation. The information students provide is voluntary and confidential. For more information, visit http://www.cod.edu/student_life/student_services/access_accommodations/index.aspx

Testing Center

The Testing Center serves students and community members to:

- satisfy course, college, or program requirements
- identify academic strengths and weaknesses
- clarify interests, values, and personality traits
- complete specialized testing needs

For more information, visit http://www.cod.edu/admission/testing/index.aspx

Information Technology Help Desk

If you have problems using the College's IT resources, knowledgeable, positive professionals staff the Information Technology Help Desk to help facilitate the resolution of technology problems. For more information, visit http://www.cod.edu./it/

WPA Outcomes Statement for First-Year Composition

(Note: This information was copied from http://www.wpacouncil.org/positions/outcomes.html on 4.21.10)

Adopted by the Council of Writing Program Administrators (WPA), April 2000; amended July 2008.

For further information about the development of the Outcomes Statement, please see

http://comppile.org/archives/WPAoutcomes/continue.html

For further information about the Council of Writing Program Administrators, please see

http://www.wpacouncil.org

A version of this statement was published in *WPA: Writing Program Administration* 23.1/2 (fall/winter 1999): 59–66

Introduction

This statement describes the common knowledge, skills, and attitudes sought by first-year composition programs in American postsecondary education. To some extent, we seek to regularize what can be expected to be taught in first-year composition; to this end the document is not merely a compilation or summary of what currently takes place. Rather, the following statement articulates what composition teachers nationwide have learned from practice, research, and theory. This document intentionally defines only "outcomes," or types of results, and not "standards," or precise levels of achievement. The setting of standards should be left to specific institutions or specific groups of institutions.

Learning to write is a complex process, both individual and social, that takes place over time with continued practice and informed guidance. Therefore, it is important that teachers, administrators, and a concerned public do not imagine that these outcomes can be taught in reduced or simple ways. Helping students demonstrate these outcomes requires expert understanding of how students actually learn to write. For this reason we expect the primary audience for this document to be well-prepared college writing teachers and college writing program administrators. In some places, we have chosen to write in their professional language. Among such readers, terms such as "rhetorical" and "genre" convey a rich meaning that is not easily simplified. While we have also aimed at writing a document that the general public can understand, in limited cases we have aimed first at communicating effectively with expert writing teachers and writing program administrators.

These statements describe only what we expect to find at the end of first-year composition, at most schools a required general education course or sequence of courses. As writers move beyond first-year composition, their writing abilities do not merely improve. Rather, students' abilities not only diversify along disciplinary and professional lines but also move into whole new levels where expected outcomes expand, multiply, and diverge. For this reason, each statement of outcomes for first-year composition is followed by suggestions for further work that builds on these outcomes.

Rhetorical Knowledge

By the end of first-year composition, students should

- Focus on a purpose
- Respond to the needs of different audiences
- Respond appropriately to different kinds of rhetorical situations
- Use conventions of format and structure appropriate to the rhetorical situation
- Adopt appropriate voice, tone, and level of formality
- Understand how genres shape reading and writing
- Write in several genres

Faculty in all programs and departments can build on this preparation by helping students learn

- The main features of writing in their fields
- The main uses of writing in their fields
- The expectations of readers in their fields

Critical Thinking, Reading, and Writing

By the end of first-year composition, students should

- Use writing and reading for inquiry, learning, thinking, and communicating
- Understand a writing assignment as a series of tasks, including finding, evaluating, analyzing, and synthesizing appropriate primary and secondary sources
- Integrate their own ideas with those of others
- Understand the relationships among language, knowledge, and power

Faculty in all programs and departments can build on this preparation by helping students learn

- The uses of writing as a critical thinking method
- The interactions among critical thinking, critical reading, and writing
- The relationships among language, knowledge, and power in their fields

Processes

By the end of first-year composition, students should

- Be aware that it usually takes multiple drafts to create and complete a successful text
- Develop flexible strategies for generating, revising, editing, and proofreading

- Understand writing as an open process that permits writers to use later invention and re-thinking to revise their work
- Understand the collaborative and social aspects of writing processes
- Learn to critique their own and others' works
- Learn to balance the advantages of relying on others with the responsibility of doing their part
- Use a variety of technologies to address a range of audiences

Faculty in all programs and departments can build on this preparation by helping students learn

- To build final results in stages
- To review work-in-progress in collaborative peer groups for purposes other than editing
- To save extensive editing for later parts of the writing process
- To apply the technologies commonly used to research and communicate within their fields

Knowledge of Conventions

By the end of first-year composition, students should

- Learn common formats for different kinds of texts
- Develop knowledge of genre conventions ranging from structure and paragraphing to tone and mechanics
- Practice appropriate means of documenting their work
- Control such surface features as syntax, grammar, punctuation, and spelling.

Faculty in all programs and departments can build on this preparation by helping students learn

- The conventions of usage, specialized vocabulary, format, and documentation in their fields
- Strategies through which better control of conventions can be achieved

Composing in Electronic Environments

As has become clear over the last twenty years, writing in the 21st-century involves the use of digital technologies for several purposes, from drafting to peer reviewing to editing. Therefore, although the *kinds* of composing processes and texts expected from students vary across programs and institutions, there are nonetheless common expectations.

By the end of first-year composition, students should:

- Use electronic environments for drafting, reviewing, revising, editing, and sharing texts
- Locate, evaluate, organize, and use research material collected from electronic sources, including scholarly library databases; other official databases (e.g., federal government databases); and informal electronic networks and internet sources
- Understand and exploit the differences in the rhetorical strategies and in the affordances available for both print and electronic composing processes and texts

Faculty in all programs and departments can build on this preparation by helping students learn

- How to engage in the electronic research and composing processes common in their fields
- How to disseminate texts in both print and electronic forms in their fields

Personal Essay

COD Student Essay
English 1101, Spring 2010

This essay was written in response to an assignment that asked students to tell a story about an experience that had a strong impact on their life and to reflect on why that experience mattered to them in a way that others could share and appreciate.

The instructor and fellow students liked this essay very much. The story is very honest, and the ending has a realistic, unresolved quality—kind of like life. The instructor wrote some critical comments about sentence-level issues, which you can see in the text of the essay (note the italicized comments, which refer to the highlighted portions).

1

Fly Away.

There was snow on the ground and Mountains in the background, the sun was shining and there I was, pulling up to my new home. After a long 14 hour ride to Denver, Colorado, I was here and pumped with adrenaline about starting this new chapter in my life, although the thought, "Am I crazy? Can I do this?" was still in the back of my mind, but it was slowly starting to fade away. *This sentence is a bit out of control . . . too many clauses strung together.*

This move all came about to me one morning when I woke up at 4 o'clock in the afternoon after a long, long night of partying, which at the time was nothing new. I was 20 years old living in Chicago, IL and I did not have a care in the world. I was living "the dream" but whose dream?

Fly Away   2

When I woke up that afternoon I thought to myself this has got to
stop, I was living on a roller coaster; I had no control over myself and
needed to change. I was miserable, don't get me wrong I had a great job,
great apartment, and made "friends" with all the right people to get me
what I wanted. I let myself sober up for a few days and decided I was
going to move and do it quickly. I applied for a job as a flight attendant
and when I was hired by United Airlines, at the interview the interviewer
said, "Denver or San Francisco, where would you like to be based?" I
thought to myself "this is it, I'm ready." Packed up my car and headed
west, to Denver. When I told my family I don't think they believed me, I
really think my sisters thought I was going crazy. My parents were very
supportive and I guess my two sisters were happy for me but I wasn't really
sure, I didn't care though, in my mind I was already gone! *Some spots here
where you should re-think the punctuation, wordiness, sentence boundaries,
etc.*

When I got to Denver I knew no one, the city was so unfamiliar, and
I felt so free. I was so anxious to just live; I didn't even know what to do
with myself! I was starting from scratch, literally. I was starting this new
job, out traveling and seeing the world which, is something I've always
wanted to do, and will continue to do for the rest of my life. While the job
was going great, besides making practically minimum wage, I wasn't just
in Denver to work, I wanted a new life. I found a bar and started working
there part time when I could and met a lot of young people you have
become some of my best friends. It was so refreshing to be able to meet
new people and have them like me and want to get to know me for me

and not because where I went to high school or what friends we had in common. It was great to open up to these people and be accepted. I took advantage of this new state and everything it had to offer, I feel in love with the outdoors, weather, and my new friends. I was having the time of my life; I was independent, cleaning up my act, making better choices and becoming a different person, and not looking back on what I left in Chicago.

Almost 2 years after being out on my own, I was broke. Reality had come and hit me hard. My job was paying my bills, *or it wasn't??this is confusing* I had to move home. I was devastated. All I could think about is how awful it was going to be coming home, knowing that my sisters will have something to say since they have the "I told you so" attitude, I'm sure they were placing bets on how long I would make it, neither of them had come to visit me while I was gone. I'm so thankful for my parents being so supportive and helpful through everything. So I found myself once again packing up my car but this time heading east.

After being home for a few months, one morning I woke up and found myself slipping back into old habits and got very scared. I had a mental breakdown. I was so unhappy and did not know what to do with myself. Once again my reality had hit me in the face. I just felt so lost and confused and started to see so much of my old self and missing the person who I had become. It was a wakeup call; I had to turn these feelings into motivation, a constant reminder as to what I am doing with my life. I know I will always have the support of my parents, on the other hand I am constantly hearing the negativity from my sisters. My whole relationship has changed since being home. I have grown very far apart from my younger sister, who before was my biggest support system. I have seen how bitter and hurtful she has become towards me since my big "failure." She sees it as me never following through on what I say. As I get older and learn, I'm finding my life isn't suppose to be what anybody else wants it to be, but what I want. Although it has been a struggle the past year, I'm getting through it and doing exactly what I see fit. Some may say that is selfish, but I firmly believe that you should live life by the lessons you learn through personal experiences, not just from what you read in a book or what is thought to us by parents, teachers, professors, and celebrities. That's what is going to make everyone their own person, unique.

Marta—See some comments marked in your text. I do like this essay and enjoyed reading it again. I would have liked it to be more carefully edited. I highlighted some major issues on the first page. Can you see the problems there; do you know how to repair them? These kinds of mistakes are distracting for readers and undermine your credibility as a writer.

Grade: B–

Persuasive Essay Responding to Readings

COD Student Essay
English 1101, Spring 2012

This essay was written as the second essay in an English 1101 class. The requirements were as follows:

- The essay should be at least four full pages (normal margins and font size).
- It must incorporate ideas and/or quotations from the assigned essays as you present your own thesis and analysis.
- It should incorporate some personal experience (your own or those of people you know) as you develop your ideas.

Here is the topic this student chose:

In "Numbers Drop for the Married-with-Children," Blaine Harden discusses how finances have impacted the decline in marriage and married-with-children households. If you agree with Harden that this is the major factor, discuss other factors that you think contribute to this decline, using your own personal observations and experiences. If you disagree with Harden, be sure to include your rebuttal as you discuss the factors you think are major contributors to this decline, and use your own personal observations and experiences as you develop your essay. Be sure to include one other assigned essay in your argument.

1

Social Change Pulls Marriage from its Moorings

Comment [1]: The metaphor you've used for your title and beginning is very effective.

There's a saying that a high tide lifts all boats. Economists, especially those of the trickle-down persuasion, use this analogy to illustrate how a robust economy improves everyone's financial standing. In his article "Numbers Drop for the Married-with-Children," journalist Blaine Harden claims the marriage rate is influenced by financial status, so the poor economy is the biggest factor behind the drop in the number of married households with children over the last 40 to 50 years. In his on-line conversation, Harden finds it "fascinating that marriage with kids became the overwhelming norm in the United States after World War II." He goes on to state how this happened during a time of unprecedented widespread prosperity, then posits that it warrants further study why the current drop in this type of household has corresponded with rising income equality (Harden 485). I would argue that Harden has it backward; it was the demographic and social changes during this time span that created the very environment that allowed people the opportunity NOT to marry (or to leave a marriage), even during bad economic times.

Comment [2]: This is a nice lead-in, which gives readers useful information about the source and author to establish credibility.

Comment [3]: Your thesis is clear, and its contrast with Harden's views suggests some deep analysis.

I submit that the effect of this unprecedented prosperity on the marriage rate would have been noticeably less without the GI bill. The GI bill contributed to individual prosperity by making both home ownership and a college education affordable, but it also changed the social dynamic of when young people marry. In those days, a man would not be considered good marriage material until he had established himself somewhat financially and could provide for a wife. A young woman lived at home until her (usually older) fiancé proved himself in his trade. The GI bill changed that -- overnight. Suddenly, thousands of young men

Comment [4]: This is an effective use of the dash for sentence variety and emphasis of your idea.

Social Change Pulls Marriage 2

(many with valuable skills) were eligible for free educations and cheap home loans. The prosperous economy contributed heavily by providing an abundance of jobs; even a cheap mortgage is not an option if you can't make the payments. But now GIs could leverage that bump in prosperity to establish themselves financially much faster than any generation before them. If a young man returning from war could afford a house and easily find a well-paying job, why wait to get married and have kids?

> **Comment [5]:** Nice use of a rhetorical question.

These GI's were the biggest reason married with kids became the most popular family configuration. The sheer number of them returning home and marrying over a relatively short period of time made marriage rates and then birth rates skyrocket. This cohort became the new norm simply because this population sector exploded and eclipsed all other household configurations. No doubt their numbers created a second wave twenty years later as their children grew up and left home, bumping these married couples into the empty-nest category, and some of them into the divorced category as well.

The marriage rate has been in steady decline since 1960, dropping nearly 15% from 1960 to 2005 (" Marriage Trends" 489). Using this data to calculate how much the rate changed from decade to decade yields:

From	1960 to 1970	-2.6%
	1970 to 1980	-3.5%
	1980 to 1990	-2.5%
	1990 to 2000	-2.8%
	2000 to 2005	-2.9%

> **Comment [6]:** This is a good analysis of the data. It's always important to not merely present it, but to analyze it as well. You've done that nicely here.

If marriage rates are driven primarily by financial security, then we would have seen the rate drop more during economic

Social Change Pulls Marriage   3

downturns and less during upturns, especially for the less
educated classes. This seems to be only partly true, so there must
be other factors at work.

Note that the rate fell considerably more (3.5%) in the 1970s.
Most of the 1970s were dominated by inflation, supporting
Harden's view, but this decade also saw dramatic shifts in the social
views of marriage as well as the enactment of laws that impacted
both the marriage and birth rates. The women's movement had
taken a firm hold, resulting in equal opportunity laws and related
laws like Title 9. The post-war boom made high-paying factory work
for women plentiful, making it possible for them to escape bad
marriages or to avoid marrying at all. No-fault divorce became law
in some states, and the stigma of divorce, while certainly still
present, was considerably weaker. Likewise, the various stigmas of
NOT being married -- living alone, remaining single and childless,
raising children as a single parent, and living out of wedlock -- also
softened. Birth control pills introduced in the early 1960s became
safer and more widely available, and the legalization of abortion in
1973 no doubt prevented at least a few shotgun weddings. The
early gay rights movement also took a tiny bite out of the married
population, as some of the bravest pioneers came out of the closet
and left their marriages, while others shunned the idea of marrying
just to hide their orientation.

The 1980s data seem especially contrary to Harden's
position. This was not a particularly good decade for those
without college degrees. They were left further behind as rust-
belt factories closed, interest rates rose, and job growth became
concentrated in the financial and technology sectors. If bad times
deter all but the professional classes from marrying, then why was

Comment [7]: I like the way you made a concession to Harden because it shows a careful analysis of his argument, but your consideration of other factors reflects your perspective examination of the situation.

Comment [8]: This paragraph provides a concise view of many important factors relating to this issue.

the drop in the 1980s the least severe (-2.5%) of those 45 years? The statistics given on page 489 are not split out by class, but since adults without degrees far outnumber the professional classes, a drop in the marriage rate of the former would more than negate any upticks of the latter. The slowing of the decline can partly be explained by the baby 'boomlet' in the 1980s as many women who had postponed marriage and childbirth in the 1970s were now deciding to do both.

Harden admits it is more than economics, but has trouble backing up some of his assertions. He says that many young people are not persuaded by "fact-based arguments that point out how marriage has a way of increasing financial stability" (484) but later states "there's very little evidence … that a desire to marry and stay married can be taught" (487). Does marriage really improve fiscal stability for people who normally wouldn't consider marriage? Marrying off the unmarried does not automatically give them more stable jobs, or, for that matter, better interpersonal skills, and it might even make them less likely to have a lasting marriage. So has Harden put the cart before the horse? Are married people better off financially because they pooled their resources, or are people who are likely to be financially responsible also more likely to choose marriage? Harden does not back up his anecdote of the Fitzhenry family (482) with any hard data. Although getting married made them both more responsible with their money, who's to say that even with their prior habits they weren't already light-years ahead of those who aren't inclined to marry?

Late in the on-line conversation, Harden concedes that cultural norms weight heavily in the decision to marry, and that

Comment [9]: It would be helpful to provide just a bit more background to remind readers about the Fitzhenrys.

"people tend to imitate in their own lives what they experience growing up" (486). Based on my parents' experiences, I would counter that sometimes people consciously choose NOT to emulate what they knew growing up, especially if what they knew was a dysfunctional family. My parents made a pact that theirs would be a healthy marriage despite all the failed marriages and out-of-wedlock children in their own working-class family trees. I take issue with Harden's statement that "it is only the best educated and the best paid who are most likely to see marriage as essential for raising kids" since my parents are neither yet both strongly feel that marriage is the best environment for childrearing.

Comment [10]: You've done a good job of weaving in your personal observations into your discussion of data, larger social trends, etc.

But if the majority of people do imitate what they grew up with, then as more people are raised in non-nuclear families, the number of adults who are disinclined to marry will continue to rise. I hope this will not mean that they are more likely to head dysfunctional households, but that their households are at least as successful as traditional married households in modeling good partnership and good parenting skills. As our former pastor is fond of saying, "Values are caught, not taught". It may come to pass that the 'marriage virus' will die out in all but those enclaves where the children are purposely exposed to it. If marriage is a cultural phenomenon mostly relevant to the upper classes, and the upper classes are predominantly white, then the decline in the number of nuclear households is certain to continue, because the proportion of whites in the United States population is currently dropping, and so is the white birth rate.

Comment [11]: Remember that commas and periods go inside quotation marks; colons and semicolons go outside (in American English).

The economy on its own won't change marriage much, but it will cause upper class couples to delay marriage and childbearing a few years. Cultural values, like acceptance of gay marriage and

Social Change Pulls Marriage   6

the further equalization of workload within the home, will impact

marriage more than the economic environment, and cultural

values take longer to evolve than an economic cycle. The post-

war prosperity was definitely the highest tide in our history, but

demographic and social changes were a tsunami that roared in

during that high tide. Its effects are still causing waves in the

landscape of marriage and childbearing in the United States.

Comment [12]: Echoing the metaphor you began with gives a wonderful sense of symmetry to your essay. Very nicely done!

Works Cited

Harden, Blaine. "Numbers Drop for the Married-with-

Children." *The Contemporary Reader*. 10th ed. Ed. Gary

Goshgarian. Boston: Pearson, 2011. 481-87. Print.

"Marriage Trends in the United States." *The Contemporary*

Reader. 10th ed. Ed. Gary Goshgarian. Boston: Pearson,

2011. 489. *Print*.

This is first-rate. You've done an excellent job of delving into
Harden's assumptions and analyzing information—not just the
assigned readings but also ideas and knowledge you've gained from
your studies and other reading you've done. Analyzing and
synthesizing ideas from a wide variety of viewpoints is the goal of
a good education, and you've demonstrated a high level of
accomplishment in this essay. You also did a nice job of weaving
in your own experiences and observations as you considered data,
historical information, and trends so that this essay is full and rich.
Great job!

A

English 1101—Evaluation Criteria for Essays

A range (90–100) The introduction leads in to the topic in a way that provides a helpful context and engages the audience in an original, insightful way. The thesis is deeply considered and well-crafted, going beyond the obvious and controlling the entire essay. Support for the thesis is specific and relevant and is presented in paragraphs which are unified and cohesive. The organization demonstrates complex relationships among ideas in the supporting paragraphs with meaningful transitions. Information from source material is skillfully integrated and well-analyzed. Sentences are skillfully worded for both clarity and effect, and there are virtually no errors in mechanics or spelling. All requirements of the assignment are met.

B range (80–89) The introduction provides a needed context and establishes an interesting focus for an audience. The thesis is clearly stated, and provides a focus that controls the essay. Support is specific and relevant, and paragraphs are generally unified and cohesive. The paragraphs are sequenced in a meaningful, logical order, and the ideas in each paragraph generally flow in a way that shows the connection to the paragraph before it to the paragraph after it with helpful transitions. Information from source material is incorporated into the essay with some helpful explanation and/or analysis. Sentences are generally varied and correct; there may be a few errors in mechanics and/or spelling, but they generally do not impede comprehension. All requirements of the assignment are met.

C range (70–79) An introduction is provided which provides some context and has a thesis. The thesis may not be sufficiently well-focused and/or may not fully control the essay. Support is provided, although examples could use more clarification or details. The organization could more effectively show the relationship among ideas in paragraphs with smoother, more meaningful transitions. Information from source material is provided, but more explanation and analysis is needed. Sentences need more variety and may occasionally have structural problems; there may also be more frequent errors in mechanics. The requirements of the assignment are met.

D range (60–69) The introduction may be skimpy; the thesis is not well-focused and does not control the essay for the most part. Support is often vague, generic, or irrelevant. The organization shows very little attempt to link ideas in paragraphs and show meaningful connections. Some information from source material may be provided, but it is not analyzed. Sentences have many structural problems, and there are serious errors in mechanics. Some of the requirements of the assignment may not be met.

F (59 or below) An introduction may not be provided, and the thesis does not control the essay. Support is greatly lacking. The organization shows no logical connections among paragraphs. There are frequent problems with sentence structure and mechanics, which hinder comprehension. Information from source material is absent. Most or all of the requirements of the assignment are unmet.

Research Paper Based on Career Topic

COD Student Essay
English 1102, Spring 2010

Students in this class were assigned to write a research essay about an issue that they will encounter in their chosen career. The essay needed to be four plus pages, with four outside sources using MLA formatting. Please note the use of the personal pronoun in this essay. Research essays can have "I" in them, despite what you may have been told. However, it is always the best policy to check with your professor in a particular class as writing conventions are fluid.

1

The Rise of Open Source

Comment [VAC1]: I don't want to start off with a grammar complaint, but notice the needlessly elevated tone here. How could you rephrase this so it's both correct grammatically (me, not I) and is more welcoming to the reader?

As a student, I have faced one common problem amongst my peers and I; having to type an essay. Composing the paper is not the problem, buying the software can be. Microsoft Office is one expensive option, yet OpenOffice, an alternative, is free. I am a computer science student, and I use OpenOffice because it is free and open source. In the near future I could be writing software that may be given away for free. The rise of open source software could drastically affect my future. Because of this, I felt compelled to explore the benefits of open source software. This software is any software in which the source code is made available online for any developer to use or edit as they please

(Weber, 54 - 64). This rough definition implies that closed source software is the exact opposite; source code is protected and kept private usually to make it more profitable. These days, more businesses and governments than ever before are making the move to open source. Individuals use open source software every day courtesy of web browser Mozilla Firefox and office suite OpenOffice, while corporations save money by using Linux or Solaris as their main server infrastructure (Casadesus-Masanell, Ghemawat; Phipps). What drives people to use this software? Besides the price tag, it tends to be better than most closed source competitors like Microsoft's Internet Explorer and Microsoft Office. Most open source software is free, however, plenty of companies have developed unique business models in order to yield a profit from their open source endeavors. Open source software is beneficial because it encourages innovation, it is more secure than closed source competitors, and it can be developed quicker, all while still allowing its creators to have a successful and profitable company. On top of all this, its free, which is ultimately what the user wants.

Security is one big advantage to open source software. Programs like VLC Media Player, OpenOffice, and countless other projects are developed very efficiently and updated frequently due to the availability of the source code (Scacchi). As a user of these applications, I find myself downloading updates on a weekly basis. It is comforting to know that people out there are working

Comment [VAC2]: Nice use of your personal ethos here.

The Rise of Open Source   3

hard to refine code and fix bugs and exploits that could harm
your computer. I believe that developers contribute to this
software because it allows them to gain experience, build a
strong resume in their free time, and give back to the community.
However, when these applications get big, one problem that can
ensue is a shortage of developers (Kessler). Popular open source
video platform VLC Media Player, an excellent example of a project
on its last limb, has millions of users, but the development cycle
has almost ceased due to a lack of developers. They do not have
the resources to keep the Macintosh version up to date which
could seriously injure the reputation that VLC has gained
(Kessler). This shortage of developers could be due to the fact
that there is no money involved with the VLC software.

This brings us to a second debate; profitability. Open source
software is often times free and this makes it hard to make
money, or a living, developing it. How can money be made off of
a product that is given away for free? As TechCrunch blogger Matt
Schonfeld has points, Mozilla, the group behind the web browser
Firefox, has crafted a partnership with search behemoth, Google.
Mozilla has a massive user base and because of this, Mozilla
brings Google a slew of search users which they can then gain
money off of in various ways (Schonfeld). A Mozilla Foundation
audit has revealed that the group earned about $66 million in
royalty fees in 2007. Thus is very remarkable considering their
entire browser is given away for free (qtd. in Schonfeld). Another

Comment [03]: I'd like a little more context here to bring the reader back to your point rather than relying on your sources to make your points.

Comment [04]: This is a good point for a transition, but in future papers think about being smoother.

The Rise of Open Source 4

company that has made millions off of open source software, IBM, has a very common, but modern, business model. Savio Rodrigues, a blogger for Infoworld and an IBM employee, notes that the main way IBM makes money revolves around giving the customer choices when buying their product; "They can have an open license, or a proprietary license. They can buy IBM support, or do it themselves. They can be passive customers, or part of the community. They can even re-sell add-ons to open source code." (qtd. in Blankenhorn). IBM has given the consumer all sorts of options causing massive enterprises to purchase what is right for them, all while enabling IBM to stay in business and turn a profit. IBM recently tried to purchase another company that has had a major part in the advance of open source; Sun Microsystems. Sun develops and allows consumers to have their entire office suite, OpenOffice, for free (Phipps). This suite is almost identical to Microsoft's office suite (Microsoft Office) yet it does not carry a price tag. Sun makes their money by selling servers to other corporations while selling support at a price, similar to IBM (Lewis). While they are not making any money off of OpenOffice (Lewis), they are running a successful business while making a difference by giving back to the user (Lewis). Writer Bernard Golden has summed the general business model up very well;

> "The professional services business model continues to be
> viable. The increasing use of open source in IT software

infrastructures will raise the demand for technical support and consulting. Entrepreneurs will find many opportunities in open source services. Open source developers themselves might choose to enter the fray; after al. who better to offer support for a product than those who built it?" (32)

All of this proves that corporations can make software, keep it open source, all while giving it away for free and being profitable.

With the rise of this software, it can also make life easier for anyone to start their own business. One company that has made their way to the top of the social website ladder is Twitter. This unique company has millions of users and has allowed many developers to make money by charging for Twitter applications (Weaver). All of this was achieved all of their success thanks to open source software (Weaver). Twitter has a wide range of developers making software for just about anything that has to do with Twitter. Evan Weaver, the infrastructure manager at Twitter, has summed up what they do on the Twitter blog; "First, we've created an open source directory for the entire company. This lists all the public software that the engineering teams have created or contributed to. Much of Twitter's success has been enabled by open-source software, and we want to give back. Everyone is welcome to use this software for their own projects, and if the project is Twitter-related, so much the better."

One of my main attractions to Twitter is the fact that everything they do is open. Without Twitter's willingness to open up their web site, they would not have as many innovative applications as they do. Regardless of

Comment [VAC5]: This is what I was talking about in the earlier comment about having more context after your source material to bring the reader back to your point.

The Rise of Open Source   6

Twitter clients, other new and interesting uses have been created because of their open system. TweetMyPC is an excellent example of this. Software developer, and creator, Shoban Kumar explains that; "TweetMyPC is a little software-application for Windows, written in VB.Net using the .Net-Framework v3.0, which allows you to control and access your computer from anywhere by simply sending a twitter-message with a special command as its content." With the opportunities to have a community create new uses for the social networking site, the company will surely be around for a long time. Regardless of all of this, Twitter is still fairly new to the industry, so predicting exactly how their business model will work out in the long run is difficult. As of now the company has had great success with the media and has been able to stay alive for a while allowing one to assume that open source does nothing but benefit them, as well as others.

Open source does not just apply to the software you use on your computer at home. Within the past couple years it has been invading mobile devices of all sorts. Android, the mobile operating system by Google, has been making a big difference for not only Google, but users and individual programmers. A statement from the *Open Handset Alliance,* a group dedicated to innovating the cell phone industry, states that many companies are dedicating themselves to open source software;

"A broad alliance of leading technology and wireless companies today joined forces to announce the development of Android, the first truly open and comprehensive platform for mobile devices. Google Inc., T-Mobile, HTC, Qualcomm, Motorola and others have collaborated on the development of Android through the Open Handset Alliance, a multinational alliance of technology and mobile industry leaders." ("Industry Leaders Announce Open Platform for Mobile Devices.")

Android is revolutionary because unlike its closed source competitor, the iPhone, software creators have total and complete control over what they can put on the Android Market (Google). According to Google's web page; "Android Market is open to all Android application developers. Once registered, developers have complete control over when and how they make their applications available to users." Selling applications on the Android platform could even make you rich over night. One developer, Edward Kim, claims that his "Car Locator" application is bringing in $13,000 a month of revenue. Kim, ecstatic about his success, has written on his blog about his achievement;

> "Clearly, I'm on cloud 9 with these numbers, but where does it go from here? Sales of about $13k/month is awesome income for any one person, so it may sound ridiculous for me to think it can go even higher. However, I still think that Android is only a fraction of what it will eventually become. Each release of a new Android handset gets me excited, as it means a wider reach for the Marketplace."

Success stories like this are becoming very common and they would not be possible without the advance of Android and open source software.

So what is the problem with open source? Companies like Microsoft want to sell people their operating system. As everybody knows, Microsoft is big for one reason; selling software. The average user will happily buy their software, but what about the huge corporation that does not want to pay millions of dollars in licensing fees? Simply put, they have a free alternative called Linux which can save not only corporations, but users, a lot of money. The official Linux web site has a bona fide summary of the operating system; "Apart from the fact that it's freely distributed, Linux's functionality, adaptability and robustness, has made it the main alternative for proprietary Unix and Microsoft operating systems.". Companies have been switching to Linux due to the zero dollar price tag it comes with. Professors Pankaj Ghemawat and Ramon Casadesus-Masanell, who teach at Harvard in the business department put it this way; "Microsoft has a great deal to lose if Linux wins the operating systems battle. Microsoft is a software company, and a defeat in operating systems would point to the vulnerability of its entire business portfolio". Their statement makes sense, Microsoft's Windows and Windows Server operating systems are what put them where they are today. Microsoft would not be happier to see Linux out of the picture. Though there is not much of a statement from Microsoft, I always think about a common combination of applications; Linux, OpenOffice, and Firefox. This combination could grow in the

Comment [VAC6]: Nice transition here, I like the way you shift from one group to another drawing connections between them.

future to put Microsoft out of power just because it is free, superb, and available to everyone.

Corporations are not the only ones who have issues with open source. The *International Intellectual Property Alliance*, a group backed by the *Recording Industry Association of America* (RIAA) and the *Motion Picture Association of America* (MPAA), has publicly opposed the rise of open source in government. Bobbie Johnson, a writer for news web site Gaurdian.co.uk, got his hands on a statement from the IIPA stating that; "Open Source software "simply weakens the software industry and undermines its long-term competitiveness" while "it fails to build respect for intellectual property rights," the IIPA recommendation says." (qtd. in Ernesto). The point of open source software is not to harm intellectual property rights. If a company wanted to protect intellectual property rights then they would copyright a closed source application. The even bigger problem is their claim that open source software does cripples long term competitiveness. When a corporation releases a product and expects users to pay money for it, they better have the better application, considering their competitor is giving their product away for free. I believe that is a great way to promote competition. All of this has started recently because the United States government has begun to consider the implementation of open source software (Vass). Other countries that have been using open source software are Indonesia, Brazil, and India (Johnson). The reasoning behind this

The Rise of Open Source   10

possible switch consists of two main components; cutting costs to the tax payers and having a more secure infrastructure (Vass). These two reasons are the most common reasons people switch to open source software so it is no surprise that our government is trying to make the switch as well.

Looking at all of the arguments used on both sides, I can only assume that a future of open source software cannot be a bad thing for business, software engineers, consumers, or governments. Whether working for Microsoft or creating the next big Android application, there will be money to be made all over the industry. Free software will be great for promoting competition in our capitalist society as well as the benefits it provides for small businesses, like faster growth (Twitter being an example). Though there may still be problems to sort out with products like Linux, or the difficulty of crafting a successful business model for an 'open' company, I can safely say that my future is not going to be harmed because of the rise in open source software. If anything, my future will be affected for the better because of the extra opportunities I have due to open source software.

Good work. I liked how you used your own experience and knowledge and supported it with your source material. I'd like to see more of that in your upcoming essays. Always remember that you're the author here, you are in control of your essay. Don't give that power to your sources.

Grade: A

Works Cited

Blankenhorn, Dana. "IBM open source strategy becomes
   clearer." *ZDNet*. CBS Interactive Inc., 20 Sept. 2007. Web.
   5 Mar. 2010.

Bloem, Jaap, Menno Van Doorn, and Erik Van Ommeren. *Open
   for Business – Open Source Inspired Innovation*. Ed.
   George Hall and Susan MacFarlane. Trans. Robert Olsen.
   N.p.: Uitgeverij kleine Uil, 2007. *ebook3000*. Web. 27
   Feb. 2010.

Board of Directors, Mozilla Foundation. *Mozilla Foundation
   and Subsidiary*. San Francisco, CA: Hood & Strong LLP,
   2008. PDF file.

Casadesus-Masanell, Ramon and Ghemawat, Pankaj.
   "Microsoft vs. Open Source: Who Will Win?" Interview by
   Sean Silverthorne. *Harvard Business School*. President
   and Fellows of Harvard College, 6 June 2005. Web. 27
   Feb. 2010.

Ernesto. "Open Source Software Turns Countries Into Pirate
   Havens." *Freakbits*. TorrentFreak, 24 Feb. 2010. Web.
   27 Feb. 2010.

Golden, Bernard. *Succeeding with Open Source*. N.p.: Addison-
   Wesley Professional, 2005. Print.

Google. "Android Market – About." *Android Market*. Google,
   2008. Web. 12 Mar. 2010.

Johnson, Bobbie. "When using open source makes you an
      enemy of the state." Editorial. *Guardian.co.uk*. Guardian
      News and Media Limited, 23 Feb. 2010. Web. 27 Feb.
      2010.

Kessler, Topher. "Mac development of VLC nearly dead." *CNET*.
      CBS Interactive, 17 Dec. 2009. Web. 27 Feb. 2010.

Kim, Edward. "An Android Success Story: $13,000/month App
      Sales." *Edward Kim*. Posterous, 1 Mar. 2010. Web.
      12 Mar. 2010.

Kumar, Shoban. "TweetMyPC." *CodePlex*. Ed. BasisBit.
      Microsoft, 17 Feb. 2010. Web. 12 Mar. 2010.

Lewis, Latif. "Sun Microsystems' profit report offers glimpse
      of what's in store for Oracle." *DailyFinance*. AOL Money
      & Finance, 28 Apr. 2009. Web. 27 Feb. 2010.

Linux. "What is Linux." *Linux.org*. Linux Online Inc., 2 July
      2007. Web. 20 Mar. 2010.

Open Handset Alliance. "Industry Leaders Announce Open
      Platform for Mobile Devices." *Open Handset Alliance*.
      Open Handset Alliance, n.d. Web. 12 Mar. 2010.

Phipps, Simon. "Interview with Simon Phipps." Interview by
      Glyn Moody. *Linux Journal* June 2007: 47-49. Print.

Schonfeld, Erick. "Google Makes Up 88 Percent Of Mozilla's
      Revenues, Threatens Its Non-Profit Status." *TechCrunch*.
      N.p., n.d. Web. 27 Feb. 2008.

Scacchi, Walt. "Is Open Source Software Development Faster, Better, and Cheaper than Software Engineering?" N.d. PDF file.

Vass, Bill. "The Open Source Coming Out Party. . . ." *Bill Vass' Weblog*. Sun Microsystems Federal, Inc., 28 Sept. 2008. Web. 1 Mar. 2010.

Weaver, Evan. "Open Engineering." Editorial. *Twitter Blog*. Twitter, 23 Feb. 2010. Web. 23 Feb. 2010.

Weber, Steven. *The Success of Open Source*. Cambridge, MA: Harvard University Press, 2004. Print.

Composing

1 Think as a Writer 2

**2 Read and View with
   a Critical Eye 4**

3 Plan and Draft 7

**4 Compose
   Paragraphs 21**

**5 Rewrite, Edit,
   and Proofread 30**

1 | Think as a Writer

1a Think About the Process of Communication

Whether you are writing a research paper for a political science course, designing a Web site for a small business, or preparing slides for a sales presentation, you are participating in a complex process. That process—communication—involves the interaction of three essential elements: the writer or speaker, the audience, and the subject. These three elements are often represented by a triangle.

Speaker, subject, and audience are each necessary for an act of communication to occur. These three elements interact with each other. Speakers make adjustments to their presentations of a subject depending on the audience (think of how you talk to small children). Just as speakers adjust to audiences, audiences continually adjust to speakers (think of how your attitude toward speakers changes when they are able to laugh at themselves).

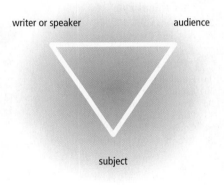

writer or speaker   audience

subject

The rhetorical triangle

1b Think About Your Audience

In college writing, you often write for readers you know directly, including your classmates and your teachers. In the workplace, you may not always know who is going to read your reports or memos. Ask yourself who will read your writing and think about what kind of information you need to provide to engage them.

WRITING SMART

Understand your audience

- Who is most likely to read what you write?
- How much does your audience know about your subject? Are there any key terms or concepts that you will need to explain?
- How interested is your audience likely to be? If they lack interest in your subject, how can you get them engaged?
- What is their attitude likely to be toward your subject? If they hold attitudes different from yours, how can you get them to consider your views?
- What would motivate your audience to want to read what you write?

1c Think About Your Credibility

Some writers have credibility because of their standing in a given field. Most writers, however, have to convince their readers to keep reading by demonstrating knowledge of their subject and concern with their readers' needs.

WRITING SMART

Build your credibility

- How can you convince your audience that you are knowledgeable about your subject? Do you need to do research?
- How can you convince your audience that you have their interests in mind?
- What strategies can you use to enhance your credibility? Should you cite experts on your subject? Can you acknowledge opposing positions, indicating that you've taken a balanced view of your subject?
- Does the appearance, accuracy, and clarity of your writing give you credibility?

2 | Read and View with a Critical Eye

2a Become a Critical Reader

You can become a more effective critical reader if you have a set of strategies and use them while you read.

Preview

No subject is ever completely new; it is likely that many people have talked about the subject before. Begin by asking the following questions.

- Who wrote this material?
- Where did it first appear? In a book, newspaper, magazine, or on-line?
- What is the topic or issue?
- Where does the writer stand on the topic or issue?
- What else has been written about the topic or issue?
- Why was it written?

Summarize

Make sure you understand exactly what is at issue. Circle any words or references that you don't know and look them up. Ask yourself

- What is the writer's main claim or question?
- If I do not find a specific claim, what is the main focus?
- What are the key ideas or concepts that the writer considers?
- What are the key terms? How does the writer define those terms?

Respond

As you read, write down your thoughts. Ask these questions:

- To what points made by the writer should I respond?
- What ideas might be developed or interpreted differently?
- What do I need to look up?

Analyze

On your second reading, analyze the structure using the following questions.

- How is the piece of writing organized?
- What does the writer assume the readers know and believe?
- Where is the evidence? Can you think of contradictory evidence?
- Does the writer acknowledge opposing views? Does the writer deal fairly with opposing views?
- What kinds of sources are cited? Are they thoroughly documented?
- How does the writer represent herself or himself?

 **2b** Become a Critical Viewer

Like critical reading, critical viewing requires you to reflect in depth on what you see. Use the following strategies.

Preview

Critical viewing requires thinking about the context first.

- Who created this image?
- Why was it created?
- Where and when did it first appear?
- What media are used?
- What has been written about the creator or the image?

Respond

Make notes as you view the image with these questions in mind:

- What was my first impression of the image?
- After thinking more—perhaps reading more—about it, how have I changed or expanded my first impression.

Analyze

The following analytical questions apply primarily to still images.

- How is the image composed or framed?
- Where do my eyes go first?
- How does the image appeal to the values of the audience?
- Was it intended to serve a purpose besides art or entertainment?

The billboard suggests that this photograph was taken when travel by train was still popular. In fact, it was taken in 1937 by Dorothea Lange (1895–1965), who gave it the title *Toward Los Angeles, California*. The lines of the shoulder of the road, the highway, and the telephone poles slope toward a vanishing point on the horizon, giving a sense of great distance. The two figures in dark clothing walking away contrast to a rectangular billboard with a white background and white frame.

Another approach to critical viewing is to analyze the purpose of the content. In 1937 the United States was in the midst of the Great Depression and a severe drought, which forced many small farmers in middle America to abandon their homes and go to California in search of work. By placing the figures and the billboard beside each other, Lange is able to make an ironic commentary on the lives of well-off and poor Americans during the Depression.

Dorothea Lange, *Toward Los Angeles, California*.

3 | Plan and Draft

QUICKTAKE

- Establish your goals (see below)
- Explore your topic (see p. 9)
- Write a working thesis (see p. 13)
- Plan a strategy (see p. 17)

3a Establish Your Goals

Your instructor will give you specific suggestions about how to think about your audience and topic. There are two ways to make your task simpler.

- Be sure you are responding to the assignment appropriately.
- Select a topic that both fits the assignment and appeals to you strongly enough to make you want to write about it.

Look carefully at your assignment

When your instructor gives you a writing assignment, look closely at what you are asked to do. Often the assignment will contain key words such as *analyze, compare and contrast, define, describe, evaluate,* or *propose* that will assist you in determining what direction to take.

- **Analyze:** Find connections among a set of facts, events, or readings, and make them meaningful.
- **Compare and contrast:** Examine how two or more things are alike and how they differ.
- **Define:** Make a claim about how something should be defined, according to features that you set out.
- **Describe:** Observe carefully and select details that create a dominant impression.
- **Evaluate:** Argue that something is good, bad, best, or worst in its class, according to criteria that you set out.
- **Propose:** Identify a particular problem and explain why your solution is the best one.

If you are unclear about what the assignment calls for, talk with your instructor.

Find a topic you care about

If you do not have an assigned topic, a good way to find one is to look first at the materials for your course. You may find something that interests you in the readings for the course or in a topic that came up in class discussion.

If your assignment gives you a wide range of options, you might write more than one list, starting with your personal interests. Think also about campus topics, community topics, and national topics that intrigue you. Your lists might resemble these:

Personal
1. Benefits of weight training
2. Wordplay in Marx brothers movies
3. History of hairstyles

Campus
1. Pros and cons of charging computer fees
2. Should my university have a foreign language requirement?
3. Affirmative action admissions policies

Community
1. Helmet laws for people who ride bicycles and motorcycles
2. Bilingual education programs
3. More bike lanes to encourage more people to ride bicycles
4. Better public transportation

Nation/World
1. Advertising aimed at preschool children
2. Censorship of the Internet
3. Effects of climate change
4. Setting aside the laws that govern police searches, in the effort to stop terrorism

Often you will find that, before you can begin writing, you need to analyze exactly what you mean by a phrase like "censorship of the Internet." For example, do you mean censorship of Web sites, or of everything that goes over the Internet, including private e-mail?

After you make a list or lists, you should review it.

- Put a checkmark beside the topics that look most interesting or the ones that mean the most to you.

- Put a question mark beside the topics that you don't know very much about. If you choose one of these issues, you will have to do research.
- Select the two or three topics that look the most promising.

3b Explore Your Topic

Once you have identified a potential topic, the next step is to determine what you already know about that topic and what you need to find out. Experienced writers use many strategies for exploring their knowledge of a topic and how interesting it really is to them. Here are a few.

Ask questions

These classic reporter's questions will assist you in thinking through a topic.

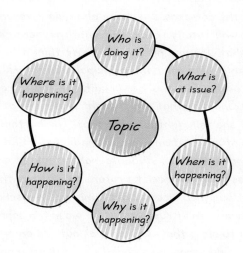

Freewrite

Another way to find out how much you know about a topic is to **freewrite**: write as quickly as you can without stopping for a set time, usually five or ten minutes. The goal of freewriting is to get as much down as possible. Don't stop to correct mistakes. The constant flow of words should generate ideas—some useful, some not.

If you get stuck, write the same sentence over again, or write about how hungry you are, or how difficult freewriting is, until thoughts on your selected topic reappear. After you've finished, read what you have written and single out any key ideas. The following freewrite was composed by Mariela Martinez on a student free speech case that wound up before the United States Supreme Court in March 2007. In 2002 in Juneau, Alaska, high school senior Joseph Frederick was suspended for ten days by principal Deborah Morse after he displayed a banner off of school property during the Winter Olympics Torch Relay. You can read Martinez's essay in Section 9d.

Freewrite on Morse v. Frederick

I did dumb stuff when I was a senior in high school. I can imagine Joe Frederick sitting around with his friends after they found out that the Winter Olympics Torch Relay would pass by his school. I can imagine what happened. Someone said it would be really cool if we held up a banner that said Bong Hits 4 Jesus in front of the cameras. Everyone else said awesome! The principal will totally freak! But what happens next? That's what Joe and his friends didn't think through. And when it happened, the principal didn't think it through either, but give her credit, she had to react on the spot. She did what she thought was right at the time, but she fell right into the trap. The bottom line is when do stupid statements become illegal? A lot of adults and high school students make stupid statements, but unless they are racist, profane, or libelous, they don't get punished. Joe did get punished. In a school he would have been disruptive, but he wasn't in school. He didn't go to class that day. He was outside on a public sidewalk. And school was called off that afternoon because of the parade. So he was just a high school student doing something dumb, not something illegal. Joe made the principal look bad, but he embarrassed his school and his parents, and my guess is that if he had it to do over again, he wouldn't have done it. Still, he shouldn't have been punished. He didn't make a serious argument in favor of doing drugs. Or ridicule Christians. The real argument is about the limits of free speech.

Ideas to Use
1. *Joe's banner was in poor taste, but poor taste doesn't meet legal requirement for censorship.*
2. *The principal was embarrassed and made a knee-jerk reaction without thinking.*
3. *The real issue is what free speech rights do young people have.*

You may want to use a key word or idea as a starting point for a second freewrite. After two or three rounds you will discover how much you already know about your topic and possible directions for developing it.

Brainstorm

An alternative method of discovery is to **brainstorm**. The end result of brainstorming is usually a list—sometimes of questions, sometimes of statements. You might come up with a list of observations and questions, such as these for the free speech case.

- *The student wasn't in the school at the time of the incident.*
- *The principal overreacted.*
- *Drugs are an excuse to give authorities more control.*
- *What is the recent history of free speech cases involving high school students?*
- *Student's citing of Jefferson resulted in more punishment—WHY???*
- *Isn't there protection for satire?*

Make an idea map

Still another strategy for exploring how much you know about a potential topic is to make an **idea map**. Idea maps are useful because they let you see everything at once, and you can begin to make connections among the different aspects of an issue—definitions, causes, effects, proposed solutions, and your personal experience. A good way to get started is to write down ideas on sticky notes. Then you can move the sticky notes around until you figure out which ideas fit together. Figure 2.1 shows what an idea map on the freedom of speech case involving Joseph Frederick might look like.

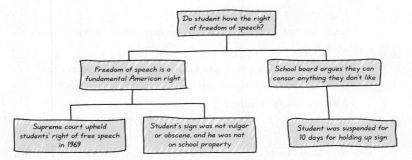

Figure 2.1   Idea map on the Juneau, Alaska, freedom of speech case

Respond to something you've read

Most of the writing you do in college will be linked to texts you are read-ing. Find time to read about your topic before writing about it. Select a book or an article that you find to be a powerful statement about your topic. You don't have to agree with the author completely; in fact, it's more productive if you can "talk back" to the author.

Imagine you are sitting down face-to-face with the author. Find places where you can write things like the following:

- *"I agree with your general point, but did you think of this other example? What would you do with it?"*
- *"Here you seem to be arguing for one side, but later you seem to contradict yourself and give credit to the other side."*
- *"Your point about one group might be applied to a different group."*
- *"I don't agree with this claim because your evidence doesn't support your assertion."*

Talking back to a text can help you find your own position: "While X sees it this way, I look at it a different way."

Talk and listen

Writing requires concentration, which for many people depends on quiet and solitude. Nevertheless, many ideas come from conversation, and all ideas are born from other ideas. When we talk and listen, we discover. Pro-ductive writers are engaged in a community where ideas are discussed. Your writing class is a writing community. To make the community as useful as possible, it is important to ask your peers for specific and genuine feedback on your drafts and to pay close attention to your classmates' writing as well.

■ You can get one-on-one help in developing your ideas, focusing your topic, and revising your paper at your writing center.

If any of your class communication is done through e-mail or online discussion, you will already have a head start on your assigned writing. E-mails and online discussions can be used the way journals and freewrites are—as material for essays. When you are planning your essay, you may find that you already have a wealth of written material to draw from.

3c Write a Working Thesis

The initial stage of the planning process involves finding ideas, expanding and broadening your thoughts, and recording ideas from written sources and conversations. The next stage of thinking, after you have decided on a general topic, is *narrowing* your focus to a specific topic. Having a specific focus is the key to writing a strong essay.

Use questions to focus a broad topic

Childhood obesity is certainly a current and interesting research topic, but it is too broad. Ask questions that will break the big topic into smaller ones.

- *Why are children becoming obese?*
- *Why are children today more obese than children of past generations?*

- How has the American food industry contributed to childhood obesity?
- What changes in American culture have contributed to childhood obesity?
- What are the adverse health effects of childhood obesity?
- What strategies are effective for preventing childhood obesity?

Consider other angles to expand a narrow topic

Too-narrow topics are rarer than topics that are too broad. Although candy consumption is certainly one factor contributing to obesity in children, this narrow focus overlooks many other factors that together lead to childhood obesity. For instance:

- Why do some children eat large amounts of candy yet maintain a healthy weight?
- Children have always eaten candy. Why are children today more obese than children of past generations?
- Even when parents keep kids away from candy, some still gain weight. Why?

If you cannot seem to find enough information on your topic to construct an argument, your topic might be too narrow.

Turn your topic into a thesis statement

Your **thesis** states your main idea. Much of the writing that you will do in college and later in your career will have an explicit thesis, usually stated near the beginning. The thesis announces your topic and indicates what points you want to make about that topic.

Your thesis should be closely tied to your purpose—to reflect on your own experience, to explain some aspect of your topic, or to argue for a position or course of action.

Reflective thesis	My experience in a government seminar where other students frequently and sometimes vehemently expressed conflicting views taught me that creating an atmosphere of tolerance can be just as important as passing laws to protect free speech.
Informative thesis	Courts in the United States have consistently upheld the right of free speech on public property if it is not obscene, threatening violence, or inciting violence.

Persuasive thesis
1. A public college or university should have the right to limit free speech in cases of overtly racist or anti-gay language because failing to address such abuses condones intolerance and threatens students' ability to learn.

2. A public college or university should not have the right to limit free speech, even when it is hateful, because speech that is not obscene or threatening violence is protected on public property.

STAYING ON TRACK

Evaluate your working thesis

Ask yourself these questions about your working thesis.

1. Is it specific?
2. Is it manageable in the length and time I have?
3. Is it interesting to my intended readers?

Consider the following examples:

Example 1

Eating disorders remain a serious problem on college campuses.

Specific? The thesis is too broad. Exactly who suffers from eating disorders? Is the problem the same for men and women?
Manageable? Because the thesis is not limited to a particular aspect of eating disorders, it cannot be researched adequately.
Interesting? The topic is potentially interesting, but most people know that many college students suffer from eating disorders. If you chose this topic, what could you tell your readers that they don't know already?

Revised thesis

Glamorous images of ultrathin people in the fashion industry, the movie industry, and other media are a contributing cause of eating disorders on college campuses because they influence young people to believe they are fat when in fact their weight is normal.

(continued on next page)

STAYING ON TRACK   *(continued)*

Example 2

> The United States entered World War II when the Japanese bombed Pearl Harbor on December 7, 1941.

Specific? The thesis is too narrow. It states a commonly acknowledged fact.

Manageable? A known fact is stated in the thesis, so there is nothing to research. The general topic of the attack on Pearl Harbor is too large for essay-length treatment.

Interesting? The attack on Pearl Harbor remains interesting to Americans (witness a recent Hollywood film that deals with the subject), but there is no topic to work from.

Revised thesis

> Although combat between the United States and Japan began at Pearl Harbor, the unofficial war began when President Roosevelt froze Japanese assets in the United States in July 1940 and later declared a commercial embargo.

These examples suggest that the key to writing an effective thesis is finding a topic that is neither too vast nor too narrow—and not obvious. You may have to adjust your working thesis more than once as you plan and begin drafting.

What makes an effective thesis statement

A thesis should not be a question. The thesis is your answer to your research question.

Not a thesis: *Why did England lose against Germany in the 2010 World Cup?* Along with being specific, manageable, and interesting, your thesis should also tell *what* you plan to argue and an indication of *how* you plan to argue without simply offering a list. Announce how you will be weighing and arranging the points in your argument.

Uninteresting: *The German team's youth, teamwork, and superior coaching led to their victory over England in the 2010 World Cup.* [the typical boring five-paragraph organization: youth, yada yada; teamwork, yada yada; *coaching*, yada yada]

Better: *Although the youth of the German players was certainly a factor in their victory over England in the 2010 World Cup, teamwork and superior coaching had a much greater role.* [arguing that one or two elements are more important breaks out of the five-paragraph formula]

Another way to narrow a potential thesis is to think about possible counterarguments. And then make sure you address these in your argument.

> *Many commentators and fans say that England would have beat*
> *Germany in the 2010 World Cup if the contested goal had been good;*
> *however, Germany's superior coaching and teamwork would have still*
> *made an English victory very difficult, if not impossible.*

A thesis should never be combative or confrontational.

> Combative: *England lost to Germany in the 2010 World Cup because*
> *the English team is made up of thugs and millionaires.*

Plan a Strategy

People who write frequently on the job or who make their living by writing have many different ways of producing a successful piece of writing.
Some may plan extensively in advance, either individually or as a team,
specifying exactly what will go in each section. Other writers find that
putting ideas into words often changes the ideas and generates new ones.
These writers know that writing drafts is a way of discovering their subject, and they count on one or two or more rewrites to get their document
into shape.

Consider making an outline

At some point in school you may have been required to produce a formal
outline to submit along with a paper. A **formal outline** typically begins
with the thesis statement, which anchors the entire outline. Each numbered or lettered item clearly supports the thesis, and the relationship
among the items is clear from the outline hierarchy.

> Thesis statement: The United States needs to take concrete steps to
> reduce obesity in children.
>
> I. A disturbing aspect of the trend of fatter Americans is that
>   children are increasingly obese.
>   A. More than one third of children 10–17 are obese.
>   B. Obese children suffer many serious health problems today.
>   C. America has had some success in addressing other teenage health
>   problems including smoking, drug use, and teen pregnancy.
> II. Many causes have been proposed for overweight America.
>   A. One proposed cause is the move to the suburbs, but the
>   population shift to the suburbs occurred before the rapid rise
>   in weight gain.
>   B. The couch potato argument is countered by increases in
>   exercise and participation in athletics.
>   C. The simple answer is that Americans consume about twice as
>   many calories per day as they need.

Consider using a working outline

A working outline is more like an initial sketch of how you will arrange the major sections. Jotting down main points and a few subpoints before you begin can be a great help while you are writing. You can read the complete essay that developed from these outlines in Section 26l.

Addressing Childhood Obesity

Section 1: Begin with a description of the problem including statistics on the rising number of obese children.

Section 2: Discuss the causes that have been proposed for childhood obesity.

Section 3: Discuss how the eating patterns of Americans have changed during the last thirty years and how portions served have increased.

Section 4: Examine how food is being marketed to children.

Section 5: Look at the role of parents and why parents often don't control much of the environment where children eat.

Section 6: Describe solutions: (1) restrict marketing of food to children, (2) educate parents and children, (3) promote healthier lifestyles.

Section 7: Discuss how these solutions can be implemented.

3e Compose a Draft

Skilled writers aim at producing a good draft—not a perfect draft. They know that they can go back and revise later.

Essays typically contain an introduction, body, and conclusion. You do not have to write these parts in that order, though. In your **introduction**, you can offer a short example that illustrates the problem being discussed. You can state a surprising fact. You can begin with a fascinating quotation. Your aim is to interest the reader and to let the reader know the topic of the paper, if not necessarily the thesis.

The **body** of the essay consists of the primary discussion. Remember to guide readers through the discussion by letting them know where you are going. Your readers need road signs to tell them where the discussion is taking them. Road signs are transition words and phrases such as *consequently*, *the third reason is . . .* , and *on the other hand*.

The last section, the **conclusion**, often repeats what has already been said. If the essay has been long and complex, sometimes this repetition is necessary, but usually the repetition is just that—annoying redundancy. The final paragraph does not have to repeat the main point. It can give a compelling last example or propose a course of action. It can ponder the larger significance of the subject under discussion. It can pose an important question for the reader to think about.

3f Write as a Member of a Team

Almost without exception, people in occupations that require a college education write frequently on the job, and much of that writing is done in collaboration rather than alone. The better you understand how to write effectively with other people, the more enjoyable and more productive the process will be for you.

Determine the goals and identify tasks and roles

- Write down the goals as specifically as you can and discuss them as a team.
- Determine what tasks are required to meet those goals. Write down the tasks and arrange them in the order they need to be completed.
- If the team does not possess the necessary skills and resources, adjust the goals to what you can realistically expect to accomplish.

Make a work plan

- Make a time line that lists the dates when specific tasks need to be completed and distribute it to all team members. Charts are useful tools for keeping track of progress.
- Assign tasks to team members.
- Revisit the team's goals often. To succeed, each team member must keep in mind what the team aims to accomplish.
- Decide on a process for monitoring progress. Set up specific dates for review and assign team members to be responsible for reviewing work that has been done.

Understand the dynamics of a successful team

- Teamwork requires some flexibility. Keep talking to each other along the way.
- It may be desirable to rotate roles during the project.

Deal with problems when they come up

- If a team member is not participating, find out why.
- If team members have different ideas about what needs to be done, find time to meet so that the team can reach an agreement.
- Get the team together if you are not meeting the deadlines you established in the work plan and devise a new plan, if necessary.

WRITING SMART

Overcome writer's block

1. **If you have an outline, put it on the computer screen or place it beside you.** The outline will give you prompts to help get you started.

2. **Begin writing what you know best.** If you don't know exactly where you are headed, the introduction can be the hardest section to write. The introduction can wait until last.

3. **Resist the urge to revise too soon.** It's more important to keep moving forward. If you stop to polish a section, you will lose momentum, and in the end you may discard that section anyway.

4. **If you get stuck, try working on another section.** Look again at your notes or outline.

5. **If you are still stuck, talk to someone about what you are trying to write.** If your campus has a writing center, talk to a consultant. Reading more about your subject can also help you to get moving again.

4 | Compose Paragraphs

QUICKTAKE

- Focus your paragraphs (see below)
- Organize your paragraphs (see p. 23)
- Make your paragraphs coherent (see p. 23)
- Write effective beginning and concluding paragraphs (see p. 26)

4a Focus Your Paragraphs

Readers expect sentences in a paragraph to be closely related to one another. Often writers will begin a paragraph with one idea, but other ideas will occur to them while they are writing. Paragraphs confuse readers when they go in different directions. When you revise your paragraphs, check for focus.

In the following example, notice how much stronger the paragraph becomes when we remove the sentences in red. They distract us from the subject, Royal Chitwan National Park in Nepal and how it is different from Western national parks.

> Like everything else in Nepal, Royal Chitwan National Park is different from Western notions of a park. It is a jungle between two rivers, with grass twenty to twenty-five feet tall growing in the swampy land along the rivers. Several rare or endangered species live in the park, including leopards, crocodiles, royal Bengal tigers, and the greater one-horned Asian rhinoceros. In fact, we saw several rhinos during our weeklong visit to the park. To my relief we saw all but one from the safety of an elephant's back. But the boundaries of the park restrict neither the Nepalis nor the animals. The Nepalis cross the river into the park to gather firewood and the tall grass, which they use to make their houses. Some even live within the park. The rhinos and deer raid the Nepalis' fields at night, and the leopards prey on their dogs and livestock. To keep the truce between these competitors, the army patrols the park, mostly to prevent poachers from killing the tigers and rhino. But confrontations do occur; the animals lose habitat and the Nepalis lose their crops and lives.

When to use explicit topic sentences

You were probably taught to begin a paragraph with a topic sentence. Topic sentences alert readers to the focus of a paragraph and help writers stay on topic. Topic sentences should explain the focus of the paragraph and situate it in the larger argument. However, topic sentences do not have to begin paragraphs, and they need not be just one sentence. You will decide what placement and length will best suit your subject.

Topic sentences at the beginning of a paragraph will quickly orient readers, preparing them for the sentences to come. Each sentence that follows elucidates the topic sentence.

Topic sentence at the beginning

We live in a world of risks so much beyond our control that it is difficult to think of anything that is risk free. Even the most basic human acts involve risk—having sex in an era of AIDS, eating in an era of genetically altered food, walking outdoors in an ozone-depleted atmosphere, drinking water and breathing air laden with chemicals whose effects we do not understand. Should we eat more fish in our daily diet? Nutritionists tell us that eating fish reduces the risk of heart disease. Other scientists, however, tell us that fish are contaminated with a new generation of synthetic chemicals.

When a paragraph builds to make a particular point, the topic sentence is more effective at the end of the paragraph.

Topic sentence at the end

We are continually being summoned to change ourselves for the better—through fitness programs, through various kinds of instruction, through advice columns, through self-help books and videos—and somehow we never quite measure up. The blame always comes back on us. If we had eaten better, or exercised more, or paid more attention to our investments, or learned a new skill, or changed our oil every 3,000 miles, then things would have turned out better. Very rarely do we ask how a different social organization might have made things better. Our society incorporates critical thinking without being much affected by the consequences of that thinking.

When to use implicit topic sentences

In some cases, particularly in narrative prose, writers omit explicit topic sentences because they would clash with the tone or style of the paragraph. Instead, these paragraphs use tightly connected, focused sentences to make the topic implicitly clear.

Implicit topic sentence

By the mid-1970s in the United States, the temporary advantage of being the only major power with its industries undamaged following World War II had evaporated, and rust-belt industries failed one after the other against competition from a revived Europe and an emergent

Asia. The United States seemed to be going the way of other historical world powers, where efficient trading nations beat out bloated military regimes. Japan appeared to be the model for a fast and light capitalism that the rest of the world would imitate. Just a few years later, however, the American decline reversed. The United States again became the economic leader of the world in the 1990s.

The implicit topic sentence is something like "The United States' economy appeared to be in rapid decline in the 1970s, only to bounce back to world leadership in the 1990s."

4b Organize Your Paragraphs

Well-organized paragraphs in essays usually follow a pattern similar to that of a well-organized paper, but in miniature. Chances are you'll use a combination of these strategies in order to get your point across.

- **Description.** Descriptive paragraphs are frequent in informative writing. The key is providing concrete details, including sights, sounds, smells, textures, and tastes.
- **Narration.** Narrative paragraphs are organized by time. They are essential for histories and any how-to writing.
- **Comparison and contrast.** Paragraphs of comparison assess one subject in terms of its relation to others, usually highlighting what they have in common. Contrasting paragraphs analyze differences between things.
- **Definition.** Paragraphs organized by definition usually begin with a term and then go on to list its defining characteristics, sometimes using examples.
- **Examples and illustrations.** Examples and illustrations make key points and ideas vivid and memorable.
- **Cause and effect.** Cause and effect paragraphs are structured in two basic ways: they can begin with causes and then state the effect or they can begin with the effect and then analyze the causes.
- **Classification and division.** Classifying places items into categories according to their similarities. Dividing takes a single item or concept and breaks it down into its component parts.

4c Make Your Paragraphs Coherent

You've no doubt heard that good writing should "flow," but what exactly does flow mean? Writing that flows is coherent, which means readers understand how sentences fit together. Repeating key phrases and signaling relationships with transitional terms help in building coherence.

Reiterate key terms and phrases

In the following paragraph, notice how the writer keeps the focus on *Facebook*, *privacy*, and *personal information* by repeating key terms.

> The value of Facebook as a corporate entity is based on its potential for advertising revenue. In November 2007, Facebook launched Beacon, an advertising system that sent targeted advertising and tracked activities of Facebook members on partner Web sites, even when the members were not logged in on Facebook. Facebook retreated to an opt-in privacy policy only after large-scale protests brought negative publicity, but activists discovered that Facebook was still collecting personal information from those who had opted out. In August 2008, the activists filed a class-action lawsuit against Facebook and its corporate marketing partners, alleging that Facebook's selling of members' personal information is a violation of federal and state privacy laws. Even though Facebook has shut down Beacon, there are no certain safeguards to protect privacy. The BBC program *Click* demonstrated that anyone with a basic knowledge of Web programming could gain access to restricted personal details on Facebook. Furthermore, the information does not go away. Facebook friends are literally friends forever because social networking sites are archived on servers.

Signal relationships with transitional terms

Transitional terms act like warning signs for readers, preparing them for what is around the bend. Notice how transitional terms signal the relationship of one sentence to the next.

> Critics of Web 2.0, including Tim Berners-Lee, who is credited with inventing the Web, dismiss the term as jargon, pointing out that the Web has always been about connecting people. Indeed, in the late 1970s and early 1980s, e-mail and hobby bulletin boards were the most popular features of the ARPANET, the predecessor of the Internet. More accurately, Web 2.0 marked a revival of the mid-1990s ebullience about the Internet as one of the greatest achievements in human history. For example, Kevin Kelly speaks of Web 2.0 in terms of religious transcendence: "The Machine provided a new way of thinking (perfect search, total recall) and a new mind for an old species. It was the Beginning."

STAYING ON TRACK

Use transitional terms

Be sure to use transitional terms accurately in order to signal the relationships between your sentences.

- **To enumerate:** again, also, and, as well, finally, furthermore, first, second, third, in addition, last, moreover, next, too

- **To generalize:** commonly, in general, for the most part, on the whole, usually, typically

- **To offer an example:** for example, for instance, indeed, in fact, of course, specifically, such as, the following

- **To situate in time:** after a month, afterward, as long as, as soon as, at the moment, at present, at that time, before, earlier, followed by, in the meantime, in the past, lately, later, meanwhile, now, preceded by, presently, since then, so far, soon, subsequently, suddenly, then, this year, today, until, when, while

- **To situate in space:** above, below, beyond, close to, elsewhere, far from, following, here, near, next to, there

- **To conclude:** as a result, hence, in conclusion, in short, on the whole, therefore, thus

- **To contrast:** although, but, even though, however, in contrast, conversely, in spite of, instead, nevertheless, nonetheless, on the one hand, on the contrary, on the other hand, still, though, yet

- **To compare:** again, also, in the same way, likewise, similarly

- **To signal cause or effect:** as a result, because, consequently, for this reason, hence, if, so, then, therefore, thus

- **To sum up:** as I said, as we have seen, as mentioned earlier, in conclusion, in other words, in short, in sum, therefore, thus

- **To concede a point:** certainly, even though, granted, in fairness, in truth, naturally, of course, to be fair, while it's true

Consider Paragraph Length

Paragraph breaks can signal various kinds of shifts:

- A new concept
- The next step in an argument
- The end of the introduction
- The beginning of the conclusion
- A new speaker in dialogue
- A shift in time or place
- A logical pause that gives the reader a breather

What is the ideal length for a paragraph? It depends on what sort of paragraphs you are writing. Business letter writers strive for short paragraphs so their readers can see the essential information at a glance. Academic writers need space to make and support arguments in depth. As a general rule, readers' eyes glaze over when they see paragraphs in an essay that stretch beyond one page. Nevertheless, too many short paragraphs are a sign that the piece lacks either weighty ideas or sufficient development.

4e Write Effective Beginning and Ending Paragraphs

Beginning and ending paragraphs of essays should behave like a smart suitor meeting "the parents" for the first time: dress well; start with a firm handshake; show you are thoughtful and personable; close on a strong note. Because readers are more likely to remember beginning and ending paragraphs, they are your best opportunity to make a good impression.

Understand what beginning paragraphs do

Effective beginning paragraphs convince the reader to read on. They capture the reader's interest and set the tone for the piece. In essays they often state the thesis and briefly map out the way the writing will progress from paragraph to paragraph. Sometimes the work of the beginning paragraph might be carried through three or four paragraphs. A writer might start with a memorable example, then use the example to launch the rest of the essay.

Start beginning paragraphs with a bang

Getting the first few sentences of an essay down on paper can be daunting. Begin with one of the following strategies to get your reader's attention:

A question

How valuable are snow leopards? The director of a zoo in Darjeeling, India, was fired when its snow leopard caught a cold and died.

A hard-hitting fact

Poaching is big business—to be exact, a six-billion-dollar business. The only illegal trade that's larger is drugs.

A pithy quotation

"That the snow leopard is," writes Peter Matthiessen, "that it is here, that its frosty eyes watch us from the mountains—that is enough." And it has to be enough because, while snow leopards are here now, they may not be here much longer.

Images

Tons of animal pelts and bones sit in storage at Royal Chitwan National Park in Nepal. The mounds of poached animal parts confiscated by forest rangers reach almost to the ceiling. The air is stifling, the stench stomach-churning.

An anecdote

The snow leopard stood so still in the frosty bushes, it wasn't until the goat squealed that we saw it. Its mottled white fur was now spattered with the goat's blood. Steam rose from the animal's wounds. We fumbled for our cameras, hoping to capture this terrible beauty.

A problem

Ecologists worry that the construction of a natural gas pipeline in Russia's Ukok Plateau will destroy the habitat of endangered snow leopards, argali mountain sheep, and steppe eagles.

A concisely stated thesis

If the governments of China and Russia don't soon act decisively, snow leopards will be extinct in a few years.

A contradiction or paradox

Snow leopards are tremendously versatile animals, strong enough to kill a horse and fast enough to chase down a hare. What they can't do is hide from poachers in Nepal and India. And this may be their downfall.

An odd, ridiculous, or unbelievable fact

Caterpillar fungus is a hot commodity. Traditional healers and their clients are willing to pay handsomely for illegally harvested ingredients for their treatments. As a result, demand for the fungus, along with other poached items like rhinoceros horns and snow leopard bones, drives a lucrative and destructive black market in endangered species.

Understand what ending paragraphs do

Ending paragraphs remind readers where they've been and invite them to carry your ideas forward. Use the ending paragraph to touch on your key points, but do not merely summarize. Leave your readers with something that will inspire them to continue to think about what you have written.

Conclude with strength

The challenge in ending paragraphs is to leave the reader with something provocative, something beyond pure summary of the previous paragraphs. The following are strategies for ending an essay:

Issue a call to action

Although ecological problems in Russia seem distant, students like you and me can help protect the snow leopard by joining the World Wildlife Fund campaign.

Discuss the implications of your argument

Even though the extinction of snow leopards would be a sad event, their end is not the fundamental problem. Instead, their precarious position is a symptom of a larger dilemma: Environmental damage throughout developing nations in Asia threatens their biodiversity.

Explain the applications of your argument

This study of snow leopard breeding behavior can inform captive breeding programs in zoos.

Make recommendations

Russia's creditors would be wise to sign on to the World Wildlife Fund's proposal to relieve some of the country's debt in order to protect the snow leopard habitat. After all, if Russia is going to be economically viable, it needs to be ecologically healthy.

Speculate about the future

Unless Nepali and Chinese officials devote more resources to snow leopard preservation, these beautiful animals will be gone in a few years.

Tell an anecdote that illustrates a key point

Poachers are so uncowed by authorities that they even tried to sell a snow leopard skin to a reporter researching a story on endangered species.

Describe a key image

As they watched the pile of confiscated furs and bones burn, Nepali forest rangers flashed proud smiles that seemed to say, "This time we mean business."

Offer a quotation that expresses the essence of your argument

Too often, developed nations impose their high-flown priorities, like protecting snow leopards and tigers, on developing nations. A Russian farmer summed up the disjunction succinctly. Tigers ate two cows in his herd of fifty. When he was compensated for the two he asked, "What's this? Can't the tiger come back and eat the remaining forty-eight?"

Ask a rhetorical question

Generally, the larger and more majestic (or better yet, cute) an endangered animal is, the better its chances of being saved. Bumper stickers don't implore us to save blind cave insects; they ask us to save the whales, elephants, and tigers. But snow leopards aren't cave bugs; they are beautiful, impressive animals that should be the easiest of all to protect. If we can't save them, do any endangered species stand a chance?

5 | Rewrite, Edit, and Proofread

QUICKTAKE

- Switch from writer to reader (see below)
- Learn strategies for rewriting (see p. 32)
- Respond to other writers' drafts (see p. 34)
- Proofread carefully (see p. 37)

5a Switch from Writer to Reader

Even the best writers often have to revise several times to get the result they want. To be able to revise effectively, you have to plan your time. You cannot revise a paper or a Web site effectively if you wait until the last minute to begin working. Allow at least a day to let what you write cool off. With a little time you will gain enough distance to "re-see" it, which, after all, is what *revision* means.

You must also have effective strategies for revising if you're going to be successful. The biggest trap you can fall into is starting off with the little stuff first. *Don't sweat the small stuff at the beginning.* When you see a word that's wrong or a misplaced comma, the great temptation is to fix it. But if you start searching for errors, it's hard to get back to the larger concerns.

Begin your revision by pretending you are someone who is either uninformed about your subject or holds an opposing view. If possible, think of an actual person and pretend to be that person. Read your draft aloud, all the way through. When you read aloud, you will probably hear clunky phrases and outright errors, but do no more at this stage than put checks in the margins so you can find these things later. Once again, you don't want to get bogged down with the little stuff.

Use these questions to evaluate your draft. Note any places where you might make improvements.

Does your paper or project meet the assignment?

- Look again at your assignment, especially at the key words, such as *analyze, define, evaluate,* and *propose.* Does your paper or project do what the assignment asks?
- Look again at the assignment for specific guidelines, including length, format, and amount of research. Does your work meet these guidelines?

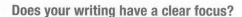

Does your writing have a clear focus?

- Does your project have an explicitly stated thesis? If not, is your thesis clearly implied?
- Is each paragraph related to your thesis?
- Do you get off the track at any point by introducing other topics?

Are your main points adequately developed?

- Do you support your main points with reasons and evidence?
- Can you add more examples and details that would help to explain your main points?
- Would additional research fill in gaps or make your case stronger?

Is your organization effective?

- Is the order of your main points clear to your reader? (You may want to make a quick outline of your draft if you have not done so already.)
- Are there any places where you find abrupt shifts or gaps?
- Are there sections or paragraphs that could be rearranged to make your draft more effective?

Do you consider your potential readers' knowledge and points of view?

- Do you give enough background if your readers are unfamiliar with your subject?
- Do you acknowledge opposing views that readers might have?
- Do you appeal to common values that you share with your readers?

Do you represent yourself effectively?

- To the extent you can, forget for a moment that you wrote what you are reading. What impression do you have of you, the writer?
- Does "the writer" create an appropriate tone?
- Has "the writer" done his or her homework?
- Is the writing project visually effective? Does "the writer" use headings and illustrations where they are helpful?

Do you conclude emphatically?

- Conclusions that only summarize tend to bore readers. Does your conclusion offer more than a review of ideas you have already fully discussed?
- Could you use your conclusion to discuss further implications?

- Could you conclude by making recommendations for change or improvement, or by urging readers to take action?
- Have you left your audience with a final provocative idea that might invite further discussion?

When you finish, make a list of your goals for the revision. You may have to write another draft before you move to the next stage.

5b Learn Strategies for Rewriting

Now it's time to go through your draft in detail. You should work on the goals you identified in your review.

1. Keep your audience in mind.   Step back and assess your paper from a reader's perspective. Paragraphs with strong, engaging openers keep an audience's attention, establish a writer's credibility, and above all intrigue readers so that they want to read on. Reread each of your paragraphs' opening sentences and ask yourself whether the language is strong and engaging enough to keep your reader interested in your argument from paragraph to paragraph.

2. Sharpen your focus wherever possible.   You may have started out with a large topic but find now that most of what you wrote concerns only one aspect of it. For example, you may have started with the large topic of privacy, but your focus now is on the current practice of some states' selling their driver's license databases to companies that build junk-mail lists. Revise your thesis and supporting paragraphs as needed.

3. Check that key terms are adequately defined.   What are your key terms? Are they defined precisely enough to be meaningful? If your argument relies on an abstract term such as *justice*, you are obligated to define it specifically.

4. Develop where necessary.   Key points and claims may need more explanation and supporting evidence. Look for opportunities to replace generalizations with specific details.

General statement	Grizzly bears and black bears look different.
Specific details	Rely on body shape rather than size and color to distinguish grizzly bears from black bears. Grizzlies have a hump above their front shoulders; black bears lack this hump. In profile, grizzlies have a depression between their eyes and nose, while black bears have a "Roman" profile with a straight line between the forehead and nose.

5. Check links between paragraphs.   Carefully crafted transitions between paragraphs accomplish two things: They explain to your reader why a paragraph logically follows the previous one, and they express the twists and turns of your thinking.

If you are struggling with your transitions, try this quick diagnostic: Underline the first and last sentences of each paragraph in your paper and then read these underlined sentences aloud to a friend. Do these sentences together make a logical and coherent argument? If not, spend more time figuring out the relationships between your ideas. Often you can express these relationships more clearly by choosing accurate transitional phrases such as *although, for example, on the other hand, in contrast, similarly,* and so on.

6. Consider your title.   An effective title makes the reader want to read what you have written. Be as specific as you can in your title, and if possible, suggest your stance. "Use of Anabolic Steroids" as a title is vague and bland, and it suggests a topic far too large to be handled well in a few pages. A stronger title would be "Is Andro a Food Supplement or a Steroid?"

7. Consider your introduction.   In the introduction you want to get off to a fast start and convince your reader to keep reading. If your subject is the use of steroids among high school students, don't start with an empty sentence like "Drugs are a big problem in today's high schools." Cut to the chase with a sentence such as "The National Institute of Drug Abuse reports that the number of high school students who abuse anabolic steroids rose steadily during the 1990s, while the perception of the risks involved declined." Then you might follow with a sentence that indicates how you will approach your topic: "My experiences as a high school athlete gave me insights into why students would risk future liver failure, cancer, strokes, heart attacks, and other serious health problems in order to gain a competitive advantage." In two sentences you have established your topic and your own authority to write about it.

8. Consider your conclusion.   Restating your claim usually isn't the best way to finish; conclusions that offer only summary tend to bore readers. The worst endings say something like "in my paper I've said this." In contrast, effective conclusions remind readers where your argument has taken them and then invite further discussion. Try to leave your reader with something interesting and provocative. Think about whether there is an implication you can draw or another example you can include that sums up your position. If you are writing a proposal, your ending might be a call for action.

9. Improve the visual aspects of your text.   Does the font you selected look attractive? Do you use the same font throughout? Are you consistent if you use more than one font? Do you include headings and subheadings to identify key sections of your argument? If you include statistical data, would presenting it in charts be effective? Would illustrations help to establish key points? For example, a map could be very useful if you are arguing about the location of a proposed new highway.

5c Respond to Other Writers' Drafts

Your instructor may ask you to review your classmates' drafts. Writing a response to the work of a fellow student may make you feel uncomfortable. You may think you don't know enough to say anything useful. Remember that you are only charged with letting the writer know how you—one of many potential readers—react.

But you do have to put forth your best effort. Responding to other people's writing requires the same careful attention you give to your own draft. To write a helpful response, you should go through the draft more than once. Before you begin, number the paragraphs if the writer has not already done so.

First reading

Read at your normal rate the first time through without stopping. When you finish you should have a clear sense of what the writer was trying to accomplish.

- **Main idea:** Write a sentence that summarizes what you think is the writer's main idea in the draft.
- **Purpose:** Write a sentence that summarizes what you think the writer was trying to accomplish in the draft.

Second reading

In your second reading, you should be most concerned with the content, organization, and completeness of the draft. Make notes as you read.

- **Introduction:** Does the writer's first paragraph effectively introduce the topic and engage your interest?
- **Thesis:** Where exactly is the writer's thesis? Note in the margin where you think the thesis is located.
- **Focus:** Does the writer maintain a focus on the thesis? Note any places where the writer seems to wander off to another topic.

- **Organization:** Are the sections and paragraphs ordered effectively? Do any paragraphs seem to be out of place? Do you note any abrupt shifts? Can you suggest a better order for the paragraphs?
- **Completeness:** Do any sections and paragraphs lack key information or adequate development? Where do you want to know more?
- **Sources:** If the draft uses outside sources, are they cited accurately? If there are quotations, are they used correctly and worked into the fabric of the draft?

Third reading

In your third reading, turn your attention to matters of audience, style, and tone.

- **Audience:** Who is the writer's intended audience? What does the writer assume the audience knows and believes?
- **Style:** Is the writer's style engaging? How would you describe the writer's voice?
- **Tone:** Is the tone appropriate for the writer's purpose and audience? Is the tone consistent throughout the draft? Are there places where another word or phrase might work better?

When you have finished the third reading, write a short paragraph on each bulleted item, referring to specific paragraphs in the draft by number. Then end by answering these two questions:

1. What does the writer do especially well in the draft?
2. What one or two things would most improve the draft in a revision?

5d Edit for Particular Goals

In your final pass through the text of your paper, you should concentrate on style and eliminate as many errors as you can.

1. Check the connections between sentences.   Notice how your sentences are connected. If you need to signal the relationship from one sentence to the next, use a transitional word or phrase.

2. Check your sentences.   If you noticed that a sentence was hard to read or didn't sound right when you read your paper aloud, think about how you might rephrase it. Often you can pick up problems with verbs, pronouns, and modifiers by reading aloud. If a sentence seems too long, you might break it into two or more sentences. If you notice a string of short sentences that sound choppy, you might combine them. If you notice run-on sentences or sentence fragments, fix them.

3. Eliminate wordiness.   Writers tend to introduce wordiness in drafts. Look for long expressions that can easily be shortened (*at this point in time* to *now*) and unnecessary repetition. Remove unnecessary qualifiers (*rather, very, somewhat, little*). See how many words you can take out without losing the meaning.

4. Use active verbs.   Any time you can use a verb other than a form of *be* (*is, are, was, were*) or a verb ending in *-ing,* take advantage of the opportunity to make your style more lively. Sentences that begin with *There is (are)* and *It is* often have better alternatives:

> **Draft**   It is true that exercising a high degree of quality control in the manufacture of our products will be an incentive for increasing our market share.

> **Revised**   If we pay attention to quality when we make our products, more people will buy them.

Notice too that the use of active verbs often cuts down on wordiness.

5. Use specific and inclusive language.   As you read, stay alert for any vague words or phrases. Check to make sure that you have used inclusive language throughout.

> ### Example of sentence-level editing to integrate quotations into your text
>
> In ~~the article,~~ "How to Feed the World," Michael Pollan ~~writes,~~ maintains that "agricultural lands make up a precious and finite resource; we should be using it to grow food for people, not for cars or cattle." ~~I definitely agree with Pollan that u~~ Using ten pounds of grain to make one pound of beef doesn't make sense when over a billion people are at the brink of starvation.
> ~~As for~~ Nevertheless, James McWilliams~~' article, he writes~~ ~~against~~ disagrees with Pollan~~'s argument.~~ about the need to feed as many people as possible. McWilliams believes that citizens shouldn't "have to give up tropical fruits altogether" just for the sake of saving resources.

5e Proofread Carefully

To proofread effectively, you have to learn to slow down. Some writers find that moving from word to word with a pencil slows them down enough to allow them to find errors. Others read backward to force themselves to concentrate on each word.

1. Know what your spelling checker can and cannot do.   Spelling checkers are the greatest invention since peanut butter. They turn up many typos and misspellings that are hard to catch. But spelling checkers do not catch wrong words (e.g., *to much* should be *too much*), missing endings (*three dog*), and other, similar errors. You still have to proofread carefully to eliminate misspellings.

2. Check for grammar and mechanics.   Nothing hurts your credibility with readers more than a text with numerous errors. Many job application letters get tossed in the reject pile because an applicant made a single, glaring error.

5f Learn to Edit the Writing of Others

Editing someone else's writing is easier than editing your own. In your own writing you know most of the time what you meant to say and often you don't notice where a reader might be stopped or jarred. But editing someone else's writing is also harder because you want to give the writer useful feedback without taking over the writer's task.

1. Make comments in the margins.   If you find a sentence hard to read, let the writer know. If you think a sentence is repetitive, let the writer know. If you think a word was left out, say so in the margin. Also let the writer know when a sentence is especially successful.

> *Word missing here?*
> *Same point as sentence 1?*
> *Can you join this sentence with the previous sentence?*
> *Vivid description!*

2. Use symbols to indicate possible problems.　Draw a wavy line under any phrase or sentence where you think there may be a problem. Even if you are not sure what the problem is, you can ask the writer to look carefully at a particular sentence. If you think a word is misspelled, draw a circle around it. If you think words can be deleted, put parentheses around them.

WRITING SMART

Standard proofreading symbols

Advanced editing requires learning standard proofreading symbols. Authors, editors, and printers use proofreader's marks to indicate changes. These marks are used in pairs: one mark goes in the text where the change is to be made and the other goes in the margin, close to the change.

Mark in the margin	Mark in the text
ℯ	Delete: take it out
◠	Close up: foot ball
∧	Caret: insert here
#	Insert a space: a word
⟋tr⟍	Transpose: the in beginning
∧	Add a comma: moreover we
∨	Add an apostrophe: Ellens books
∨ / ∨	Add double quotation marks: James Joyce's Clay
:	Add a colon: 3 45 p.m.
;	Add a semicolon: concluded however, we
⊙	Add a period: last call Next we
¶	Begin a new paragraph
No ¶	No new paragraph
sp	Spell out: 7 dwarfs => seven dwarfs
stet	Ignore correction: in the beginning

2 Analyzing, Reflecting, Informing, Arguing

You **can learn more and do more** with MyCompLab and with the eText version of *The Penguin Handbook*. To find resources in MyCompLab that will help you successfully complete your assignment, go to

Resources

Writing

● **Writing Purposes**
Writing to Analyze | Writing to Reflect | Writing to Inform | Writing to Argue or Persuade

● **Writing and Visuals**

Review the tutorials (Read, Watch, Listen) within each topic, then complete the Exercises and click on the Gradebook to measure your progress.

In the **eText version** of *The Penguin Handbook*, you will also find audio commentary provided by Lester Faigley for the sample student papers in this Part, as well as extra writing assignments.

6 | Write an Analysis

QUICK*TAKE*

- Analyze the context and the text (see below)
- Organize and write a rhetorical analysis (see p. 45)
- Analyze images and other kinds of visual texts (see p. 53)

6a Understand the Goal of a Rhetorical Analysis

The goal of a **rhetorical analysis** is to understand how a particular act of writing or speaking influenced particular people at a particular time. Rhetorical analysis is not limited to speaking and writing. The tools of rhetorical analysis have been applied to understanding how meaning is made by other human creations, such as art, buildings, photographs, dance, memorials, Web sites, music, advertisements—any kind of symbolic communication.

Writing a rhetorical analysis (also called "critical analysis" or "textual analysis") is frequently an assignment in college. A rhetorical analysis requires you to step back from a text and consider it from multiple perspectives. Writing a rhetorical analysis can give you a heightened awareness of a text and a better appreciation of what the author accomplished.

Understanding how communication works or fails to work is a worthy goal by itself, but rhetorical analysis has other benefits. It enables you to think about a text in more depth, to better understand the arguments it makes, and to appreciate how it is put together. In turn, this knowledge helps you in writing your own text. You will have a much better sense of what has been said and written about your subject and where you have opportunities to contribute your own ideas.

6b Analyze the Context and the Text

A rhetorical analysis begins with a text to analyze. If your instructor does not assign a text, select a text that has significance for you, either because it was important when it was written or it is about a subject that is important to you.

Think of your analysis as running on a continuum between considering the **context**—the relationship between the piece of writing or speaking and the larger society surrounding it—and the **text** itself—what it is about

The Gettysburg Address

■ Broader context

Executive Mansion.

Washington, 180

Four score and seven years ago our fathers brought forth, upon this continent, a new nation, conceived in liberty, and dedicated to the proposition that "all men are created equal"

Now we are engaged in a great civil war, testing whether that nation, or any nation so conceived, and so dedicated, can long endure. We are met on a great battle field of that war. We have come to dedicate a portion of it, as a final resting place for those who died here, that the nation might live. This we may, in all propriety do. But, in a larger sense, we can not dedicate — we can not consecrate — we can not hallow, this ground — The brave men, living and dead, who struggled here, have hallowed it, far above our poor power to add or detract. The world will little note, nor long remember what we say here; while it can never forget what they did here.

It is rather for us, the living, to stand here,

■ Text

■ Immediate context

and how it is designed. We can think of the context, which lies at one end of the continuum, in two senses. First, the **immediate context** refers to where the text was written and read or heard. For example, Abraham Lincoln delivered his 10-sentence, 272-word Gettysburg Address on November 19, 1863, at the dedication ceremony of a national cemetery, where he followed a speaker who had talked for two hours. Second, the **broader context** refers to the larger cultural and historical circumstances in which a text is produced and read. The broader context of the Gettysburg Address was, of course, the American Civil War, which had taken thousands of lives and was far from over at the time Lincoln spoke. Lincoln's brief remarks have been immortalized because he could envision an end to the war and a healing process.

At the other end of the continuum lies the text itself. We can consider a text as if it were a piece in a museum, where we closely scrutinize it. For example, if you look carefully at the language of the Gettysburg Address, you'll begin to appreciate Lincoln's tactics and skill. He says of his purpose: "We have come to dedicate a portion of that field, as a final resting place for those who here gave their lives that that nation might live."

But then he immediately turns this purpose on its head: "But in a larger sense, we can not dedicate—we can not consecrate—we can not hallow—this ground. The brave men, living and dead, who struggled here, have consecrated it, far above our poor power to add or detract." Lincoln's words become powerful because they defy expectation: we cannot consecrate the field because the field is already consecrated. Lincoln does not once refer to "the enemy" in the Gettysburg Address. Instead he says, "The brave men, living and dead, who struggled here." Even though the cemetery was a burying ground for Union soldiers, Lincoln's language invokes the heroism and sacrifice of both sides.

Often in the back and forth movement between text and context, you gain surprising insights about how a text achieves certain effects. These questions will help you get started in composing a rhetorical analysis.

Analyze the immediate context
Examine the author

- What is the author's purpose: to change beliefs? to inspire action? to teach about a subject? to praise or blame? to amuse?
- How did the author come to this subject?
- What else did the author write?

Examine the audience

- Who was the intended audience?
- What were their attitudes and beliefs about the subject?
- What were their attitudes and beliefs about the author?
- What does the author assume about the audience?

Analyze the broader context

Examine the larger conversation

- Why did this text appear at this particular time?
- What else has been said or written about this subject?
- What was going on at the time that influenced this text?

Examine the larger society

- What social, political, and economic influences can you find in the text?

Analyze the text

Examine the kind of text

- What kind of text is it: speech? essay? letter? editorial? advertisement?
- What is the medium: print? Web site? voice recording?

Summarize the content

- What is the author's main claim or main idea?
- How is the main claim or main idea supported?
- How is the text organized?

Examine the appeals

- *Ethos:* How does the author represent himself or herself? How does the author build or fail to build trust?
- *Logos:* What kinds of facts and evidence does the author use?
- *Pathos:* How does the author appeal to values shared with the audience?

Examine the language and style

- Is the style formal? informal? academic?
- Does the author use humor or satire?
- What metaphors are used?

6c Organize and Write a Rhetorical Analysis

When you have completed your initial analysis, you are ready to begin writing. Expect to discover additional ideas you can use in the analysis while you are writing and to go back and forth with your analysis.

---

1 Before you write

Take stock of your initial analysis
- If your selected text isn't working for the assignment, find one that works better.
- Look at your notes on the author, the audience, the circumstances of original publication or delivery, what other texts the author was responding to, and what else was going on at the time.
- Spend some time thinking about how to organize your analysis.

Think about your readers
- How much do readers know about your text? the author? the events surrounding the text? other texts like it?
- What will readers gain from reading your analysis?

---

2 Write an introduction

Begin your analysis by giving the necessary background
- Inform your readers about the author and why the author selected this particular topic.
- Tell readers about the original audience and the conversation about the topic that was going on at the time the text was written.

Make a claim
- Make a claim about how the text you are analyzing uses rhetoric for particular purposes.

3 | **Organize and write the body of your paper**

Support your claim with your detailed analysis of the text and context

- Give examples from the text to show how the author builds credibility with the audience, appeals to their values and beliefs, and convinces them with facts and evidence.
- Analyze the author's style, tone, and language, including metaphors.
- Analyze how the author responded to the immediate context and to the broader context.

4 | **Write a conclusion**

End with more than a summary

- Draw larger implications from your analysis.
- End with a vivid example from the text.

5 | **Revise, revise, revise**

Evaluate your draft

- Make sure your analysis meets the requirements of the assignment.
- Consider where you might provide more information about the context.
- Consider where you might provide more evidence supporting your claim about the text.
- When you have finished revising, edit and proofread carefully.

6d **Sample Rhetorical Analysis**

Jackson 1

Samantha Jackson

Professor Janis

English 100

4 May 2009

Rhetorical Strategies in Sojourner Truth's
"Ain't I a Woman?"

Sojourner Truth was born into slavery in 1797 and given the name Isabella Baumfree. Between 1797 and her escape from slavery in 1827, Isabella was "owned" by five different masters. Her last owner, John Dumont, sometimes bragged that she could "do a good family's washing in the night and be ready to go into the field the next morning, where she would do as much raking and binding as his best hands" (Washington 15). However, in 1817, the New York Legislature had passed a law that slavery in New York would end ten years later, on July 4, 1827. With this date fast approaching, Dumont decided to strike a deal with Isabella: he would release her one year early if she worked hard throughout 1826. Isabella agreed, but at the end of the year Dumont refused to release her. Enraged, Isabella escaped. After experiencing mystical visions from God on June 1, 1843, at the age of forty-six, Isabella changed her name to Sojourner Truth and pledged to "'sojourn' the land and speak the 'truth' of God's word" (Washington 15).

Jackson's opening provides background to help readers understand why Truth's personal history is relevant.

Jackson 2

This paragraph uses examples to show how slavery and the Women's Suffrage movement shaped the rhetorical situation.

As debates over slavery raged, Sojourner was sometimes harassed. Once she was told that a building she was scheduled to speak in would be burned down if she lectured there. She replied, "Then I will speak to the ashes" (Washington 11). As the Women's Suffrage movement became more popular in the late 1840s, Truth took notice. In 1851 she traveled to Akron, Ohio, to attend a women's rights convention aimed at getting Ohio to add more rights for women in its state constitution. Many Ohioans were against this goal. Many local men, including several ministers, attended the convention just to heckle speakers. Sojourner Truth delivered her famous "Ain't I a Woman?" speech in this intense atmosphere. In her spontaneous lecture, Truth used her own physical and intellectual credibility to make powerful emotional appeals and convincing logical claims. Her arguments redefined the word "womanhood" and made direct connections between women's rights and the abolition of slavery for an all-white audience. Her powerful speech was so successful that her words are the main reason this convention is remembered today.

In these two sentences, Jackson makes a claim about the persuasive power of Truth's speech.

Jackson demonstrates how Truth established her relationship to her audience in the opening of her speech.

When Truth began to speak, her words displayed her experience and wisdom. Rather than addressing her audience as "Ladies and gentlemen," or, "Members of the convention," Truth begins this way: "Well children, when there is so much racket there must be something out of kilter" (268). By using the word "children" to address her adult, white audience, Truth draws attention to her age and wisdom, and at the same time proves

Jackson 3

that she is equal to, not subservient to, these white adults. She also refers to the heated arguments between the women and men attending the convention as "so much racket," a statement that takes her out of the arguments she is witnessing and therefore makes her seem like a voice of reason in a chaotic environment.

Another reason Truth was such an effective speaker at this convention was how she used humor to break down arguments against women's rights. Just after she notes that the convention has become a "racket," she offers a tongue-in-cheek observation: "I think that 'twixt the negroes of the South and the women at the North, all talking about rights, the white men will be in a fix pretty soon" (268). Although Truth is making the serious point that when white women and African Americans get equal rights, white men will be less powerful, she uses humor to break up some of the tension of the moment.

> Jackson discusses the humor employed by Truth to defuse tension and put her audience at ease.

Once Truth has her audience listening through this light tone, she begins to use her status as a former slave woman to bring out feelings of guilt and shame in her audience. She builds her argument slowly. First, she shows the fallacy in the argument that women do not need rights because male chivalry protects them from harm and guarantees them protection. Truth restates this argument: "That man over there says that women need to be helped into carriages, and lifted over ditches, and to have the best place everywhere." She points out that as a poor, black woman, she is excluded from this definition of womanhood: "Nobody ever helps

> This paragraph demonstrates how Truth built her argument by drawing on personal experience and by using emotional appeals to her audience's sense of shame.

Jackson 4

me into carriages, or over mud puddles, or gives me any
best place! And ain't I a woman?" (268).

She next shows the connection between women's
rights and abolition by referring to the unique horrors
of womanhood under slavery: "I could work as much
and eat as much as a man—when I could get it—and
bear the lash as well! And ain't I a woman? I have
borne thirteen children, and seen them most all sold
off to slavery, and when I cried out with a mother's
grief none but Jesus heard me" (268-69). By using
emotional appeals to produce shame in her audience,
Truth connects women's rights and abolition. She
argues that people who believe women should be
protected and treated to "the best" are obliged to treat
all women, black and white, with "chivalry."

Jackson analyzes
Truth's use of logic
to expose fallacies
in common argu-
ments against
women's rights.

Although Truth is appealing to her audience's
shame here, and asking them to reconsider their
positions on women's rights and abolition, her main
way of arguing is through logic. Truth tries to expose
the flaws in arguments against women's rights, and also
in arguments against equal rights for African Americans.
First, Truth points out that claiming that chivalry makes
rights unnecessary for women is illogical because her
audience's definition of "woman" is flawed. Women, she
argues, are not only people who need assistance getting
into fancy carriages, or those who wear expensive
clothes that must be protected from mud puddles.
Women are also people like her, who "have ploughed
and planted, and gathered into barns" (268).

Jackson 5

Truth's most powerful logical argument for this audience of mostly religious men is her argument about God, Eve, and women's rights. She first restates their argument: that "women can't have as much rights as men, 'cause Christ wasn't a woman." Then she exposes the flaws in that argument: she asks, "Where did your Christ come from?" and answers, "From God and a woman. Man had nothing to do with Him." Then, turning to her audience's argument that women should not have rights because of Eve's sins, she asks, "If the first woman God ever made was strong enough to turn the world upside down all alone, these women together ought to be able to turn it back, and get it right side up again!" She is arguing here that if these men credit the first woman, Eve, with such a huge amount of power, then they should see that other women are equally powerful and should be given equal rights. If Eve turned the world upside down, these women can turn it right-side up again. Truth argues: "And now they is asking to do it, the men better let them."

Finally, Truth addresses the topic of intelligence: "Then they talk about this thing in the head; what's this they call it?" (269). An audience member reminds her that the word is "intellect," and she replies, "That's it, honey." She then asks, "What's that got to do with women's rights or negro's rights?" (269). This question is deceptive. Although at first it seems like Truth is agreeing with sexist notions when she characterizes women's minds as capable of "hold[ing]

> Jackson describes the process Truth used to counter arguments that the Bible authorized male supremacy.

Jackson 6

Jackson concludes with a powerful example of Truth's wit.

but a pint" while male minds can "hold a quart," it becomes clear that she is using flattery as a manipulative tool: "if my cup won't hold but a pint, and yours holds a quart, wouldn't you be mean not to let me have my little half measure full?" Clearly, a speaker who can develop such convincing logical arguments is just as intelligent as the audience members whose arguments she exposed as flawed. It is for this reason that Sojourner Truth's "Ain't I a Woman?" speech made such an impression then, and continues to do so today.

Jackson 7

Works Cited

Truth, Sojourner. "Ain't I a Woman?" *Argument in America: Essential Issues, Essential Texts*. Ed. Jack Selzer. New York: Longman, 2004. 268-69. Print.

Washington, Margaret, ed. *The Narrative of Sojourner Truth*. New York: Random, 1993. Print.

To hear audio commentary on this piece of writing, visit this page of the eText at **www.mycomplab.com**.

6e   Analyze Images and Other Kinds of Visual Texts

The word *text* typically brings to mind words on a printed page. But in the sense that anything that can be "read" can be a text, then nearly everything is a text. We see hundreds of visual texts every day distributed on television, the Web, films, newspapers, advertisements, product labels, clothing, signs, buildings—indeed, on nearly everything. We can analyze how these images create meaning by the same means we use to analyze verbal texts—by examining the relationship between the text and its contexts.

Some culturally significant images, significant at least at the time they were created, are public art and public sculpture. On one of the bridge houses of the Michigan Avenue Bridge crossing the Chicago River in downtown Chicago is a large relief sculpture depicting the massacre of settlers fleeing Fort Dearborn in 1812. The size of the sculpture and its placement on the busiest and most famous street in Chicago attests to its significance at the time it was commissioned.

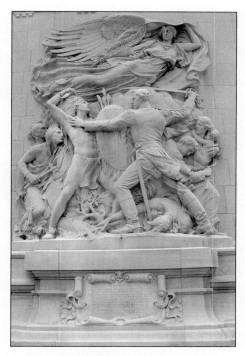

■ Relief sculpture of the Fort Dearborn Massacre, on the Michigan Avenue Bridge, Chicago

Two central figures—an American soldier and a Potawatomi Indian—battle as an angel hovers above. On the left another Indian is stealthily approaching, crouched with a tomahawk in hand. On the right a man shields a woman and a child from the threat. The sculpture uses a familiar stereotype of American Indians to make a visual argument: The Indians are attacking because they are bloodthirsty and sneaky; the innocent settlers bravely resist. The sculpture does not speak to the circumstances of the massacre: The Potawatomis allied with the British during the War of 1812 to resist settlers who were taking their land, and the settlers waited too long to evacuate Fort Dearborn in the face of growing numbers of Indians surrounding the fort.

It's not surprising that the sculpture represents the settlers as heroic. The bridge and monument were part of a grand plan, begun in 1909, to enhance Chicago's waterfront. Thus, the monument plays its part in obscuring the actual history of the area. Viewers who are unaware of the facts may feel a sense of patriotic pride in the actions of the soldier and the woman. Viewers who are familiar with the whole story may take a different view.

7 | Write a Reflection

QUICK*TAKE*

- Find a topic that has special significance for you (see below)
- Identify a focus for your reflection (see p. 56)
- Write a title, write an introduction, and determine your organization (see p. 56)

Find a Reflective Topic

Reflecting on experience

Reflections, whether they appear in print, video, or any other medium, often deal with personal and private experiences, but they do not have to be based on explicitly personal topics. In some cases, being too personal or confessional can limit a writer's ability to connect to his or her audience. The goal of reflection should not be simply to vent pent-up feelings or to expose secrets. Instead, the goal should be to allow the audience to share with the writer his or her discovery of the significance of an experience.

Discovering a reflective topic

Listing is a good way to identify possibilities for reflective essays based on memories.

- List five people who have been significant in your life.
- List five events that have been important in your life. Think about one-time events, such as getting a scholarship, and recurring events, such as a yearly family get-together.
- List five places that have been important in your life.
- Now look through your lists and check the items that are especially vivid.

Another set of possibilities can be drawn from looking at family photographs (see Melissa Dodd's reflection on a family photograph in Section 7d). You can also write about objects that have special significance for your family or just for you, such as a scrapbook that you kept in elementary school.

Not all reflective topics are about the past. You can visit a place or go to an event and focus on your interaction with the place or event instead of on the place or event itself.

7b Identify a Focus

Reflections do not often have a formal thesis, but they typically have a **focus** that makes the reflection coherent by communicating a central idea to readers. Why is this experience important? Why is it memorable? In short, why is it worth writing about? Often the focus comes not in the big idea but in the small details that call for reflection.

7c Organize and Write a Reflection

When you have a topic and a focus that communicates the importance of the experience or event to your readers, then it's time to write your reflection. You might not follow this order as writing is often a back-and-forth process.

1 | **Before you write**

Think about your readers
- What attitudes are your readers likely to have about your subject?
- How can you make readers care about your subject?
- What will readers gain from reading your reflection?

2 | **Write an introduction**

Engage your readers quickly
- Choose a title that will interest readers.
- Start with the incident, place, or person that is the focus.

3 Organize and write the body of your paper

Should you use a chronological organization?
- Use chronological order to let readers re-live events with you.

Should you use a conceptual organization?
- Use conceptual order to show connections and links between ideas.

Communicate experiences with details
- Give specifics such as dates and names to provide background information.
- Augment visual details with other sensory details (smells, sounds, tastes, tactile feelings).
- Choose specific words to convey details.
- Identify people by more than how they look. Think about typical mannerisms, gestures, and habits.
- If people interact, use dialogue to convey the interaction.

Consider your voice and tone
- Your writing should sound like you. Be yourself.
- If your writing sounds like the voice that makes announcements in the airport, try rewriting as you would talk.
- Let yourself go in the first draft. If you become excessive, you can adjust the language when you revise.

4 Write a conclusion

End by inviting further reflection
- Share any discoveries you made in the process of reflecting.
- Avoid a simple moral lesson, but your conclusion should help your readers to make sense of your reflection.

5 Revise, revise, revise

Evaluate your draft
- Make sure your reflection meets the requirements of the assignment.
- Consider how you might sharpen the focus and significance of your reflection.
- Consider where you might provide more details, dialogue, or background information.
- When you have finished revising, edit and proofread carefully.

7d Sample Reflective Essay

In her film studies class, Melissa Dodd was asked to read excerpts from Michelle Citron's *Home Movies and Other Necessary Fictions*, in which Citron asks why home movies of her childhood do not correspond with her memories of her family. For a course assignment, Melissa Dodd decided to write her own reflection on a family snapshot. The focus of Dodd's reflection is that the objects in a photograph give clues not only to the dynamics of the moment the photo claims to capture, but also to what is missing.

Dodd 1

Melissa Dodd

Professor Mendoza

Introduction to Film

25 April 2009

My Sister and Me on Grandma's Lap

This picture was taken at my paternal grandmother's house in Enid, Oklahoma. I'm on Grandma's lap, and my sister Rhonda is on the floor.

Dodd begins with a descriptive paragraph, bringing the reader into the photo.

Dodd 2

I believe this picture was taken around 1989 or 1990 because I look about two or three years old. It is after supper, and Grandma is reading to me.

This photograph is interesting to me because it reflects two points that Michelle Citron makes in her book, *Home Movies and Other Necessary Fictions*. First, the person taking the picture is asserting control over the interpretation of the memory. Second, there are clues within the frame that signify what has actually been left out of the frame. The item missing from this picture is my mother.

The summary of Citron's *Home Movies* is used to pose a question about why Dodd's mother was missing from the photo.

My father took the picture in order to show me wearing the moccasins my maternal grandfather had just bought for me when we visited him in Holdenville, Oklahoma. My mother had remained there, while we went on to Enid. She rarely came with us to visit Grandma because they did not get along. Like her own mother, my mother could be moody, distant, and bad-tempered. Grandma, on the other hand, was somewhat meddlesome, but affectionate, and over-indulgent with us kids. Consequently, they argued over how we should be treated.

A detail in the photo, the moccasins, leads to a description of conflict between mother and grandmother.

Grandma is pointing to the moccasins, which signify my mother's absence. In some ways, the photo is a conciliatory gesture; my father is acknowledging his in-laws' contribution to my happiness and well being. In another, less obvious way, it is an act of spite. Since my mother refused to be there, my father replaced her with his own mother in this happy family scene he has created.

Dodd steps back to reflect on the photograph in the context of what was happening in the family.

Dodd 3

Dodd examines how her sister was affected by family conflicts by contrasting her appearance in this photo with her appearance in others.

Her absence is also highlighted by the presence of my sister, Rhonda, who was about nine or ten. When I was a baby, Rhonda and I were always in pictures together. Usually she's playing "mommy" and holding me on her lap. She was very protective of me and would not let me out of her sight. Taking the role of my guardian often got her in trouble, especially when my mother's temper flared. Here, she looks silly and relaxed, more childlike than she does in other family pictures.

Citron argues that since they are selective and often taken by men, home movies and family photographs assert a balance of power within the family and strive to promote the "good" memory of family: "parents in control, men in charge, families together" (15). What she does not overtly mention, however, is that these created memories are also punitive. It is the people, things, or events that disrupt the image of the ideal family that are banished from the frame. Importantly, my mother's temper and her refusal to make peace with my grandmother led to her omission from my father's carefully constructed scene of domestic tranquillity.

Dodd moves one step further to explore how good memories are manufactured in family photographs by banishing what is disruptive.

In the end, what is most significant is the fact that this manufactured memory works. Until I began to look at this picture through Citron's eyes, I simply had a memory of my Grandma's house—its warmth, and that it always smelled like bacon and Dr. Pepper. Unfortunately, this is not the whole picture. But this pleasant memory does not have to go away just because I now see things in more detail.

Dodd 4

By recognizing what is missing, I hope I can work to
reconcile the fiction to the reality and come to a more
complete understanding of my family's dynamics.

Dodd 5

Work Cited

Citron, Michelle. *Home Movies and Other Necessary
Fictions*. Minneapolis: U of Minnesota P, 1999 Print.

*To hear audio commentary on this piece of writing, visit this page
of the eText at* **www.mycomplab.com.**

8 | Write an Informative Essay

QUICKTAKE

- Find a topic that explains or one that explores questions and problems (see below)
- Narrow your topic and write a thesis (see p. 63)
- Identify your main points and decide how to best present them (see p. 64)

Find an Informative Topic

Many of the writing tasks assigned in college are informative—from lab reports and essay exams to analyses of literature, research papers, and case studies. Look at your assignment for key words such as *study, analyze, explain*, and *explore*, which indicate what kind of writing you are expected to produce. Informative writing has four primary functions: to report new or unfamiliar information; to analyze for meaning, patterns, and connections; to explain how to do something or how something works; and to explore questions and problems.

Reporting information

Reporting information takes many forms, ranging from reports of experimental research and reports of library research to simple lists of information. In one sense, writing to reflect (Chapter 7) and writing to persuade (Chapter 9) also report information. The main difference is that the focus of a report and other informative kinds of writing is on the subject, not on the writer's reflections or on changing readers' minds or on getting them to take action. Writers of reports usually stay in the background and keep their language as neutral as possible.

Analyzing meaning, patterns, and connections

Writers not only report what they read and observe. They often construct meaning through selecting what and what not to include and in organizing that information. Sometimes this construction of meaning is made explicit as **analysis**. The complexity of the world we live in requires making connections. For example, advertisers know that certain kinds of ads (for example, ads that associate drinking beer with social life) sell the product, but often they do not know exactly how these ads work or why some ads are more effective than others.

Explaining how

Often what you know well is difficult to explain to others. You may know how to solve certain kinds of difficult problems, such as how to fix a problem in your car's electrical system, but if you have to tell a friend how to do it over the phone, you may quickly become very frustrated. Often you have to break down a process into steps that you can describe in order to explain it. Explaining a process sometimes requires you to think about something familiar in a new way.

Exploring questions and problems

Not all informative writing is about topics with which you are familiar or ones that you can bring to closure. Often college writing involves issues or problems that perplex us and for which we cannot come to a definitive conclusion. The goal in such writing is not the ending but the journey. Tracing the turns of thought in a difficult intellectual problem can result in writing far beyond the ordinary. Difficult issues often leave us conflicted; readers appreciate it when we deal honestly with those conflicts.

Finding a topic

When your general subject is specified in your assignment, you can make your work more enjoyable by choosing a specific topic that is either more familiar to you or that you find particularly interesting. Your level of engagement in a topic can have a real impact on your readers' level of interest. Here are guidelines you can use when choosing a topic.

- Choose a topic you will enjoy writing about.
- Choose a topic that readers will enjoy reading about.
- Choose a topic for which you can make a contribution of your own, perhaps by viewing something familiar in a new way.
- If you choose an unfamiliar topic, you must be strongly committed to learning more about it.

8b Narrow Your Topic and Write a Thesis

A central difficulty with writing to inform is determining where to stop. For any large subject, even a lifetime may be insufficient. The key to success is to limit the topic. Find a topic you can cover thoroughly in the space you have. Broad, general topics are nearly impossible to cover in an essay of five pages. Look for ways of dividing large topics such as *the use of steroids among college students* into smaller categories and select one that is promising. *Why college athletes ignore the risks of steroids* is a topic that you are more likely to be able to cover in a short paper.

Often your readers will lack initial interest in your topic. If you ignore their lack of interest, they in turn will likely ignore you. Instead, you can take your readers' knowledge and interest into account when you draft your thesis. For example, someone who knows a lot about birds in the parks of your city might write this informative thesis:

> Watching birds in urban areas is interesting because unusual birds often show up in city parks.

It doesn't sound like a topic that most college students would find as interesting as the writer does. But if the writer puts the audience's attitude in the foreground, challenging them to consider a subject they have likely not thought much about, a college audience might read beyond the title:

> Although most college students think of bird watching as an activity for retired people, watching birds gives you a daily experience with nature, even in urban areas.

This thesis also gives the writer a stance from which to approach the topic.

8c Organize and Write an Informative Essay

Successful reporting of information requires a clear understanding of the subject and a clear presentation. How much information you need to include depends on your readers' knowledge of and potential interest in your topic. You might not follow this order as writing is often a back-and-forth process.

---

1 | **Before you write**

Think about your readers
- What do your readers already know about the subject?
- What questions or concerns might they have about your subject?
- What is their attitude toward the subject? If it is different from yours, how can you address the difference?

Review your thesis and scope
- When you learn more about your topic, you should be able to identify one aspect or concept that you can cover thoroughly.

2 | Write an introduction

Engage your readers quickly
- Write a title and an introduction that will make readers take an interest in your topic.

3 | Organize and write the body of your paper

Think about your main points
- Use an idea map to organize your main points (see Section 2b).
- Make a working outline to identify your main points and the relationships among them.

Decide how your points are best ordered
- Chronological organization often works best for a topic that occurs over time.
- Conceptual organization focuses on how important concepts are related.
- Compare and contrast organization helps to show how two things are similar or different.

4 | Write a conclusion

End with more than a summary
- Make a point that readers can take away.
- Raise an interesting question.
- End with a vivid example.

5 | Revise, revise, revise

Evaluate your draft
- Examine the order of your ideas and reorganize if necessary.
- Add detail or further explanation where needed.
- When you have finished revising, edit and proofread carefully.

WRITING SMART

Use visuals to report information

Complex statistical data can often be presented effectively in a table or a chart. Other visuals such as maps and photos can help readers to understand your subject. Be sure to provide the sources of your data and the source of any visual that you do not create.

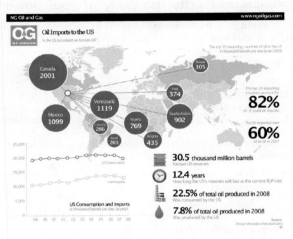

■ *O&G* magazine published this graphic created by BP's Energy Information Administration. Why do you think BP created this graphic? Is the purpose to persuade as well as to inform?

8d ## Sample Informative Essay

Haddad 1

Akilah Haddad

Professor Swift

English 1102

5 October 2010

Protecting Your Privacy on the Internet:

Is There an App for That?

Early in 2010, Google and Facebook found themselves in trouble for breaching the public's trust with their privacy policies. Google caught the attention of privacy regulators for collecting data as they

Haddad's title, given as a question, piques reader interest.

Haddad 2

captured images for its Street View project. Facebook
enraged its users by not only altering its privacy
controls to make more of its users' personal data
public by default, but also by creating a
complicated interface for changing privacy
options (Hartley). In addition, Facebook unveiled
a service called "Instant Personalization," which
automatically shares information about customers with
external sites unless the customer opts out, site by site
(Manjoo). The result of these two events is a revival of
the fear that, as the *Economist* puts it, "online privacy
is being trampled underfoot as Internet behemoths
race to grab as much data as possible" ("Dicing").
And the behemoths want these data because of the
potential for huge profits, especially for Facebook,
which generates most of its revenue from targeted
advertisements based on users' demography (Robinson).

Haddad's thesis
is given in the
last two sen-
tences of the
first paragraph.

    The debates about Internet privacy are nothing
new; they have been raging since Web sites started
leaving "cookies" on users' hard drives to trace their
Internet behavior. At the center of this debate has
been the question of who is responsible for making
sure that information collected by Web sites is not
misused—the government, the Internet companies, or
consumers themselves. Vice President Albert Gore was
an early advocate of government intervention, and he
announced an "Electronic Bill of Rights" in 1998,
defining privacy as a basic human right protected by
the Constitution and numerous federal laws (Broder).
In light of the recent Google and Facebook scandals,

Haddad 3

other people, such as social-networking expert Danah
Boyd, are again thinking that the Internet should be
regulated by the government, perhaps as a utility.

    Advocates of self-regulation believe that since
Internet companies are financially motivated to make
consumers feel secure about their Internet use, they
should be trusted to police themselves. However,
if self-regulation is to work, there have to be
consequences for bad behavior, which leads to the next
question: How can self-regulation be enforced? TRUSTe,
a program operated by a nonprofit that grants certificates
to Web sites posting a privacy statement that meets
TRUSTe's standards and submitting to an audit, was
created as a partial solution to this issue ("Tailed").

    In addition, companies have to recognize their
culpability, which they are often reluctant to do. Google,
for example, apologized for its mistake, but the data
collection had been going on for several years. Google
did not admit to violating laws until German officials
asked them to come clean (Heining). The CEO of
Facebook, Mark Zuckerberg, was also reluctant to accept
blame for his company's actions, arguing that Facebook
should be entirely public. He believes that most users are
agreeable to Facebook being open by default because, as
he says, "people have really gotten comfortable not only
sharing information and different kinds, but more openly
and with more people. That social norm is just something
that has evolved over time" (Kirkpatrick).

    These controversies have spurred discussion about
whether or not the idea of privacy itself has changed,

*Haddad
provides an
analysis of the
problems of
regulating the
Internet.*

Haddad 4

and consequently, how responsible consumers are for
protecting themselves. Like Zuckerberg, Facebook's
Barry Schnitt believes that the world is becoming
more open, as evidenced by Twitter, My Space, and
reality TV (Kirkpatrick). In his book *Delete*, Viktor
Mayer-Schönberger warns of the costs of what he calls
the "digital panopticon," in which every move and
decision is recorded into digital memory, incapable of
being forgotten. Thus, compromising photos, candid
statements about our jobs, embarrassing searches,
and controversial acts can be used against us in a
variety of contexts (11). Since users voluntarily
disclose information about themselves every day, "in
that strict sense, they bear responsibility for the
consequences of their disclosures" (5). However, there
are also times when users disclose without knowing,
as is the case with the recent Facebook and Google
privacy scandals. Are users then still responsible for
not adequately securing their networks, as in the case
with Google, or not being vigilant enough about their
privacy settings, as in the case with Facebook?

These questions still consider privacy a matter
of culture, however. Issues become more thorny when
privacy enters the legal realm. Helen Nissenbaum
in *Privacy in Context* argues that the changes to the
Internet have happened too fast for us to be able to
accurately assess how harmful the aggregation and
dissemination of information will be. In particular,
increasing sophistication of both software and users
has made what was once rather boring and disconnected

A conceptual
organization has
been used to
explain the threats
to privacy and
how both Face-
book and Google
have responded
to critics of the
policies.

Haddad 5

information gathering dust in databases vulnerable to being "remixed" into full, recognizable profiles of individuals by savvy programmers and hackers (17). In addition, some of Google's new Map features have raised unexpected questions in law enforcement. Specifically, why do you need a warrant to search a property for drugs when Google Earth and Street View can show you what's growing in someone's yard? And is evidence gathered in this way admissible in court (Morozov)?

As the Internet continues to grow and change, these debates over responsibility will continue. Regarding government intervention, experts agree that it is unlikely that the Internet will be regulated as a utility since sites such as Facebook and Google are not essential services, nor do they enjoy a monopoly. In addition, regulating the Internet in this way could restrict further innovation ("Dicing"). What will probably happen in the next two years, however, is some form of FCC regulation ("Price"). As for the companies themselves, it is in their best interest to keep consumers happy, which was certainly the case for Facebook. Even though the activist-initiated "Quit Facebook Day" only saw 31,000 users out of 450 million follow through on their pledge to quit the site on May 31, 2010, it was still enough to convince Zuckerberg to address publicly its new privacy policies and make changes, including creating one single page where users can control who sees their information. In addition, Facebook also enabled users to block

Haddad 6

outside software developers from accessing users'
personal information (Hartley). In fact, according to
Tom Spring in *PC World* magazine, on several other
occasions from 2007 to the present, public pressure has
led Facebook to change policies and page layouts. But
the problem still remains that, despite these lessons,
Facebook continues to engage in practices that enrage
consumers. As Spring points out, Facebook would
be "well served to be more pro-active about
communicating changes to its terms and services rather
than reactive." Until that happens, it remains the user's
job to police what is being made of his or her
information online.

Haddad con-
cludes with a key
point for readers
to take away—
namely it is up to
each of us to
safeguard our
privacy on the
Internet.

Haddad 7

Works Cited

Boyd, Danah. "Facebook Is a Utility; Utillities Get
Regulated." *apophenia*. N.p., 15 May 2010. Web.
13 Sept. 2010.

Broder, John M. "Gore to Announce 'Electronic Bill of
Rights' Aimed at Privacy." *New York Times* 14 May
2010, late ed.: 16. *LexisNexis Academic*. Web. 15
Sept. 2010.

"Dicing with Data: Facebook, Google and Privacy."
Economist 22 May 2010, US ed.: 16. *LexisNexis
Academic*. Web. 15 Sept. 2010.

Haddad 8

Manjoo, Farhad. Interview with Neal Conan. *Talk of the Nation*. NPR, 12 May 2010. Radio.

Hartley, Matt. "Facebook Founder Mark Zuckerberg to Blame for Privacy Mess." *National Post*. National Post, 28 May 2010. Web. 14 Sept. 2010.

Heining, Andrew. "What's So Bad about the Google Street View Flap?" *The Christian Science Monitor*. csmonitor.com, 15 May 2010. Web. 16 Sept. 2010.

Kirkpatrick, Marshall. "Facebook's Zuckerberg Says that the Age of Privacy is Over." *ReadWriteWeb*. N.p., 9 Jan. 2010. Web. 14 Sept. 2010.

Mayer-Schönberger, Viktor. *Delete: The Virtue of Forgetting in the Digital Age*. Princeton: Princeton UP, 2009. Print.

Morozov, Evgeny. "e-outed." Rev. of *Privacy in Context* by Helen Nissenbaum. *Times Literary Supplement* 12 Mar. 2010: 8. Print.

"The Price of Privacy." *On the Media*. Natl. Public Radio. WNYC New York, 28 May 2010. Web. 14 Sept. 2010.

Robinson, James. "Facebook Users Revolt Against Mark Zuckerman Over Privacy." *Guardian*. Guardian.co.uk, 23 May 2010. Web. 15 Sept. 2010.

Spring, Tom. "Quit Facebook Day Was a Success Even as It Flopped." *PC World*. pcworld.com, 1 June 2010. Web. 14 Sept. 2010.

"You Are Being Tailed." *Economist* 27 June 1998, US ed.: 62. *LexisNexis Academic*. Web. 15 Sept. 2010.

To hear audio commentary on this piece of writing, visit this page of the eText at **www.mycomplab.com**.

9 | Write a Position Argument

QUICK*TAKE*

- Find and narrow a topic (see below)
- Make sure your arguments are convincing (see p. 77)
- Acknowledge opposing viewpoints (see p. 78)

9a Position Arguments and Proposal Arguments

When you imagine an argument, you might think of two people with different views, engaged in a heated debate—maybe even shouting slogans. In college courses, in public life, and in professional careers, written arguments are meant to persuade readers who refuse to accept a **claim** when it is expressed as a slogan. Extended written arguments attempt to change people's minds by convincing them that a new idea or point of view is valid, or that a particular course of action is the best one to take.

Written arguments

- offer evidence and reason,
- examine the assumptions on which the evidence and reason are based,
- explore opposing arguments, and
- anticipate objections.

How you develop a written argument depends on your goals. You may want to convince your readers to change their way of thinking about an issue or perhaps get them to consider the issue from your perspective. Or you may want your readers to take some course of action based on your argument. These two kinds of arguments can be characterized as **position** and **proposal arguments**.

9b Find an Arguable Topic and Make a Claim

In a position argument you make a claim about a controversial issue. You

- define or rebut the issue,
- take a clear position,

- make a convincing argument, and
- acknowledge opposing views.

Position arguments often take two forms—definition arguments and rebuttal arguments.

Definition arguments. People argue about definitions (for example, is graffiti vandalism or is it art?) because of the consequences of something being defined in a certain way. If you can get your audience to accept your definition, then usually your argument will be successful.

Definition arguments take the form shown here.

Something is (or is not) _____ because it has (or does not have) Criteria A, Criteria B, and Criteria C (or more).

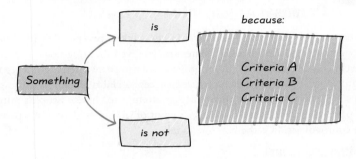

Graffiti is art because it is a means of self-expression, it shows an understanding of design principles, and it simulates both the senses and the mind.

Rebuttal arguments take the opposite position. You can challenge the criteria a writer uses to make a definition or you can challenge the evidence that supports the claim. Often the evidence presented is incomplete or wrong. Sometimes you can find counterevidence. Often when you rebut an argument, you identify one or more fallacies in that argument.

Rebuttal arguments take this form.

The opposing argument has serious shortcoming that undermine the claim because

flawed reason 1

flawed reason 2

because:

| Something | is not | flawed reason 1 <br> flawed reason 2 |

The great white shark gained a false reputation as a "man eater" from the 1975 movie Jaws, but in fact attacks on humans are rare and most bites have been "test bites," which is a common shark behavior with unfamiliar objects.

Finding an arguable topic

Probably you know people who will argue about almost anything. Some topics, however, are much better suited than others for writing an extended argument. One way to get started is to make a list of topics you care about. Below are examples of other starting points.

Think about issues that are debated on your campus

- Should admissions decisions be based solely on academic achievement?
- Should varsity athletes get paid for playing sports that bring in revenue?

Think about issues that are debated in your community

- Should people who ride bicycles and motorcycles be required to wear helmets?
- Should the public schools be privatized?

Think about national and international issues

- Should advertising be banned on television shows aimed at preschool children?
- Should capital punishment be abolished?

Read about your issue

- What are the major points of view on your issue?
- Who are the experts on this issue? What do they have to say?
- What major claims are being offered?
- What reasons are given to support the claims?
- What kinds of evidence are used to support the reasons?
- How can you add to what has been said about your subject?

Supporting claims with reasons

The difference between a slogan, such as *Oppose candidate X*, and an arguable claim, such as *Oppose candidate X because she will not lower taxes and not improve schools*, is the presence of a reason linked to the claim. A reason is typically offered in a **because** **clause**, a statement that begins with the word *because* and provides a supporting reason for the claim. The word *because* signals a **link** between the reason and the claim.

Claims must be specific and contestable

In addition to being supported by reasons that are appropriately linked to it, your claim must also be *specific*. Broad general claims such as *The United States has become too crowded* are nearly impossible to argue effectively. Often general claims contain more restricted claims that can be argued, such as *The United States should increase its efforts to reduce illegal immigration* or *The amount of land in national parks should be doubled to ensure adequate wild spaces for future generations*.

Your claim must also be contestable. Your claim that you like sour cream on a baked potato is specific, but not contestable. No matter how often you are told that a baked potato is less fattening without sour cream, the fact that you like sour cream won't change. You may stop eating the sour cream, but you won't stop wanting to eat it.

9c Organize and Write a Position Argument

Thinking of reasons to support a claim is not hard. What *is* hard is convincing your audience that your reasons are good ones. Imagine you will have critical readers. Whenever you put forward a reason, they will ask *So what?* You will have to have evidence, and you will have to link that evidence to your claim in ways they will accept if they are to agree that your reason is a good reason. Be open to new ideas while you are writing. Often you will go back and forth in developing a position argument.

1 Before you write

Think about your readers
- What do your readers already know about the subject?
- What is their attitude toward the subject? If it is different from your position, how can you address the difference?
- What are the chances of changing the opinions and beliefs of your readers? If your readers are unlikely to be moved, can you get them to acknowledge that your position is reasonable?
- Are there any sensitive issues you should be aware of?

2 Write an introduction

Engage your readers quickly
- Get your readers' attention with an example of what is at stake.
- Define the subject or issue.
- State your thesis to announce your position.

3 | Organize and write the body of your paper

Develop reasons
* Can you argue from a definition? Is _____ a _____?

EXAMPLES

> Are cheerleaders athletes?
>
> Are zoos guilty of cruelty to animals?

* Can you compare and contrast? Is _____ like or unlike _____?
* Can you argue that something is good (better, bad, worse)?
* Can you argue that something caused (or may cause) something else?
* Can you refute objections to your position?

Support reasons with evidence
* Can you support your reasons by going to a site and making observations?
* Can you find facts, statistics, or statements from authorities to support your reasons?

Consider opposing views
* Acknowledge other stakeholders for the issue, and consider their positions.
* Explain why your position is preferable.
* Make counterarguments if necessary.

4 | Write a conclusion

End with more than a summary
* Think of a strong way to end by offering more evidence in support of your thesis, reinforcing what is at stake, or giving an example that gets at the heart of the issue.

5 | Revise, revise, revise

Evaluate your draft
* Make sure your position argument meets the assignment requirements.
* Can you sharpen your thesis to make your position clearer?
* Can you add additional reasons to strengthen your argument?
* Can you supply additional evidence?
* Examine your language for bias and emotionally loaded words and reword if needed.
* When you have finished revising, edit and proofread carefully.

9d Sample Position Argument

Martinez 1

Mariela Martinez
Professor Barnes
English 102
13 April 2009

Should Students Have the Right
of Freedom of Speech?

In January 2002, students at Juneau-Douglas
High School in Juneau, Alaska, were dismissed from
classes for a parade sponsored by a local business for the
Winter Olympic Torch Relay, which passed in front of
the school. Across the street and off of school grounds,
high school senior Joseph Frederick, who had not
attended school that day, and his friends waited until
the torch and cameras approached. They then unfurled
a banner that read "Bong Hits 4 Jesus." The outraged
school principal, Deborah Morse, ran across the street
and seized the banner. She then suspended Frederick
for five days and later increased the penalty to ten
days when Frederick quoted Thomas Jefferson on the
right of freedom of speech (Sherman).

Frederick appealed to the Superintendent and the
Juneau School Board, which denied his appeal. He then
filed suit against Morse and the school board, claiming
they had violated his First Amendment right to freedom
of speech. The federal district court ruled in favor of
Morse and the school board. The United States Court of

The first and
second paragraphs
give the back-
ground of an issue
that likely is
unfamiliar to most
readers.

Martinez 2

Appeals for the Ninth Circuit, however, reversed the
district court in a unanimous decision, ruling that
Frederick's right to freedom of speech had been violated
(Hussain). The Juneau School Board then took the case
to the United States Supreme Court, which heard oral
arguments on March 19, 2007. Kenneth Starr, the
Whitewater prosecutor during the Clinton administration,
presented the case for the school board.

At first glance the incident seems blown
enormously out of proportion, certainly unworthy
of consuming many hours of a federal judge's time.
Frederick's banner was a stupid prank done in poor
taste by an adolescent. He is far from the ideal poster
child for free speech. But the underlying issue is huge.
I maintain that there is no reason to restrict
the First Amendment rights of students when they are
not disrupting the school. To give school authorities
the right to control anything a student says anywhere
far exceeds any reasonable interpretation of our
Constitution.

Attorney Kenneth Starr argued before the
Supreme Court that Morse's censorship of Frederick
was justified because of the precedent set in Bethel
School District v. Fraser. In that 1986 case, the
Supreme Court ruled that public schools could limit
student speech at a school assembly. Vulgar or
obscene speech could be censored. The court decided
that "[T]he undoubted freedom to advocate unpopular
and controversial views in schools and classrooms

In the third
paragraph
Martinez gives
her interpretation
that the event
was not worthy
of the attention it
received. Then
she states her
thesis that
students' rights
to freedom of
speech should be
protected.

Martinez
examines the
opposing position.
She concludes
that the evidence
cited by the
opposition does
not apply to the
Juneau case.

Martinez 3

must be balanced against the society's countervailing interest in teaching students the boundaries of socially appropriate behavior." But that case involved a school assembly on school property. Starr argued that Frederick v. Morse is comparable because students had been collectively released from school to watch the Olympic torch pass by and were accompanied by their teachers.

The case Morse v. Frederick is not, as Starr maintained, about protecting young people from "the scourge of drugs." The drug reference is a red herring. Frederick described the words as nonsense meant to get the attention of the television cameras (Biskupic). The banner was not pornographic or obscene. The banner did not incite violence. The only violent act was the principal's seizing the banner. Neither could it be interpreted as attacking Christianity. Organizations that litigate on behalf of the religious right including the Christian Legal Society and the American Center for Law and Justice, founded by the Rev. Pat Robertson, have sided with Frederick (Greenhouse).

Instead the case is an effort by school administrators supported by their professional organizations to get the Supreme Court to allow them to censor anything they disagree with. This effort is chilling because they currently have the power to censor obscene, violent, and libelous speech. It is an attempt to use the public's fear about illegal drugs to justify heavy-handed authoritarian control of student

Martinez argues that Frederick's banner neither broke any laws nor did it insult Christian organizations because the religious right sided with Frederick.

Martinez 4

expression, whether on or off campus. Morse and Starr
may not like to admit it, but the First Amendment
does apply in our nation's public schools. The U.S.
Supreme Court decided in 1969, in the case of Tinker
et al. v. Des Moines Independent Community School
District, that students do have the right of political
expression. The court ruled that as long as the
student's expression does not disrupt the educational
environment, officials cannot suppress it (Haynes).
The Supreme Court has long maintained that speech
that is unpleasant or uncomfortable is nonetheless
protected.

Frederick's prank was stupid and boorish, but
imagine that Frederick held up a banner protesting
racial segregation in the South in 1961. We would now
see his act as courageous. Indeed, students were at
the forefront of the Civil Rights movement, and many
school administrators opposed their actions. Principal
Morse was not wrong to disagree with Frederick's
message, but she was wrong to censor it. The Supreme
Court declared in its Tinker ruling in 1969 that
students do not "shed their constitutional rights to
freedom of speech or expression at the 'schoolhouse
gate.'" The First Amendment is fundamental to our
sense of what the United States is about, and we
should always be vigilant when those in power seek
to limit freedom of speech.

Martinez supplies evidence that students do have the right of political expression when they are not disruptive.

In her conclusion, Martinez reiterates that she does not think Frederick's prank was a good idea, but the principal was wrong to deny his right to freedom of speech off of school property. She gives additional evidence that the Supreme Court has ruled in the past that students do have freedom of speech.

Martinez 5

Works Cited

Bethel School Dist. v. Fraser. 478 US 675. Supreme
    Court of the US. 1986. *Supreme Court Collection*.
    Legal Information Inst., Cornell U Law School, n.d.
    Web. 3 Apr. 2009.

Biskupic, Joan. "Justices Debate Student's Suspension
    for Banner." *USA Today*. 20 Mar. 2007: 3A. Print.

Greenhouse, Linda. "Free Speech Case Divides Bush and
    Religious Right." *New York Times*. 18 Mar. 2007,
    final ed.: A22. Print.

Haynes, Charles C. "T-shirt Rebellion in the Land of the
    Free." *First Amendment Center*. First Amendment
    Center, Vanderbilt U, 14 Mar. 2004. Web. 4 Apr. 2009.

Hussain, Murad. "The 'Bong' Show: Viewing Frederick's
    Publicity Stunt Through Kulmeier's Lens." *Yale Law
    Journal Pocket Parts*. Yale U Law School, 9 Mar.
    2007. Web. 2 Apr. 2009.

Sherman, Mark. "'Bong Hits 4 Jesus' Banner Case Reaches
    Supreme Court." *Lansing State Journal*. Lansing State
    Journal, 16 Mar. 2007. Web. 2 Apr. 2009.

Tinker et al. v. Des Moines Independent Community
    School Dist. 393 US 503. Supreme Court of the US.
    1969. *Supreme Court Collection*. Legal Information
    Inst., Cornell U Law School, n.d. Web. 3 Apr. 2009.

*To hear audio commentary on this piece of writing, visit this page
of the eText at* **www.mycomplab.com**.

10 | Write for Online Courses

10a Use Courseware

Whatever course management system your school uses, take advantage early in the semester of tutorials and help documents that guide you in how to e-mail, post to a discussion, or submit an assignment for your course. After the course begins, you will want to be comfortable with these features. Even if you may not be face-to-face with your instructor, you'll need to know when to ask for help.

10b Keep Track of Online Coursework

Plan your time

Online courses require self-discipline and strong organization to keep your work on track. At the beginning of the term, use the course syllabus or online course schedule to create your own detailed schedule to be sure you keep up with reading and assignments. Some students choose to use a traditional planner; others do well using an online calendar or other reminders. The important thing is to stay on top of due dates.

Then stick to the schedule you have outlined. Know the course policy for late assignments, for written work, and other participation. The sooner you start the work for the course the better. As in any other class, keeping up with reading and due dates is essential. Many students who take online courses report that it is especially important not to fall behind. Without the reminders that face-to-face interaction in the classroom can provide, it is up to you to remember what you should be working on and when.

Stay organized

Hard drive failure or Internet service interruptions tend to happen when it is least convenient. As in any course, be sure you back up files as a regular part of your routine. Technical problems will not excuse you from online work. Plan to have alternative ways to access the Internet, e-mail, and your course materials if your usual means of access is down.

Staying connected also means keeping up communication with your instructor and participating in required discussion forums. Regardless of whether your class meets online or both online and face-to-face, success in online courses comes when you participate fully in the community and discussions.

10c Participate in Online Course Discussions

Your instructor will likely give specific instructions for how often you are required to participate in online discussion forums and may also specify the number and kinds of posts you must make. Once the class has begun, read earlier posts carefully as you choose how to make a point in a class discussion.

When you are posting the first entry in a discussion thread, give your post a clear, specific subject line that lets readers know what you are writing about before they open it. For new or response posts, offer the context (the assignment or reading name), the date and name of a previous post, or other background.

Discussion post assignment

Discussion #2: Visual signs

Think of some clothing or style that is popular among friends of yours: tattoos, baseball caps, piercings, jewelry, sneakers, and so on. Interview a friend who wears the item and photograph him or her, focusing on the item. Upload the photo to the discussion board. Write a post of 250–400 words about the significance of the item and what it says about the generation who values it.

Discussion post

Clear subject
line repeats
assignment
language.

Thread: Style or clothing? Magenta Chucks with Cartoon Laces

Author: Lindsey Rodriguez

Posted Date: Thursday, January 27, 2011 4:54:31 PM CST

Edited Date: Thursday, January 27, 2011 4:58:23 PM CST

Shoes are a versatile type of clothing because the wearer can consciously choose the look of the statement they make. People can pick a pair of subtle shoes that complement their outfit or wear a pair for their functionality. Alternatively, shoes may also serve as a statement—accessories that make a jarring contrast against the rest of the outfit or even serve as the focal point.

Photograph
responds to
assignment and
shows details
described in
post.

For example, a pair of well-worn, magenta Converse sneakers with mismatching laces can only be meant to generate intrigue as a clothing choice. While a magenta pair of Converses with Hello-Kitty and Spiderman laces would seem odd for the typical male, Rick Wang's closet is a sea of black, white, and shades of purple with the occasional ironic or vintage T-shirt lying on the floor. Rick is unlike any person I've ever met. For his senior yearbook portrait, he wore the same rented tux that was required for all guys with one exception: after much convincing of the photographer, on his shoulder sat the turtle beanie-baby he named Cornelius Alfonso Laramy Galileo III Esq. His eighteenth birthday party was held at Chuck E. Cheese's, where he gallivanted around with the cape and Chuck E. Cheese mask given to all birthday children. Like many of his generation, the shoes convey his embrace of the strange, fun, and colorful without any regard to dignity. The cartoon shoelaces are a display of his eccentricity and still lively inner-child.

Post relates results of interview.

As the technological revolution gave power and prestige to nerds, Converse's "Chucks" became popular among the generation that values socially awkward yet intelligent and quirky individuals. Crazy colored shoes have also grown in popularity because they express creativity and individualism for a generation that resists becoming boring.

Post length is appropriate to assignment.

10d Observe Netiquette

In online courses your discussion posts, wiki entries, and other written work speak for and create an impression of you. Your instructor and classmates will rely on your comments and conversations in writing to relate to you and assess your ideas. Follow commonsense rules of netiquette.

- **Remember your classmates are people like you.** Address them by name if possible, and sign your post with your name. Don't say things online that you would not say to a classmate face-to-face.
- **Be aware of tone.** Often sarcasm and attempts at humor come off badly when you are having a discussion online.
- **Be a forgiving reader.** You don't need to point out every minor error. If you feel strongly about a mistake, send the writer a private e-mail rather than communicating with the entire class.
- **Keep the discussion civil.** Often a reply like "what a stupid idea" leads to a flame war with name calling, and the possibility of exploring an issue ends.
- **Don't spam your classmates.** Refrain from sending off-topic messages to everyone. Your classmates have enough to sort through without having to deal with frivolous messages.
- **Make yourself credible.** Check for punctuation, grammar, and spelling errors before you post.

PART 3

Planning Research and Finding Sources

RESEARCH MAP: CONDUCTING RESEARCH

College research writing requires that you

- determine your goals,
- find a topic,
- ask a question about that topic,
- find out what has been written about that topic,
- evaluate what has been written about that topic, and
- make a contribution to the discussion about that topic.

Here are the steps in planning research and finding sources.

1 | Plan the research project

First, analyze what you are being asked to do; go to Section 11a.

Ask a question about a topic that interests you and narrow that topic. Go to 11b.

Determine what kinds of research you will need; go to 11c.

Conduct field research if it is appropriate for your project. See strategies for

- **CONDUCTING INTERVIEWS**; go to 14b.
- **ADMINISTERING SURVEYS**; go to 14c.
- **MAKING OBSERVATIONS**; go to 14d.

2 | Draft a working thesis

Draft a working thesis. Go to 11d.

Create a working bibliography. Go to 11e.

3 | Find and track sources

Consult with a research librarian if possible, and determine where and how to start looking.

Find sources online and in print:

- for sources in **DATABASES**, go to 12b.
- for sources on the **WEB**, go to 12c.
- for **VISUAL** sources, go to 12d.
- for **PRINT** sources, go to 12e.

Keep track of sources. Go to 12f.

4 | Evaluate sources

Decide which sources are going to be useful for your project. For each source you'll need to determine the

- **RELEVANCE** to your research question; go to 13a.

Evaluate the different types of sources you are using:

- **DATABASE** and **PRINT SOURCES**; go to 13b.
- **WEB SOURCES**; go to 13c.

11 | Plan Your Research

11a Analyze the Research Task

If you have an assignment that requires research, look closely at what you are being asked to do.

Look for words that signal what is expected

- An *analysis* or *examination* asks you to look at an issue in detail, explaining its history, the people and places affected, and what is at stake.
- A *review of scholarship* requires you to summarize what key scholars and researchers have written about the issue.
- An *evaluation* requires you to make critical judgments.
- An *argument* requires you to assemble evidence in support of a claim you make.

Identify your potential readers

- How familiar are your readers with your subject?
- What background information will you need to supply?
- If your subject is controversial, what opinions or beliefs are your readers likely to hold?
- If some readers are likely to disagree with you, how can you convince them?

Assess the project's length, scope, and requirements

- What kind of research are you being asked to do?
- What is the length of the project?
- What kinds and number of sources or field research are required?
- Which documentation style—such as MLA or APA—is required?

11b Find and Narrow a Topic

You might begin by doing one or more of the following.

- **Visit "Research by Subject" on your library's Web site.** Clicking on a subject such as "African and African American Studies" will take you to a list of online resources. Often you can find an e-mail link to a reference librarian who can assist you.
- **Look for topics in your courses.** Browse your course notes and readings. Are there any topics you might want to explore in greater depth?
- **Browse a Web subject directory.** Web subject directories, including Yahoo Directory (dir.yahoo.com), are useful when you want to narrow a topic or learn what subcategories a topic might contain. In addition to the Web subject directories, the Library of Congress Virtual Reference Shelf (www.loc.gov/rr/askalib/virtualref.html) may help you identify sites relevant to your topic.
- **Consult a specialized encyclopedia.** Specialized encyclopedias focus on a single area of knowledge, go into more depth about a subject, and often include bibliographies. Check if your library database page has a link to the Gale Virtual Reference Library, which offers entries from many specialized encyclopedias and reference sources.
- **Look for topics as you read.** When you read actively, you ask questions and respond to ideas in the text. Review what you wrote in the margins or the notes you have made about something you read that interested you. You may find a potential topic.

It can be tricky to find a balance between what you want to say about a topic and the amount of space you have to say it in. Usually your instructor will suggest a length for your project, which should help you decide how to limit your topic. If you suspect your topic is becoming unmanageable and your project may be too long, look for ways to narrow your focus.

Off track	A 5-page paper on European witch hunts
On track	A 5-page paper tracing two or three major causes of the European witch hunts of the fifteenth and sixteenth centuries

Off track	A 10-page paper on accounting fraud
On track	A 10-page paper examining how a new law would help prevent corporate accounting fraud

11c Determine What Kind of Research You Need

When you begin your research, you will have to make a few educated guesses about where to look. Ask these questions before you start.

- How much information do you need? The assignment may specify the number of sources you should consult.
- Are particular types of sources required? If so, do you understand why those sources are required?
- How current should the information be? Some assignments require you to use the most up-to-date information you can locate.

Secondary research

Most people who do research rely partly or exclusively on the work of others as sources of information. Research based on the work of others is called **secondary research**. Chapter 13 explains in detail how to find and evaluate database, Web, and print sources.

Primary research

Much of the research done at a university creates new information through **primary research**: experiments, data-gathering surveys and interviews, detailed observations, and the examination of historical documents. Chapter 14 explains how to plan and conduct three types of field research: interviews (14b), surveys (14c), and observations (14d).

11d Draft a Working Thesis

If you ask a focused and interesting research question, your answer will be your **working thesis**. This working thesis will be the focus of the remainder of your research and ultimately your research project.

Ask questions about your topic

When you have a topic that is interesting to you, manageable in scope, and possible to research using sources or doing field research, then your next task is to ask researchable questions.

Explore a definition

- While many (most) people think X is a Y, can X be better thought of as a Z?

  Most people think of deer as harmless animals that are benign to the environment, but their overpopulation devastates young trees in forests, leading to loss of habitat for birds and other species that depend on those trees.

Evaluate a person, activity, or thing

- Can you argue that a person, activity, or thing is either good, better, or best (or bad, worse, or worst) within its class?

  Fender Stratocasters from the 1950s remain the best electric guitars ever made because of their versatility, sound quality, and player-friendly features.

Examine why something happened

- Can you argue that while there were obvious causes of Y, Y would not have occurred had it not been for X?

  College students are called irresponsible when they run up high credit card debts that they cannot pay off, but these debts would not have occurred if credit card companies did not aggressively market cards and offer high lines of credit to students with no income.

- Can you argue for an alternative cause rather than the one many people assume?

  The defeat of the Confederate Army at the Battle of Gettysburg in July 1863 is often cited as the turning point in the Civil War, but in fact the South was running out of food, equipment, and soldiers, and it lost its only real chance of winning when Great Britain failed to intervene on its side.

Counter objections to a position

- Can the reverse or opposite of an opposing claim be argued?

  New medications that relieve pain are welcomed by runners and other athletes, but these drugs also mask signals that our bodies send us, increasing the risk of serious injury.

Propose a solution to a problem

- Can you propose a solution to a local problem?

  The traffic congestion on our campus could be eased by creating bike lanes on College Drive, which would encourage more students, faculty, and staff to commute by bicycle.

Turn your answers into a working thesis

Topic	Reading disorders
Researchable question	Why do some people learn to read top-to-bottom Chinese characters more easily than left-to-right alphabetic writing?
Working thesis	The direction of text flow may be an important factor in how an individual learns to read.

11e Create a Working Bibliography

When you begin to collect your sources, make sure you get full bibliographic information for everything you might want to use in your project: articles, books, Web sites, and other materials. Decide which documentation style you will use. If your instructor does not tell you which style is appropriate, ask. (The major documentation styles—MLA, APA, CMS, and CSE—are dealt with in detail in Chapters 18–21.)

Find the necessary bibliographic information

Chapter 12 gives instructions on what information you will need to collect for each kind of source. In general, as you research and develop a working bibliography, the rule of thumb is to write down more information rather than less. You can always delete unnecessary information when it comes time to format your citations according to your chosen documentation style (APA, MLA, CMS, or CSE), but it is time-consuming to go back to sources to find missing bibliographic information.

11f Create an Annotated Bibliography

A working bibliography is an alphabetized list of sources with complete publication information that you collect while researching your topic. An **annotated bibliography** builds on the basic citations of a working bibliography by adding a brief summary or evaluation of each source. Annotated bibliographies must include

- a complete citation in the documentation style you are using (MLA, APA, CMS, CSE).
- a concise summary of the content and scope.

In addition, your instructor may ask you to include one or more of the following:

- a comment on the relevance of the source to your research topic.
- an evaluation of the background and qualifications of the author.
- a comparison to another work on your list.

Writer at Work

Lopez 1

Gabriella Lopez

Professor Kimbro

English 1102

15 Apr. 2010

Annotated Bibliography

Bartholemew, Mel. *All New Square Foot Gardening: Grow More in Less Space*. Franklin, TN: Cool Spring P, 2006. Print.

Mel Bartholemew is the expert on square foot gardening. This book explains everything you need to know about constructing and maintaining a square-foot garden. It will help me show not only how to create small campus gardens, but all of the options available and how easy and inexpensive it will be.

Berman, Jillian. "Sustainability Could Secure a Good Future: College Students Flock to "Green" Degrees, Careers." *USA Today* 3 Apr. 2009, final ed.: 7D. *LexisNexis Academic*. Web. 6 Apr. 2010.

This article describes how the growth in "green" jobs is making students seek colleges that provide them with opportunities to learn about sustainability. This trend will be useful in helping me argue that our college needs to offer students opportunities to learn about sustainability in real ways.

Lopez 2

Lewington, Jennifer. "Lean Green Campus Machines:

Students Are at the Forefront of a Grassroots

Environmental Revolution As They Coax—and

Sometimes Embarrass—Administrators into Walking

the Walk with Them." *The Globe and Mail* [Toronto] 23

Oct. 2008: 14. *LexisNexis Academic*. Web. 8 Apr. 2010.

This article talks about how students in Canada are

getting administrators to support sustainability. It shows

how a new kind of collaborative, rather than

confrontational, student activism works.

Rozin, Paul, Rebecca Bauer, and Dana Catanese. "Food

and Life, Pleasure and Worry, among American

College Students: Gender Differences and Regional

Similarities." *Journal of Personality and Social

Psychology* 85.1 (2003): 132–141. *PsycARTICLES*.

Web. 10 Apr. 2010.

This scientific article describes a study of how students think

about food. It not only complements Michael Pollan's

argument that we have developed an unhealthy relationship

with food, but it also shows how important the college years

are for establishing that relationship.

"Starting a College Farm: Stories from the Yale Sustainable

Food Project." *Yale Sustainable Food Project*. Yale

Sustainable Food Project, n.d. Web. 9 Apr. 2010.

This document is invaluable in showing how Yale

students gained and maintain support for the

Sustainable Food Project. It is written by students who

work in that program.

12 | Find Sources

12a Develop Strategies for Finding Sources

Libraries still contain many resources not available on the Web. Even more important, libraries have professional research librarians who can help you locate sources quickly.

Learn the art of effective keyword searches

Keyword searches take you to the sources you need. Start with your working thesis and generate a list of possible keywords for researching your thesis.

First, think of keyword combinations that make your search **more specific**. For example, a search for sources related to youth voter participation might focus more specifically on young adults *and*

> voter registration
> historical participation rates
> voter turnout

Also think about **more general** ways to describe what you are doing—what synonyms can you think of for your existing terms? Instead of relying on "young adult," try keywords like

> under 30
> Generation Y
> college students

Many databases have a thesaurus that can help you find more keywords.

WRITING SMART

Find the right kinds of sources

Type of source	Type of information	How to find them
Scholarly books	Extensive and in-depth coverage of nearly any subject	Library catalog
Scholarly journals	Reports of new knowledge and research findings by experts	Online library databases
Trade journals	Reports of information pertaining to specific industries, professions, and products	Online library databases
Popular magazines	Reports or summaries of current news, sports, fashion, entertainment subjects	Online library databases
Newspapers	Recent and current information; foreign newspapers are useful for international perspectives	Online library databases
Government publications	Government-collected statistics, studies, and reports; especially good for science and medicine	Library catalog and city, state, and federal government Web sites
Videos, audios, documentaries, maps	Information varies widely	Library catalog, Web, and online library databases

12b Find Sources in Databases

Sources found through library databases have already been filtered for you by professional librarians. They will include some common sources like popular magazines and newspapers, but the greatest value of database sources are the many journals, abstracts, studies, e-books, and other writing produced by specialists whose work has been scrutinized and commented upon by other experts.

Use databases

Your library has a list of databases and indexes by subject. If you can't find this list on your library's Web site, ask a reference librarian for help. Follow these steps to find articles.

1. Select a database appropriate to your subject. (For example, if you are researching multiple sclerosis, you might start with *Health Reference Center*, *MEDLINE*, *PsycINFO,* or *PubMed*.)
2. Search the database using your list of keywords. (You could start with *multiple sclerosis* and then combine *MS* with other terms to narrow your search.)
3. Once you have chosen an article, print or e-mail to yourself the complete citation to the article. Look for the e-mail link after you click on the item you want.
4. Print or e-mail to yourself the full text if it is available. The full text is better than cutting and pasting because you might lose track of which words are yours, leading to unintended plagiarism.
5. If the full text is not available, check the online library catalog to see if your library has the journal.

WRITING SMART

Know the advantages of database versus Web sources

	Library database sources	Web sources
Speed	✓ Users can find information quickly	✓ Users can find information quickly
Accessibility	✓ Available 24/7	✓ Available 24/7
Organization	✓ Materials are organized for efficient search and retrieval	User must look in many different places for related information
Consistency and quality	✓ Librarians review and select resources	Anyone can claim to be an "expert," regardless of qualifications
Comprehensiveness	✓ Collected sources represent a wide and representative body of knowledge	No guarantee that the full breadth of an issue will be represented
Permanence	✓ Materials remain available for many years	Materials can disappear or change in an instant
Free of overt bias	✓ Even sources with a definite agenda are required to meet certain standards of documentation and intellectual rigor	Sources are often a "soapbox" for organizations or individuals with particular agendas and little knowledge or experience
Free of commercial slant	✓ Because libraries pay for their collections, sources are largely commercial-free	Sources are often motivated primarily by the desire to sell you something

Common Databases

Academic OneFile	Indexes periodicals from the arts, humanities, sciences, social sciences, and general news, with full-text articles and images.
Academic Search Premier and Complete	Provide full-text articles for thousands of scholarly publications.
ArticleFirst	Indexes journals in business, the humanities, medicine, science, and social sciences.
Business Search Premier	Provides full-text articles in all business disciplines.
EBSCOhost Research Databases	Gateway to a large collection of EBSCO databases, including *Academic Search Premier* and *Complete*, *Business Source Premier* and *Complete*, *ERIC*, and *Medline*.
Google Books	Allows you to search within books and gives you snippets surrounding search terms for copyrighted books. Many books out of copyright have the full text. Available for everyone.
Google Scholar	Searches scholarly literature according to criteria of relevance. Available for everyone.
General OneFile	Contains millions of full-text articles about a wide range of academic and general-interest topics.
JSTOR	Provides scanned copies of scholarly journals.
LexisNexis Academic	Provides full text of a wide range of newspapers, magazines, government and legal documents, and company profiles from around the world.
ProQuest Databases	Like EBSCOhost, ProQuest is a gateway to a large collection of databases with over 100 billion pages, including the best archives of doctoral dissertations and historical newspapers.

12c Find Sources on the Web

The Web offers you some resources for current topics that would be difficult or impossible to find in a library. The key to success is knowing where you are most likely to find current and accurate information about the particular question you are researching, and knowing how to access that information.

Use search engines wisely

Search engines designed for the Web work in ways similar to library databases and your library's online catalog but with one major difference. Databases typically do some screening of the items they list, but search engines potentially take you to everything on the Web—millions of pages in all.

Most search engines offer you the option of an advanced search, which gives you the opportunity to limit numbers. The advanced searches on *Google* and *Yahoo!* give you the options of using a string of words to search for sites that contain (1) all the words, (2) the exact phrase, (3) any of the words, or (4) that do not contain certain words. They also allow you to specify the site, the date range, the file format, and the domain. For example, if you want to limit a search for *multiple sclerosis* to government Web sites such as the National Institutes of Health, you can specify the domain as **.gov**.

Find online government sources

The federal government has made many of its publications available on the Web. Often the most current and most reliable statistics are government statistics. Among the more important government resources are the following.

- **Bureau of Labor Statistics** (www.bls.gov). Source for official U.S. statistics on employment, wages, and consumer prices
- **Census Bureau** (www.census.gov). Contains a wealth of links to sites for population, social, economic, and political statistics, including the *Statistical Abstract of the United States* (www.census.gov/compendia/statab)
- **Centers for Disease Control** (www.cdc.gov). Authoritative and trustworthy source for health statistics

- **CIA World Factbook** (www.cia.gov/library/publications/the-world-factbook). Resource for geographic, economic, demographic, and political information on the nations of the world
- **Library of Congress** (www.loc.gov). Many of the resources of the largest library in the world are available on the Web.
- **National Institutes of Health** (www.nih.gov). Extensive health information including MedlinePlus searches
- **NASA** (www.nasa.gov). A rich site with much information and images concerning space exploration and scientific discovery
- **Thomas** (thomas.loc.gov). The major source of legislative information, including bills, committee reports, and voting records of individual members of Congress
- **USA.gov** (www.usa.gov). The place to start when you are not sure where to look for government information

Find online reference sources

Your library's Web site may have a link to **reference sites**, either on the main page or under another heading like **research tools**.

Reference sites are usually organized by subject, and you can find resources under the subject heading.

- **Business information** (links to business databases and sites like *Hoover's* that profile companies)
- **Dictionaries** (including the *Oxford English Dictionary* and various subject dictionaries and language dictionaries)
- **Education** (including *The College Blue Book* and others)
- **Encyclopedias** (including *Britannica Online* and others)
- **Reference books** (commonly used books like atlases, almanacs, biographies, handbooks, and histories)

Search interactive media

Several search engines have been developed for interactive media. Facebook and Twitter also have search engines for their sites.

WRITING SMART

Know the limitations of *Wikipedia*

Wikipedia is a valuable resource for current information and for popular culture topics that are not covered in traditional encyclopedias. You can find out, for example, that SpongeBob SquarePants's original name was "SpongeBoy," but it had already been copyrighted.

Nevertheless, many instructors and the scholarly community in general do not consider *Wikipedia* a reliable source of information for a research project. The fundamental problem with *Wikipedia* is stability, not whether the information is correct or incorrect. *Wikipedia* and other wikis constantly change. The underlying idea of documenting sources is that readers can consult the same sources that you consulted. To be on the safe side, treat *Wikipedia* as you would a blog. Consult other sources to confirm what you find on *Wikipedia*, and cite those sources.

Discussion list search engines

- **Big Boards** (www.big-boards.com). Tracks over 2,000 of the most active discussion forums
- **Google Groups** (groups.google.com). Archives discussion forums dating back to 1981
- **Yahoo Groups** (groups.yahoo.com). A directory of groups by subject

Blog search engines

- **Google Blog Search** (blogsearch.google.com). Searches blogs in several languages besides English
- **IceRocket** (blogs.icerocket.com). Searches blogs, MySpace, and Twitter
- **Technorati** (www.technorati.com). Searches blogs and other user-generated content

12d Find Multimedia Sources

Massive collections of images; audio files, including podcasts; videos; maps; charts; and other resources are now available on the Web.

Find images

The major search engines for images include the following.

- **Bing Images** (www.bing.com/images)
- **Google Image Search** (images.google.com)
- **Picsearch** (www.picsearch.com)
- **Yahoo! Image Search** (images.search.yahoo.com)

Libraries and museums also offer large collections of images.

Find videos

- **Bing Videos** (www.bing.com/videos)
- **Google Videos** (video.google.com)
- **Yahoo! Video Search** (video.search.yahoo.com)
- **YouTube** (www.youtube.com)

Find podcasts

- **iTunes Podcast Resources** (www.apple.com/itunes/podcasts)
- **PodcastDirectory.com** (http://www.podcastdirectory.com)

Find charts, graphs, and maps

You can find statistical data represented in charts and graphs on many government Web sites.

- **Statistical Abstract of the United States** (www.census.gov/compendia/statab)
- **Google Earth** (earth.google.com)
- **National Geographic Map Machine** (mapmachine. nationalgeographic.com)
- **Perry Casteñada Map Collection, University of Texas** (www.lib.utexas.edu/maps/map_sites/map_sites.html)

Respect copyright

Just because images, videos, and other multimedia files are easy to download from the Web does not mean that everything is available for you to use. Look for the creator's copyright notice and suggested credit line. This notice will tell you if you can reproduce the multimedia file.

12e   Find Print Sources

No matter how current the topic you are researching, you will likely find information in print sources that is simply not available online. Print sources have other advantages as well.

- Books are shelved according to subject, allowing easy browsing.
- Books often have bibliographies, directing you to other research on the subject.
- You can search for books in multiple ways: author, title, subject, or call letter.
- The majority of print sources have been evaluated by scholars, editors, and publishers, who decided whether they merited publication.

Find books

The floors of your library where books are shelved are referred to as the stacks. The call number will enable you to find the item in the stacks. You will need to consult the locations guide for your library, which gives the level and section where an item is shelved.

Find journal articles

Like books, scholarly journals provide in-depth examinations of subjects. The articles in scholarly journals are written by experts, and they usually contain lists of references that can guide you to other research on a subject.

Some instructors frown on using popular magazines, but these journals can be valuable for researching current opinion on a particular topic. Databases increasingly contain the full text of articles, allowing you to read and copy the contents onto your computer.

12f   Keep Track of Sources

As you begin to collect your sources, make sure you get full bibliographic information for everything you might want to use in your project. Decide which documentation style you will use. (The major documentation styles—MLA, APA, CMS, and CSE—are dealt with in detail in Chapters 17–21.)

Locate elements of a citation in database sources

For any source you find on a database, MLA style requires you to provide the full print information, the name of the database in italics, the medium of publication (*Web*), and the date you accessed the database. If page numbers are not included, use *n. pag.* Do *not* include the URL of the database.

Author's name	Shefner, Ruth
Title of article	"Politics Deserve Teens' Attention"
Publication information	
Name of periodical	*Post-Standard* [Syracuse]
Date of publication (and edition for newspapers)	28 Nov. 2006, final ed.
Section and page number	B3
Database information	
Name of database	*LexisNexis Academic*
Date you accessed the site	28 Apr. 2010

The citation would appear as follows in an MLA-style works-cited list (see Section 17g).

> Shefner, Ruth. "Politics Deserve Teens' Attention." *Post-Standard* [Syracuse] 28 Nov. 2006, final ed.: B3. *LexisNexis Academic*. Web. 28 Apr. 2010.

APA style no longer requires listing the names of common databases or listing the date of access, unless the content is likely to change (see Section 18e). If you name the database, do not list the URL.

> Shefner, R. (2006, November 28). Politics deserve teens' attention. *The Post-Standard*, p. B3. Retrieved from LexisNexis Academic database.

Locate elements of a citation in Web sources

As you conduct your online research, make sure you collect the necessary bibliographic information for everything you might want to use as a source. Because of the potential volatility of Web sources (they can and do disappear overnight), their citations require extra information. Depending on the citation format you use, you'll arrange this information in different ways.

Collect the following information about a Web site:

Author's name, if available (if not, use the associated institution or organization)	Samadzadeh, Nozlee
Title of article	"Farm Update: The Third Annual Jack Hitt Annual Last Day of Classes Pig Roast"
Publication information	
Name of site or online journal	*Yale Sustainable Food Project Student Blog*
Publisher or Sponsor of the site (for MLA style)	Yale Sustainable Food Project
Date of publication (for an article) or of site's last update	3 May 2010
Date you accessed the site	10 May 2010
URL (for some APA formats including blogs)	http://yalesustainablefood project.wordpress.com/ 2010/05/03/farm-update- the-third-annual-jack-hitt- annual-last-day-of-classes- pig-roast/

An MLA works-cited entry for this article would look like this:

Samadzadeh, Nozlee. "Farm Update: The Third Annual Jack Hitt Annual Last Day of Classes Pig Roast." *Yale Sustainable Food Project Student Blog*. Yale Sustainable Food Project, 3 May 2010. Web. 10 May 2010.

In an APA references list, the citation would look like this:

Samadzadeh, N. (2010, May 3). Farm update: The Third Annual Jack Hitt Annual Last Day of Classes Pig Roast. Message posted to http://yalesustainablefoodproject.wordpress.com /2010/05/03/farm-update-the-third-annual-jack -hitt-annual-last-day-of-classes-pig-roast/

Locate elements of a citation in print sources

For books you will need, at minimum, the following information, which can typically be found on the front and back of the title page.

Author's name	Ojito, Mirta
Title of the book	*Finding Manaña: A Memoir of a Cuban Exile*
Publication information	
Place of publication	New York
Name of publisher	Penguin
Date of publication	2005
Medium of publication	Print

Here's how the book would be cited in an MLA-style works-cited list.

Ojito, Mirta. *Finding Manaña: A Memoir of a Cuban Exile*. New York: Penguin, 2005. Print.

Here's the APA citation for the same book.

Ojito, M. (2005). *Finding manaña: A memoir of a Cuban exile*. New York, NY: Penguin.

You will also need the page numbers if you are quoting directly or referring to a specific passage, and the title and author of the individual chapter if your source is an edited book with contributions by several people.

For journals you will need the following:

Author's name	Romano, Susan
Title of article	"'Grand Convergence' in the Mexican Colonial Mundane: The Matter of Introductories"
Publication information	
Name of journal	*Rhetoric Society Quarterly*
Volume number and issue number	40.1
Date of publication (and edition for newspapers)	2010
Page numbers of the article	71–93
Medium of publication	Print
Document Object Identifier (DOI), if available, for APA	10.1080/02773940903413407

An entry in an MLA-style works-cited list would look like this:

Romano, Susan. "'Grand Convergence' in the Mexican Colonial Mundane: The Matter of Introductories." *Rhetoric Society Quarterly* 40.1 (2010): 71-93. Print.

And in APA style, like this:

Romano, S. (2010). "Grand convergence" in the Mexican colonial mundane: The matter of introductories. *Rhetoric Society Quarterly, 40,* 71–93. doi: 10.1080/02773940903413407

13 | Evaluate Sources

13a Determine the Relevance of Sources

Use these guidelines to determine the importance and relevance of your sources to your research question.

- Does your research question require you to consult primary or secondary sources?
- Does a source you have found address your question?
- Does a source support or disagree with your working thesis? (You should not throw out work that challenges your views. Representing opposing views accurately enhances your credibility.)
- Does a source add significant information?
- Is the source current? (For most topics, try to find the most up-to-date information.)
- What indications of possible bias do you note in the source?

13b Evaluate Database and Print Sources

Books are expensive to print and distribute, so book publishers generally protect their investment by providing some level of editorial oversight. Printed and online materials in your library undergo another review by professional librarians who select them to include in their collections. Library database collections, which your library pays to access, are also screened, which eliminates many poor-quality sources.

This initial screening doesn't free you, however, from the responsibility of evaluating the quality of the sources. Many printed and database sources contain their share of inaccurate, misleading, and biased information. Also, all sources carry the risk of being outdated when you are looking for current information.

WRITING SMART

Checklist for evaluating database and print sources

Over the years librarians have developed a set of criteria for evaluating sources, and you should apply them in your research.

1. **Source.** Who published the book or article? Enter the publisher's name on Google or another search engine to learn about the publisher. Scholarly books and articles in scholarly journals are generally more reliable than popular magazines and books, which tend to emphasize what is sensational or entertaining at the expense of accuracy and comprehensiveness.

2. **Author.** Who wrote the book or article? What are the author's qualifications? Enter the author's name on Google or another search engine to learn more about him or her. Does the author represent an organization?

3. **Timeliness.** How current is the source? If you are researching a fast-developing subject such as treating ADHD, then currency is very important, but even historical topics are subject to controversy or revision.

4. **Evidence.** Where does the evidence come from—facts, interviews, observations, surveys, or experiments? Is the evidence adequate to support the author's claims?

5. **Biases.** Can you detect particular biases of the author? How do the author's biases affect the interpretation offered?

6. **Advertising.** For print sources, is advertising a prominent part of the journal or newspaper? How might the ads affect the credibility or the biases of the information that gets printed?

13c Evaluate Web Sources

Nearly every large company and political and advocacy organization has a Web site. We expect these sites to represent the company or the point of view of the organization. Many sites on the Web, however, are not so clearly labeled.

WRITING SMART

Checklist for evaluating Web sources

Use these criteria for evaluating Web sites.

1. **Source.** What organization sponsors the Web site? Look for the site's owner at the top or bottom of the home page or in the Web address. Enter the owner's name on Google or another search engine to learn about the organization. If a Web site doesn't indicate ownership, then you have to make judgments about who put it up and why.

2. **Author.** Is the author identified? Look for an "About Us" link if you see no author listed. Enter the author's name on Google or another search engine to learn more about the author. Often Web sites give no information about their authors other than an e-mail address, if that. In such cases it is difficult or impossible to determine the author's qualifications. Be cautious about information on an anonymous site.

3. **Purpose.** Is the Web site trying to sell you something? Many Web sites are infomercials that might contain useful information, but they are no more trustworthy than other forms of advertising. Is the purpose to entertain? To inform? To persuade?

4. **Timeliness.** When was the Web site last updated? Look for a date on the home page. Many Web pages do not list when they were last updated; thus you cannot determine their currency.

5. **Evidence.** Are sources of information listed? Any factual information should be supported by indicating where the information came from. Reliable Web sites that offer information will list their sources.

6. **Biases.** Does the Web site offer a balanced point of view? Many Web sites conceal their attitude with a reasonable tone and seemingly factual evidence such as statistics. Citations and bibliographies do not ensure that a site is reliable. Look carefully at the links and sources cited, and peruse the "About Us" link if one is available.

14 | Plan Field Research

14a Know What You Can Obtain from Field Research

Even though much of the research you do for college courses will be secondary research conducted at a computer or in the library, some topics do call for primary research, requiring you to gather information on your own. Field research of this kind can be especially important for exploring local issues. It is also used extensively in professions that you may be joining after college.

Be aware that the ethics of conducting field research require you to inform people about what you are doing and why you are gathering information. If you are uncertain about the ethics of doing field research, talk to your instructor.

Three types of field research that can usually be conducted in college are **interviews, surveys,** and **observations.**

- **Interviews.** Interviewing experts on your research topic can help build your knowledge base. You can use interviews to discover what the people most affected by a particular issue are thinking and feeling.
- **Surveys.** Small surveys can often provide insight on local issues.
- **Observation.** Local observation can be a valuable source of data. For example, if you are researching why a particular office on your campus does not operate efficiently, observe what happens when students enter and how they are handled by the staff.

14b Conduct Interviews

Before you contact anyone to ask for an interview, think carefully about your goals; knowing what you want to find out through your interviews will help you determine whom you need to interview and what questions you need to ask.

- Decide what you want or need to know and who best can provide that for you.
- Schedule each interview in advance, and let the person know why you are conducting the interview.
- Plan your questions in advance. Write down a few questions and have a few more in mind. Listen carefully so you can follow up on key points.
- Come prepared with a notebook and pencil or laptop for taking notes and jotting down short quotations. Note the date, time, place, and subject of the interview. A recording device can sometimes intimidate the person you are interviewing. If you want to use a recorder, ask for permission in advance.
- When you are finished, thank your subject and ask his or her permission to get in touch again if you have additional questions.
- When you are ready to incorporate the interview into a paper or project, think about what you want to highlight from the interview and which direct quotations to include.

14c Administer Surveys

Use surveys to find out what large groups of people think about a topic (or what they are willing to admit they think). Surveys need to be carefully designed.

- Write a few specific questions. To make sure your questions are clear, test them on a few people before you conduct the survey.
- Include one or two open-ended questions, such as "What do you like about X?" "What don't you like about X?" Open-ended questions can be difficult to interpret, but sometimes they turn up information you had not anticipated.
- Decide whom you need to survey and how many people to include. If you want to claim that the results of your survey represent the views of residents of your dormitory, your method of selecting respondents should give all residents an equal chance to be selected. Don't select only your friends.

- Decide how you will contact participants in your survey. If you are going to mail or e-mail your survey, include a statement about what the survey is for and a deadline for returning it. You may need to get permission to conduct a survey in a public place.
- Think about how you will interpret your survey. Multiple-choice formats make data easy to tabulate, but often they miss key information. Open-ended questions will require you to figure out a way to analyze responses.
- When writing about the results, be sure to include information about who participated in the survey, how the participants were selected, and when and how the survey was administered.

14d Make Observations

Simply observing what goes on in a place can be an effective research tool. Your observations can inform a controversy or topic by providing a vivid picture of real-world activity.

- Choose a place where you can observe with the least intrusion. The less people wonder about what you are doing, the better.
- Carry a notebook and write extensive field notes. Get down as much information as you can, and worry about analyzing it later.
- Record the date, exactly where you were, exactly when you arrived and left, and important details like the number of people present.
- Write on one side of your notebook so you can use the facing page to note key observations and analyze your data later.

At some point you have to interpret the data. When you analyze your observations, think about what constitutes normal and unusual activities for this place. What can you determine about the purposes of these activities?

PART 4 Incorporating and Documenting Sources

15 | Understand and Avoid Plagiarism

15a What Is Plagiarism?

Plagiarism means claiming credit for someone else's intellectual work no matter whether it's to make money or get a better grade. Intentional or not, plagiarism has dire consequences. A number of famous people have had their reputations tarnished by accusations of plagiarism, and several prominent journalists have lost their jobs and careers for copying the work of other writers and passing it off as their own.

Deliberate plagiarism

If you buy a paper on the Web, copy someone else's paper word for word, or take an article off the Web and turn it in as yours, it's plain stealing, and people who take that risk should know that the punishment can be severe—usually failure for the course and sometimes expulsion. Deliberate plagiarism is easy for your instructors to spot because they recognize shifts in style, and it is easy for them to use search engines to find the sources of work stolen from the Web.

Patch plagiarism

The use of the Web has increased instances of plagiarism in college. Some students view the Internet as a big free buffet where they can grab anything, paste it in a file, and submit it as their own work. Other students intend to submit work that is their own, but they commit patch plagiarism because they aren't careful in taking notes to distinguish the words of others from their own words.

What you are not required to acknowledge

Fortunately, common sense governs issues of academic plagiarism. The standards of documentation are not so strict that the source of every fact you cite must be acknowledged. You do not have to document the following.

- **Facts available from many sources.** For example, many reference sources report that the death toll of the sinking of the *Titanic* on April 15, 1912, was around 1,500.

- **Results of your own field research.** If you take a survey and report the results, you don't have to cite yourself. You do need to cite individual interviews.

What you are required to acknowledge

The following sources should be acknowledged with an in-text citation and an entry in the list of works cited (MLA style) or the list of references (APA style).

- **Quotations.** Short quotations should be enclosed within quotation marks, and long quotations should be indented as a block. See Section 16b for how to integrate quotations with signal phrases.
- **Summaries and paraphrases.** Summaries represent the author's argument in miniature as accurately as possible. Paraphrases restate the author's argument in your own words.
- **Facts that are not common knowledge.** For facts that are not easily found in general reference works, cite the source.
- **Ideas that are not common knowledge.** The sources of theories, analyses, statements of opinion, and arguable claims should be cited.
- **Statistics, research findings, examples, graphs, charts, and illustrations.** As a reader you should be skeptical about statistics and research findings when the source is not mentioned. When a writer does not cite the sources of statistics and research findings, there is no way of knowing how reliable the sources are or whether the writer is making them up.

COMMON ERRORS

Plagiarism in college writing

If you find any of the following problems in your academic writing, you may be guilty of plagiarizing someone else's work. Because plagiarism is usually inadvertent, it is especially important that you understand what constitutes using sources responsibly. Avoid these pitfalls.

- **Missing attribution.** Make sure the author of a quotation has been identified. Include a lead-in or signal phrase that provides attribution to the source, and identify the author in the citation.

(Continued on next page)

COMMON ERRORS *(Continued)*

- **Missing quotation marks.** You must put quotation marks around words quoted directly from a source.
- **Inadequate citation.** Give a page number to show where in the source the quotation appears or where a paraphrase or summary is drawn from.
- **Paraphrase relies too heavily on the source.** Be careful that the wording or sentence structure of a paraphrase does not follow the source too closely.
- **Distortion of meaning.** Don't allow your paraphrase or summary to distort the meaning of the source, and don't take a quotation out of context, resulting in a change of meaning.
- **Missing works-cited entry.** The Works Cited page must include all the works cited in the project.
- **Inadequate citation of images.** A figure or photo must appear with a caption and a citation to indicate the source of the image. If material includes a summary of data from a visual source, an attribution or citation must be given for the graphic being summarized.

15b Avoid Plagiarism When Taking Notes

The best way to avoid unintentional plagiarism is to take care to distinguish source words from your own words. Don't mix words from the source with your own words. Create a folder for your research project and clearly label the files.

- **Create a working bibliography and make separate files for content notes.** Create a file for each source. If you work on paper, use a separate page for each source. Also write down all the information you need for a list of works cited or a list of references in your working bibliography.
- **If you copy anything from a source when taking notes, place those words in quotation marks and note the page number(s) where those words appear.** If you copy words from an online

source, take special care to note the source. You could easily copy online material and later not be able to find where it came from.

- **Print out the entire source so you can refer to it later.** Having photocopies or complete printed files allows you to double-check later that you haven't used words from the source by mistake and that any words you quote are accurate.

15c Avoid Plagiarism When Quoting Sources

Most people who get into plagiarism trouble lift words from a source and use them without quotation marks. Where the line is drawn is easiest to illustrate with an example. In the following passage, Nell Irvin Painter discusses the African Diaspora, the dispersion of African people from their native lands in Africa.

> The three centuries separating African Americans from their immigrant ancestors profoundly influenced their identity. A strong case can be made for seeing African Americans as a new, Creole people, that is, as a people born and forged in the Western Hemisphere. Language provides the most obvious indicator: people of African descent in the Diaspora do not speak languages of Africa as their mother tongue. For the most part, they speak Portuguese, Spanish, English, and French as a mother tongue, although millions speak Creole languages (such as Haitian Creole and South Carolinian Gullah) that combine African grammars and English vocabulary.
>
> As the potent engine of culture, language influences thought, psychology, and education. Language boundaries now divide descendants whose African ancestors may have been family and close neighbors speaking the same language. One descendant in Nashville, Tennessee, may not understand the Portuguese of her distant cousin now living in Bahia, Brazil. Today, with immigrants from Africa forming an increasing proportion of people calling themselves African American, the woman in Nashville might herself be an African immigrant and speak an African language that neither her black neighbors in Tennessee nor her distant cousin in Brazil can understand.

> —Nell Irvin Painter, *Creating Black Americans: African-American History and Its Meanings, 1619 to the Present* (New York: Oxford University Press, 2006), 5.

If you were writing a paper that concerned African American cultural heritage, you might want to refer to Painter's arguments about cultural differences resulting from different languages. Your options are to paraphrase the source or to quote it directly.

If you quote directly, you must place quotation marks around all words you take from the original:

> One scholar notes the numerous linguistic differences among Americans of African descent: "[P]eople of African descent in the Diaspora do not speak languages of Africa as their mother tongue. For the most part, they speak Portuguese, Spanish, English, and French as a mother tongue" (Painter 5).

Notice that the quotation is introduced and not just dropped in. This example follows MLA style, where the citation goes outside the quotation marks but before the final period. In MLA style, source references are made according to the author's last name, which refers you to the full citation in the works-cited list at the end. Following the author's name is the page number where the quotation can be located.

If the author's name appears in the sentence, cite only the page number, in parentheses:

> According to Nell Irvin Painter, "people of African descent in the Diaspora do not speak languages of Africa as their mother tongue" (5).

If you want to quote material that is already quoted in your source, use single quotes for that material:

> Nell Irvin Painter traces a long history of African American interest in Egyptian culture: "Hoping that past greatness portended future glory, black Americans often recited a verse from the Bible that inspired this hope: 'Princes shall come out of Egypt; Ethiopia shall soon stretch forth her hands unto God' (Psalms 63:31)" (7).

15d Avoid Plagiarism When Summarizing and Paraphrasing

Summarize

When you summarize, you cite your source but, instead of quoting it directly, you state the major ideas of the entire source, or part of a source, in a paragraph or perhaps even a sentence. The key is to put the summary in your own words.

Plagiarized summary

Nell Irvin Painter argues in *Creating Black Americans* that we should consider African Americans as a new Creole people, born and forged in the Western Hemisphere (5).

Most of the words of this example of patch plagiarism are lifted directly from the original.

Acceptable summary

Nell Irvin Painter argues in *Creating Black Americans* that African Americans' experiences in the Western Hemisphere made them so culturally different from their ancestors that we can think of them as a separate people (5).

Paraphrase

When you paraphrase, you represent the idea of the source in your own words at about the same length as the original. You still need to include the reference to the source of the idea. The following paraphrase is an example of patch plagiarism.

Plagiarized paraphrase

Nell Irvin Painter contends that cultural factors like language and religion divide African Americans from their ancestors. People of African descent no longer speak the languages of Africa as their first language. Since language is a potent engine of culture, the thought, psychology, and education of contemporary African Americans is radically different from that of their ancestors (5).

Even though the source is listed, this paraphrase is unacceptable. Too many of the words in the original are used directly here, including much or all of entire phrases. When a string of words is lifted from a source and inserted without quotation marks, the passage is plagiarized. Changing a few words in a sentence is not a paraphrase. Likewise, it is unacceptable to keep the structure of the sentence and change a few words.

A true paraphrase represents an entire rewriting of the idea from the source.

Acceptable paraphrase

Nell Irvin Painter contends that cultural factors like language and religion divide African Americans from their ancestors. Black Americans speak a wide variety of languages, but usually these are not African. Painter notes how important language is in shaping our cultural identity; it dictates in large part how we think and feel. Linguistic differences create significant boundaries between peoples (5).

Even though there are a few words from the original in this paraphrase, such as *identity* and *language*, these sentences are original in structure and wording while accurately conveying the meaning of the source.

16 | Use Sources Effectively

Decide When to Quote and When to Paraphrase

Use sources to support what you say; don't allow them to say it for you. Next to plagiarism, the worst mistake you can make with sources is to string together a series of long quotations. This strategy leaves your readers wondering whether you have anything to say.

When to quote and when to paraphrase

The general rule in deciding when to include direct quotations and when to paraphrase lies in the importance of the original wording.

- If you want to refer to an idea or a fact and the original wording is not critical, make the point in your own words.
- Save direct quotations for language that is memorable or conveys the character of the source.

WRITING SMART

Use quotations effectively

Quotations are a frequent problem area in research projects. Review every quotation to ensure that each is used effectively and correctly.

- **Limit the use of long quotations.** If you have more than one block quotation on a page, look closely to see whether one or more can be paraphrased or summarized. Use direct quotations only when the original wording is important.
- **Check that each quotation is supporting your major points rather than making major points for you.** If the ideas rather than the original wording are what's important, paraphrase the quotation and cite the source.
- **Check that each quotation is introduced and attributed.** Each quotation should be introduced and the author or title named. Check for verbs that signal a quotation: Smith *claims*, Jones *argues*, Brown *states*.
- **Check that each quotation is properly formatted and punctuated.** Prose quotations longer than four lines (MLA) or forty words (APA) should be indented ten spaces in MLA style or five spaces in APA style. Shorter quotations should be enclosed within quotation marks.
- **Check that you cite the source for each quotation.** You are required to cite the sources of all direct quotations, paraphrases, and summaries.
- **Check the accuracy of each quotation.** It's easy to leave out words or mistype a quotation. Compare what is in your project to the original source. If you need to add words to make the quotation grammatical, make sure the added words are in brackets. Use ellipses to indicate omitted words.
- **Read your project aloud to a classmate or a friend.** Each quotation should flow smoothly when you read your project aloud. Put a check beside rough spots as you read aloud so you can revise later.

16b   Integrate Quotations

All sources should be well integrated into the fabric of your project. Introduce quotations by attributing them in your text:

> Even those who fought for the United States in the U.S.-Mexican War of 1846 were skeptical of American motives: "We were sent to provoke a fight, but it was essential that Mexico should commence it" (Grant 68).

The preceding quotation is used correctly, but it loses the impact of the source. Compare it with the following:

> Many soldiers who fought for the United States in the U.S.-Mexican War of 1846 were skeptical of American motives, including Civil War hero and future president Ulysses S. Grant, who wrote: "We were sent to provoke a fight, but it was essential that Mexico should commence it" (68).

Use signal phrases

Signal verbs often indicate your stance toward a quotation. Introducing a quotation with "X says" or "X believes" tells your readers nothing. Find a livelier verb that suggests how you are using the source. For example, if you write "X contends," your reader is alerted that you likely will disagree with the source. Be as precise as possible.

Signal phrases that report information or a claim

X argues that . . .
X claims that . . .
X observes that . . .
As X puts it, . . .
X reports that . . .

Signal phrases when you agree with the source

X affirms that . . .
X has the insight that . . .
X points out insightfully that . . .
X theorizes that . . .
X verifies that . . .

Signal phrases when you disagree with the source

X complains that . . .

X contends that . . .

X denies that . . .

X disputes that . . .

X overlooks that . . .

X rejects that . . .

Signal phrases in the sciences

Signal phrases in the sciences often use the past tense, especially for inter-pretations and commentary.

X described . . .

X found . . .

X has suggested . . .

Introduce block quotations

Long direct quotations, called **block quotations**, are indented from the margin instead of being placed in quotation marks. In MLA style, a quotation longer than four lines should be indented 1 inch. A quotation of forty words or longer is indented 1/2 inch in APA style. In both MLA and APA styles, long quotations are double-spaced. You still need to integrate a block quotation into the text of your project by mentioning who wrote or said it.

- No quotation marks appear around the block quotation.
- Words quoted in the original retain the double quotation marks.
- The page number citation appears after the period at the end of the block quotation.

It is a good idea to include at least one or two sentences following the quotation to describe its significance to your thesis.

Double-check quotations

Whether they are long or short, you should double-check all quotations you use to be sure they are accurate and that all words belonging to the original are set off with quotation marks or placed in a block quotation. If you wish to leave out words from a quotation, indicate the omitted words with an ellipsis (. . .), but make sure you do not alter the meaning of the original quote.

17 | MLA Documentation

Research writing requires you to document the sources of all of your information that is not common knowledge. The style developed by the Modern Language Association (MLA) requires you to document each source in two places: an in-text citation in the body of your project, and a list of all works cited at the end.

MLA DOCUMENTATION MAP

1 | Collect the right Information

For every source you need to have

- the name of the author or authors,
- the full title, and
- complete publication information.

For instructions, go to the illustrated examples in section 17d of the four major source types:

- **PRINTED ARTICLE**
- **PRINTED BOOK**
- **DATABASE PUBLICATION**
- **WEB PUBLICATION**

For other kinds of sources such as visual and multimedia sources, see the Index of Works-Cited Entries on pp. 148–149.

2 | Cite sources in two places

Remember, this is a two-part process.

To create citations

a) in **the body of your paper**, go to 17a and 17c.
b) in a **List of Works Cited at the end of your paper**, go to 17b.

If you have questions that the examples in this chapter do not address, consult the *MLA Handbook for Writers of Research Papers*, seventh edition (2009), and the *MLA Style Manual and Guide to Scholarly Publishing*, third edition (2008).

3 | Find the right model citations

You'll find **illustrated examples of sources** in 17d.

Once you match your source to one of those examples, you can move on to more specific examples:

- **PRINTED ARTICLE,** go to 17e.
- **PRINTED BOOK** or parts of a book, go to 17f.
- **ONLINE:** was the source
  a) in a **library database**?
     Go to 17g.
  b) from **another Web source**?
     Go to 17h.

A complete list of examples is found in the Index of Works-Cited Entries on pp. 148–149.

4 | Format your paper

You will find a **sample research paper in MLA style** and instructions on formatting the body of your paper and your works-cited list in Section 17k.

A note about footnotes:
MLA style does not use footnotes for documentation. Use in-text citations instead (see Sections 17a and 17c). The only use of footnotes in MLA style is for providing additional information.

17a Citing Sources in an MLA-style Project

Gabriella Lopez chose to make a proposal argument for a campus garden as her research project. You can see the complete paper in Section 17k at the end of this chapter.

How to quote and cite a source in the text of an MLA-style paper

Gabriella searched for an article on the *LexisNexis Academic* database using the search terms "green" and "college." She found the article below, and she printed a copy.

Name of Database

LexisNexis® *Academic*

Results List | Edit Search |

Show Full with Indexing ▼   Search within results [   ] [GO]

◀ 1 of 1 ▶

ⓘ Find a green college: Check!; Princet...

Journal Title

USA TODAY

Date

April 20, 2010 Tuesday
FINAL EDITION

Find a green college: Check!;
Princeton Review helps applicants who seek sustainability

Title of Article

BYLINE: Betty Klinck   **Author**

SECTION: LIFE; Pg. 7D   **Page Number**

LENGTH: 675 words

For the past 19 years, The Princeton Review ▽ has been helping students shop for colleges by creating guidebooks that look at a dizzying array of factors, from academics to campus life. So why would it add yet another factor to the checklist of items for college applicants to consider?

Put simply, because students are going green and care about a college's commitment to sustainability.

"This is going to be a major issue for our generation," says Lily Twining, a junior at Yale University in New Haven, Conn. She co-chairs the Yale Student Environmental Coalition.

The Princeton Review ▽ surveys students and parents every year, and in 2008, it added a "green question" to its College Hopes and Worries Survey, says publisher Rob Franek. The company found that 63% of the 10,300 high school-age college applicants and parents surveyed said they would find information about a college's dedication to the environment useful in their college selection process. In 2009, it was 66%.

To support her argument that many students consider a college's commitment to sustainability when selecting a college, she wanted to quote the statistic that 66% of students and parents surveyed would find it useful to have information about a college's dedication to the environment.

Gabriella can either (a) mention Betty Klinck in the text of her paper with a signal phrase (see pages 128–129) or (b) place the author's name inside parentheses following the quotation. Either with or without the signal phrase, in most cases she must include inside parentheses the page number where she found the quotation. Gabriella could omit the page number for this source because MLA does not require the page number for in-text citations of one-page sources.

Author's name in signal phrase

Betty Klinck reports that in 2009, the *Princeton Review* found that 66% of high school-age college applicants and parents surveyed "would find information about a college's dedication to the environment useful in their college selection process" (7D).

OR

Author's name in parenthetical citation

In 2009, the *Princeton Review* found that 66% of high school-age college applicants and parents surveyed "would find information about a college's dedication to the environment useful in their college selection process" (Klinck 7D).

If Gabriella includes a quotation that is four lines or longer, she must doublespace and indent the quotation in her paper 1 inch (see example on pp. 167–68).

Include in-text citations for summaries and paraphrases

In another paragraph, Gabriella summarized Bartholomew's recommendations and gave the page numbers from that source.

The size of each square in the grid depends on what plants are planted there; certain plants require larger and deeper grids (Bartholomew 15-16). The main benefit of square-foot gardening is that one can grow the same amount of produce in a 140-square-foot grid that is typically grown in the average 700 square foot, single-row garden (Bartholomew 42).

17b Creating the List of Works Cited

Gabriella is ready to create an entry for the List of Works Cited at the end of her paper.

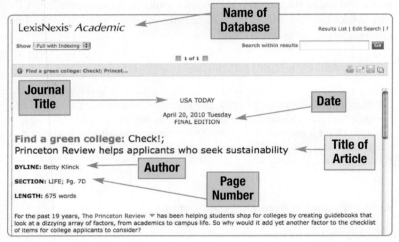

Gabriella asked herself a series of questions to create an entry for this source in her List of Works Cited.

1. What information do I need to pull from this screenshot?

For a source like this article from an online database, she needs to know five things: (1) what type of source it is; (2) the author; (3) the title; (4) the publication information; and (5) information about the online database.

2. I know this is from my library's online database, but that could be one of several different types of sources. What kind of source is this?

Gabriella selected newspapers for the source type in her *LexisNexis Academic* search; thus she knew that her source type would be a newspaper article.

3. Now how do I find the author's name?

Look for a bold heading that says something like "AUTHOR" or "BYLINE." If more than one author is listed, take note of all names listed.

4. What is the title of my source?

If the title is not immediately evident, look for a heading that says "TITLE" or "HEADLINE."

5. Where do I find the publication information?

The name and date of the periodical are usually listed at the top of the page but are sometimes found at the bottom. In this case the page number is listed beside "SECTION."

6. Where do I find the name of the database?

For databases distributed by EBSCO, you have to look for the name of the database. EBSCO is the vendor who sells access to many databases such as *Academic Search Complete*. LexisNexis is the vendor that distributes access to *LexisNexis Academic* and other LexisNexis databases.

Gabriella listed the information.

AUTHOR	Klinck, Betty
TITLE OF ARTICLE	"Find a Green College: Check! Princeton Review Helps Applicants Who Seek Sustainability"
PUBLICATION INFORMATION	
Name of periodical	USA Today
Date of publication	20 Apr. 2010, final ed.
Section and page number	7D
DATABASE INFORMATION	
Name of database	LexisNexis Academic
Date the site was accessed	20 Apr. 2010

Then she used the instructions on page 145 to format her citation.

Lopez 10

Works Cited

Klinck, Betty. "Find a Green College: Check! Princeton Review Helps Applicants Who Seek Sustainability." *USA Today* 20 Apr. 2010, final ed.: 7D. *LexisNexis Academic*. Web. 20 Apr. 2010.

17c In-text Citations in MLA Style

Index of in-text citations

1. Author named in a signal phrase

Put the author's name in a signal phrase in your sentence.

Sociologist Daniel Bell called this emerging U.S. economy the "postindustrial society" (3).

2. Author not named in your text

In 1997, the Gallup poll reported that 55% of adults in the United States think secondhand smoke is "very harmful," compared to only 36% in 1994 (Saad 4).

3. Work by one author

The author's last name comes first, followed by the page number. There is no comma.

(Bell 3)

4. Work by two or three authors

The authors' last names follow the order of the title page. If there are two authors, join the names with *and*. If there are three, use a comma between the first two names and a comma with *and* before the last name.

(Francisco, Vaughn, and Lynn 7)

5. Work by four or more authors

You may use the phrase *et al.* (meaning "and others") for all names but the first, or you may write out all the names. Make sure you use the same method for both the in-text citations and the works-cited list.

(Abrams et al. 1653)

6. Author unknown

Use a shortened version of the title that includes at least the first important word. Your reader will use the shortened title to find the full title in the works-cited list.

A review in the *New Yorker* of Ryan Adams's new album focuses on the artist's age ("Pure" 25).

Notice that "Pure" is in quotation marks because it is the shortened title of an article. If it were a book, the short title would be in italics.

7. Quotations longer than four lines

NOTE: When using indented ("block") quotations that are longer than four lines, the period appears *before* the parentheses enclosing the page number.

In her article "Art for Everybody," Susan Orlean attempts to explain the popularity of painter Thomas Kinkade:

> People like to own things they think are valuable. . . . The high price of limited editions is part of their appeal: it implies that they are choice and exclusive, and that only a certain class of people will be able to afford them. (128)

This same statement could also explain the popularity of phenomena like PBS's *Antiques Road Show*.

8. **Two or more works by the same author**

Use the author's last name and then a shortened version of the title of each source.

The majority of books written about coauthorship focus on partners of the same sex (Laird, *Women* 351).

Note that *Women* is italicized because it is the title of a book.

9. **Different authors with the same last name**

Include the initial of the first name in the parenthetical reference.

Web surfing requires more mental involvement than channel surfing (S. Johnson 107).

10. **Two or more sources within the same citation**

If two sources support a single point, separate them with a semicolon.

(McKibbin 39; Gore 92)

11. Work quoted in another source

When you do not have access to the original source of the material you wish to use and only an indirect source is available, put the abbreviation *qtd. in* ("quoted in") before the information about the indirect source.

> National governments have become increasingly what Ulrich Beck, in a 1999 interview, calls "zombie institutions"—institutions which are "dead and still alive" (qtd. in Bauman 6).

12. One-page source

A page reference is unnecessary when you are citing a one-page work.

> Economists agree that automating routine work is the broad goal of globalization (Lohr).

13. Web sources including Web pages, blogs, podcasts, wikis, videos, and other multimedia sources

MLA prefers that you mention the author in your text instead of putting the author's name in parentheses.

> Andrew Keen ironically used his own blog to claim that "blogs are boring to write (yawn), boring to read (yawn) and boring to discuss (yawn)."

14. Classic works

To supply a reference to classic works, you sometimes need more than a page number from a specific edition. Readers should be able to locate a quotation in any edition of the book. Give the page number from the edition that you are using, then a semicolon and other identifying information.

> "Marriage is a house" is one of the most memorable lines in *Don Quixote* (546; pt. 2, bk. 3, ch. 19).

17d Illustrated Samples and Index of Works Cited Entries in MLA Style

Printed Article

Scholarly journals usually list the publication information at the top or bottom of the first page. Popular magazines often do not list volume and issue numbers. You can find the date of publication on the cover.

> **Name of Journal, Volume Number, Issue Number, Date of Publication, Page Numbers**

Ecological Applications, 17(6), 2007, pp. 1742–1751
© 2007 by the Ecological Society of America

A CROSS-REGIONAL ASSESSMENT OF THE FACTORS AFFECTING ECOLITERACY: IMPLICATIONS FOR POLICY AND PRACTICE

SARAH PILGRIM, DAVID SMITH, AND JULES PRETTY[1]   **Authors**

Centre for Environment and Society, Department of Biological Sciences, University of Essex, Wivenhoe Park, Colchester CO4 3SQ United Kingdom

Title of Article

Abstract. The value of accumulated ecological knowledge, termed ecoliteracy, is vital to both human and ecosystem health. Maintenance of this knowledge is essential for continued support of local conservation efforts and the capacity of communities to self- or co-manage their local resources sustainably. Most previous studies have been qualitative and small scale, documenting ecoliteracy in geographically isolated locations. In this study, we take a different approach, focusing on (1) the primary factors affecting individual levels of ecoliteracy, (2) whether these factors shift with economic development, and (3) if different knowledge protection strategies are required for the future. We compared non-resource-dependent communities in the United Kingdom with resource-dependent communities in India and Indonesia (n = 1250 interviews). We found that UK residents with the highest levels of ecoliteracy visited the countryside frequently, lived and grew up in rural areas, and acquired their knowledge from informal word-of-mouth sources, such as parents and friends, rather than television and schooling. The ecoliteracy of resource-dependent community members, however, varied with wealth status and gender. The least wealthy families depended most on local resources for their livelihoods and had the highest levels of ecoliteracy. Gender roles affected both the level and content of an individual's ecoliteracy. The importance of reciprocal oral transfer of this knowledge in addition to direct experience to the maintenance of ecoliteracy was apparent at all sites. Lessons learned may contribute to new local resource management strategies for combined ecoliteracy conservation. Without novel policies, local community management capacity is likely to be depleted in the future.

Key words: ecoliteracy; India; Indonesia; knowledge; natural resource; oral traditions; resource management; sustainable management; United Kingdom.

Citation in the List of Works Cited

> Pilgrim, Sarah, David Smith, and Jules Pretty. "A Cross-Regional Assessment of the Factors Affecting Ecoliteracy: Implications for Policy and Practice." *Ecological Applications* 17.6 (2007): 1742-51. Print.

Elements of the citation

Author's Name

The author's last name comes first, followed by a comma and the first name.

For two or more works by the same author, see page 154.

Title of Article

Use the exact title and put it inside quotation marks. If a book title is part of the article's title, italicize the book title.

Publication Information

Name of journal or newspaper
Italicize the title of the journal or newspaper.

Abbreviate the title if it commonly appears that way.

Volume, issue, and page numbers
For scholarly journals give the volume number and issue number. Place a period between the volume and issue numbers: "55.3" indicates volume 55, issue 3.

Some scholarly journals use issue numbers only.

Give the page numbers for the entire article, not just the part you used.

Medium of publication
Print.

Find the right example for your model (you may need to refer to more than one model)

What type of article do you have?

A scholarly journal article?
Go to page 151, #22–23.

A newspaper article, review, editorial, or letter to the editor?

- For a newspaper article, go to pages 152–153, #27–31.
- For a review, go to page 153, #32.
- For an editorial, go to page 153, #34.
- For a letter to the editor, go to page 153, #33.

A government document?
Go to page 153, #35–36.

How many authors are listed?

- One, two, or more authors: go to page 150, #15–17.
- Unknown author: go to page 150, #18.

What kind of pagination is used?

- For a scholarly journal, go to page 151, #22.
- For a journal that starts every issue with page 1, go to page 151, #23.

Printed Book

Find the copyright date on the copyright page, which is on the back of the title page. Use the copyright date for the date of publication, not the date of printing.

IN DEFENSE OF FOOD ← Book Title

AN EATER'S MANIFESTO

EAT FOOD. NOT TOO MUCH. MOSTLY PLANTS.

Author → MICHAEL POLLAN

AUTHOR OF
THE OMNIVORE'S DILEMMA

Citation in the List of Works Cited

Pollan, Michael. *In Defense of Food: An Eater's Manifesto*. New York: Penguin, 2008. Print.

Elements of the citation

Author's or Editor's Name
The author's last name comes first, followed by a comma and the first name.

For edited books, put the abbreviation *ed.* after the name, preceded by a comma:
Kavanagh, Peter, ed.

Book Title
Use the exact title, as it appears on the title page (not the cover).

Italicize the title.

Publication Information

Place of publication
If more than one city is given, use the first.

For cities outside the U.S., add an abbreviation of the country or province if the city is not well known.

Publisher
Omit words such as *Publisher* and *Inc*.

For university presses, use *UP*: New York UP

Shorten the name. For example, shorten *W. W. Norton & Co.* to *Norton*.

Date of publication
Give the year as it appears on the copyright page.

Otherwise, put n.d. ("no date"): Boston: Harvard UP, n.d.

Medium of publication
Print.

Find the right example for your model (you may need to refer to more than one model)

How many authors are listed?

- One, two, or more authors: go to page 154, #38–41.
- Unknown author: go to page 155, #42.
- Group or organization as the author: go to page 155, #43.

Do you have only a part of a book?

- For an introduction, foreword, preface, or afterword, go to page 155, #44.

- For a chapter in an anthology or edited collection, go to page 155, #45.

- For more than one selection in an anthology or edited collection, go to page 155, #46.

Do you have two or more books by the same author?

- Go to page 154, #39.

Library Database Publication

You will find library databases linked off your library's Web site.

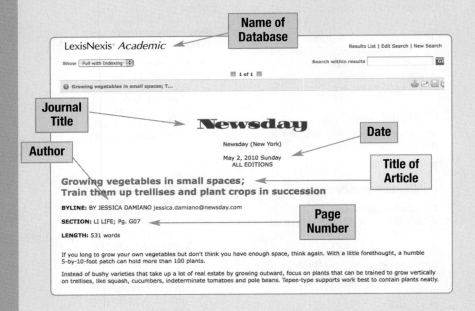

Citation in the List of Works Cited

> Damiano, Jessica. "Growing Vegetables in Small Spaces: Train Them up Trellises and Plant Crops in Succession." *Newsday* 2 May 2010: G107. *LexisNexis Academic.* Web. 8 Apr. 2010.

Take Note

Don't confuse the name of the vendor—the company that sells access to the database—with the name of the database. For example, EBSCO or EBSCO Host is not the name of a database but the name of the vendor that sells access to databases such as *Academic Search Complete.*

Elements of the citation

Start with the citation with the exact format for a print citation. Replace the word *Print* at the end with the name of the database, the medium (*Web*), and the date you accessed the source.

Author's Name

The author's last name comes first, followed by a comma and the first name.

Title of Source

Use the exact title and put it inside quotation marks.

Publication Information for an Article

Name of journal or newspaper
Italicize the title of the journal or newspaper. Abbreviate the title if it commonly appears that way.

Volume, issue, date, and page numbers
List the same information you would for a print item. If there are no page numbers, put *n. pag.* where the page numbers would ordinarily go.

Database Information

Name of the database
Italicize the name of the database, followed by a period.

Medium of publication
For all database sources, the medium of publication is *Web*.

Date of access
List the date you accessed the source (day, month, year).

Find the right example for your model (you may need to refer to more than one model)

Most databases allow you to search by document type, such as scholarly journal, newspaper article, financial report, legal case, or abstract. Use these categories to identify the type of publication.

What kind of publication do you have?

- For an article in a scholarly journal, go to page 157, #55
- For a magazine article, go to page 157, #56
- For a newspaper article, go to page 157, #58
- For a legal case, go to page 157, #59

Do you have a publication with an unknown author?
Go to page 157, #57.

Web Publication

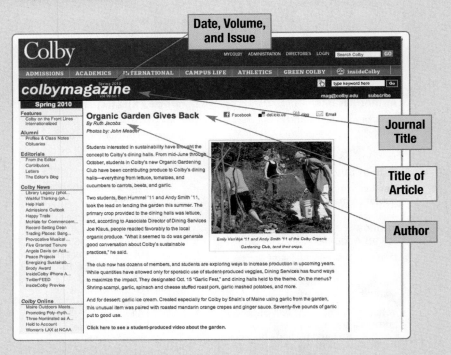

Date, Volume, and Issue

Journal Title

Title of Article

Author

Citation in the List of Works Cited

Jacobs, Ruth. "Organic Garden Gives Back." *Colby Magazine* 99.1 (2010): n. pag. Web. 2 Apr. 2010.

When Do You List a URL?

MLA style no longer requires including URLs of Web sources. URLs are of limited value because they change frequently and they can be specific to an individual search. Include the URL as supplementary information only when your readers probably cannot locate the source without the URL.

Elements of the citation

Author's Name

Authorship is sometimes hard to discern for online sources. If you know the author or creator, follow the rules for books and journals.

If the only authority you find is a group or organization, list its name after the date of publication or last revision.

Title of Source

Place the title of the work inside quotation marks if it is part of a larger Web site.

Untitled works may be identified by a label (e.g., *Home page, Introduction*). List the label in the title slot without quotation marks or italics.

Italicize the name of the overall site if it is different from the work. The name of the overall Web site will usually be found on its index or home page.

Some Web sites are updated, so list the version if you find it (e.g., *Vers. 1.2*).

Publication Information for Web Sources

List the publisher's or sponsor's name followed by a comma. If it isn't available, use *N.p.*

List the date of publication by day, month, and year if available. If you cannot find a date, use *n.d.*

Give the medium of publication (*Web*).

List the date you accessed the site by day, month, and year.

Find the right example for your model (you may need to refer to more than one model)

Do you have a Web page or an entire Web site?

- For an entire Web site, go to page 158, #61
- For a page on a Web site, go to page 158, #60

What kind of publication do you have, and who is the author?

- For a known author, go to page 158, #62
- For a group or organization as the author, go to page 158, #63
- For a publication with print publication data, go to page 158, #64
- For a PDF or digital file, go to page 159, #65
- For an article in a scholarly journal, newspaper, or magazine, go to page 159, #66–68

Do you have a source that is posted by an individual?

- For e-mail or text messaging, go to page 161, #73
- For a post to a discussion list, go to page 161, #74
- For a personal home page, go to page 161, #76
- For a blog, go to page 161, #77

Index of Works Cited Entries

17e Journals, Magazines, Newspapers, and Other Print Sources

JOURNAL AND MAGAZINE ARTICLES

15. Article by one author

> Bhabha, Jacqueline. "The Child—What Sort of Human?"
>   *PMLA* 121.5 (2006): 1526-35. Print.

16. Article by two or three authors

The second and subsequent authors' names are printed first name first.

> Kirsch, Gesa E., and Jacqueline J. Royster. "Feminist Rhetorical
>   Practices: In Search of Excellence." *CCC* 61.4 (2010): 640-72.
>   Print.

Notice that a comma separates the authors' names.

17. Article by four or more authors

You may use the phrase *et al.* (meaning "and others") for all authors but the first, or you may write out all the names.

> Breece, Katherine E., et al. "Patterns of mtDNA Diversity in
>   Northwestern North America." *Human Biology* 76.5 (2004):
>   33-54. Print.

18. Article by an unknown author

Begin the entry with the title.

> "The Fire Next Time." *Newsweek* 5 July 2010: 83. Print.

19. Article with a title within a title

If the title of the article contains the title of another short work, include it in single quotation marks. Italicize a title or a word that would normally be italicized.

> Happel, Alison, and Jennifer Esposito. "Vampires, Vixens, and
>   Feminists: An Analysis of *Twilight*." *Educational Studies* 46.5
>   (2010): 524-31. Print.

MONTHLY, WEEKLY, AND BIWEEKLY MAGAZINES

20. Monthly or seasonal magazines or journals

Use the month (or season) and year in place of the volume. Abbreviate the names of all months except May, June, and July.

> Huang, Yasheng. "China's Other Path." *Wilson Quarterly* Spring
> 2010: 58-64. Print.

21. Weekly or biweekly magazines

For weekly or biweekly magazines, give both the day and month of publication, as listed on the issue.

> Toobin, Jeffrey. "Crackdown." *New Yorker* 5 Nov. 2001: 56-61. Print.

DIFFERENT TYPES OF PAGINATION

22. Article in a scholarly journal

List the volume and issue numbers after the name of the journal.

> Duncan, Mike. "Whatever Happened to the Paragraph?" *College
> English* 69.5 (2007): 470-95. Print.

23. Article in a scholarly journal that uses only issue numbers

If a journal begins each issue on page 1, list the issue number after the name of the journal.

> McCall, Sophie. "Double Vision Reading." *Canadian Literature* 194
> (2007): 95-97. Print.

REVIEWS, EDITORIALS, LETTERS TO THE EDITOR

24. Review

Provide the title, if given, and name the work reviewed. If there is no title, just name the work reviewed. For film reviews, name the director.

> Mendelsohn, Daniel. "The Two Oscar Wildes." Rev. of *The
> Importance of Being Earnest*, dir. Oliver Parker. *New York
> Review of Books* 10 Oct. 2002: 23-24. Print.

25. Letter to the editor

Add the word *Letter* after the name of the author.

> Patai, Daphne. Letter. *Harper's Magazine* Dec. 2001: 4. Print.

26. Editorial

If the editorial is unsigned, put the title first. Add the word *Editorial* after the title.

> "Stop Stonewalling on Reform." Editorial. *Business Week* 17 June
>   2002: 108. Print.

NEWSPAPER ARTICLES

27. Article by one author

> Rojas, Rick. "For Young Sikhs, a Tie That Binds Them to Their
>   Faith." *Washington Post* 20 June 2010, final ed.: C03. Print.

28. Article by two or three authors

The second and subsequent authors' names are printed in regular order, first name first:

> Chazen, Guy, and Dana Cimilluca. "BP Amasses Cash for Oil-Spill
>   Costs." *Wall Street Journal* 26 June 2010: A1. Print.

Notice that a comma separates the authors' names.

29. Article by four or more authors

You may use the phrase *et al.* (meaning "and others") for all authors but the first, or you may write out all the names. Use the same method in the in-text citation as you do in the works-cited list.

> Watson, Anne, et al. "Childhood Obesity on the Rise." *Daily
>   Missoulian* 7 July 2003: B1. Print.

30. Article by an unknown author

Begin the entry with the title.

> "Democratic Candidates Debate Iraq War." *Austin American-
>   Statesman* 19 Jan. 2004: A6. Print.

31. **Article that continues to a nonconsecutive page**

    Add a plus sign after the number of the first page.

    > Kaplow, Larry, and Tasgola Karla Bruner. "U.S.: Don't Let Taliban Forces Flee." *Austin American-Statesman* 20 Nov. 2001, final ed.: A11+. Print.

NEWSPAPER REVIEWS, EDITORIALS, LETTERS TO THE EDITOR

32. **Review**

    List the reviewer's name and the title of the review. Then write *Rev. of* followed by the title of the work, the word *by*, and the author's name.

    > Garner, Dwight. "Violence Expert Visits Her Dark Past?" Rev. of *Denial: A Memoir of Terror*, by Jessica Stern. *New York Times* 25 June 2010: 28. Print.

33. **Letter to the editor**

    > Leach, Richard E. Letter. *Boston Globe* 2 Apr. 2007, first ed.: A10. Print.

34. **Editorial**

    If the editorial is unsigned, put the title first.

    > "High Court Ruling Doesn't Mean Vouchers Will Work." Editorial. *Atlanta Journal and Constitution* 28 June 2002, home ed.: A19. Print.

GOVERNMENT DOCUMENTS

35. **Government document**

    > United States. General Services Administration. *Consumer Action Handbook*. Washington: GPO, 2008. Print.

36. *Congressional Record*

    > Cong. Rec. 8 Feb. 2000: 1222-46. Print.

DISSERTATIONS

37. Published dissertation or thesis

> Mason, Jennifer. *Civilized Creatures: Animality, Cultural Power, and American Literature, 1850-1901*. Diss. U of Texas at Austin, 2000. Ann Arbor: UMI, 2000. Print.

17f Books

ONE AUTHOR

38. Book by one author

> Mayer-Schönberger, Viktor. *Delete: The Virtue of Forgetting in the Digital Age*. Princeton: Princeton UP, 2009. Print.

39. Two or more books by the same author

In the entry for the first book, include the author's name. In the second entry, substitute three hyphens and a period for the author's name. List the titles of books by the same author in alphabetical order.

> Krakauer, Jon. *Into the Wild*. New York: Villard, 1996. Print.

> ---. *Where Men Win Glory: The Odyssey of Pat Tillman*. New York: Doubleday, 2009. Print.

MULTIPLE AUTHORS

40. Book by two or three authors

The second and subsequent authors' names appear first name first.

> Burger, Edward B., and Michael Starbird. *Coincidences, Chaos, and All That Math Jazz*. New York: Norton, 2006. Print.

41. Book by four or more authors

You may use the phrase *et al.* (meaning "and others") for all authors but the first, or you may write out all the names. Use the same method in the in-text citation as you do in the works-cited list.

> North, Stephen M., et al. *Refiguring the Ph.D. in English Studies*. Urbana: NCTE, 2000. Print.

ANONYMOUS AND GROUP AUTHORS

42. Book by an unknown author

Begin the entry with the title.

Encyclopedia of Americana. New York: Somerset, 2001. Print.

43. Book by a group or organization

Treat the group as the author of the work.

United Nations. *The Charter of the United Nations: A Commentary*. New York: Oxford UP, 2000. Print.

PARTS OF BOOKS

44. Introduction, foreword, preface, or afterword

Benstock, Sheri. Introduction. *The House of Mirth*. By Edith Wharton. Boston: Bedford-St. Martin's, 2002. 3-24. Print.

45. Chapter in an anthology or edited collection

Sedaris, David. "Full House." *The Best American Nonrequired Reading 2004*. Ed. Dave Eggers. Boston: Houghton, 2004. 350-58. Print.

46. More than one selection from an anthology or edited collection

Multiple selections from a single anthology can be handled by creating a complete entry for the anthology and shortened cross-references for individual works in that anthology.

Adichie, Chimamanda Ngozi. "Half of a Yellow Sun." Eggers 1-17.

Eggers, Dave, ed. *The Best American Nonrequired Reading 2004*. Boston: Houghton, 2004. Print.

Sedaris, David. "Full House." Eggers 350-58.

47. Article in a reference work

"Utilitarianism." *The Columbia Encyclopedia*. 6th ed. 2001. Print.

THE BIBLE AND OTHER SACRED TEXTS

48. Sacred texts

> *The New Oxford Annotated Bible*. Ed. Bruce M. Metzger and Roland
>   E. Murphy. New York: Oxford UP, 1991. Print.

Use a period to separate the chapter and verse in the in-text note:
(John 3.16)

EDITIONS, TRANSLATIONS, AND ILLUSTRATED BOOKS

49. Book with an editor—focus on the editor

> Lewis, Gifford, ed. *The Big House of Inver*. By Edith Somerville and
>   Martin Ross. Dublin: Farmar, 2000. Print.

50. Book with an editor—focus on the author

> Somerville, Edith, and Martin Ross. *The Big House of Inver*. Ed.
>   Gifford Lewis. Dublin: Farmar, 2000. Print.

51. Book with a translator

> Mallarmé, Stéphane. *Divagations*. Trans. Barbara Johnson.
>   Cambridge: Harvard UP, 2007. Print.

52. Second or subsequent edition of a book

> Hawthorn, Jeremy, ed. *A Concise Glossary of Contemporary Literary
>   Theory*. 3rd ed. London: Arnold, 2001. Print.

53. Illustrated book or graphic narrative

After the title of the book, give the illustrator's name, preceded by the
abbreviation *Illus*. If the emphasis is on the illustrator's work, place the illustrator's name first, followed by the abbreviation *illus.*, and list the author
after the title, preceded by the word *By*.

> Strunk, William, Jr., and E. B. White. *The Elements of Style
>   Illustrated*. Illus. Maira Kalman. New York: Penguin, 2005. Print.

MULTIVOLUME WORKS

54. One volume of a multivolume work

Samuel, Raphael. *Theatres of Memory*. Vol. 1. London: Verso, 1999. Print.

17g Library Database Sources

Give the print citation followed by the name of the database in italics, the medium (Web), and the date you accessed the database. You do not need to list the URL of common library databases.

55. Scholarly journal article from a library database

Klesges, Robert C., Mary L. Shelton, and Lisa M. Klesges. "Effects of Television on Metabolic Rate: Potential Implications for Childhood Obesity." *Pediatrics* 91 (1993): 281-86. *Academic Search Complete*. Web. 14 Nov. 2010.

56. Magazine article from a library database

"The Trouble with Immortality: If We Could Live Forever, Would We Really Want To?" *Newsweek* 5 July 2010, US ed.: 78. *Academic Search Complete*. Web. 9 Dec. 2010.

57. Article with unknown author from a library database

"Dicing with Data: Facebook, Google and Privacy." *Economist* 22 May 2010, US ed.: 16. *LexisNexis Academic*. Web. 15 Sept. 2010.

58. Newspaper article from a library database

Franciane, Valerie. "Quarter Is Ready to Rock." *Times-Picayune* [New Orleans] 3 Apr. 2007: 1. *LexisNexis Academic*. Web. 23 Jan. 2010.

59. Legal case from a library database

Bilski v. Kappos. US 08-964. Supreme Court of the US. 28 June 2010. *LexisNexis Academic*. Web. 28 June 2010.

17h Web Sources and Other Online Sources

WEB SITES

60. Page on a Web site

The basic format for citing a Web page includes the author or editor, the title of the page, the title of the site (in italics), the sponsor or publisher of the site, the date of publication, the medium (*Web*), and the date you accessed the site.

> Boerner, Steve. "Leopold Mozart." *The Mozart Project: Biography.*
> Mozart Project, 21 Mar. 1998. Web. 30 Oct. 2010.

61. Entire Web site

> Boerner, Steve. *The Mozart Project.* Mozart Project, 20 July 2007.
> Web. 30 Oct. 2010.

PUBLICATIONS ON THE WEB

62. Publication by a known author

> Samadzadeh, Nozlee. "Farm Update: The Third Annual Jack Hitt
> Annual Last Day of Classes Pig Roast." *Yale Sustainable Food
> Project Student Blog.* Yale Sustainable Food Project, 3 May
> 2010. Web. 10 May 2010.

63. Publication by a group or organization

If a work has no author's or editor's name listed, begin the entry with the title.

> "State of the Birds." *Audubon.* Natl. Audubon Society, 2010. Web.
> 19 Aug. 2010.

64. Publication on the Web with print publication data

Include the print publication information. Then give the name of the Web site or database in italics, the medium of publication (*Web*), and the date of access (day, month, and year).

Kirsch, Irwin S., et al. *Adult Literacy in America*. Darby: Diane,
1993. *Google Scholar*. Web. 30 Oct. 2010.

65. PDFs and digital files

Glaser, Edward L., and Albert Saiz. "The Rise of the Skilled City."
Discussion Paper No. 2025. Harvard Institute of Economic
Research. Cambridge: Harvard U, 2003. PDF file.

PERIODICALS ON THE WEB

66. Article in a scholarly journal on the Web

Some scholarly journals are published on the Web only. List articles by
author, title, name of journal in italics, volume and issue number, and year
of publication. If the journal does not have page numbers, use *n. pag.* in
place of page numbers. Then list the medium of publication (*Web*) and the
date of access (day, month, and year).

Fleckenstein, Kristie. "Who's Writing? Aristotelian Ethos and the
Author Position in Digital Poetics." *Kairos* 11.3 (2007): n.
pag. Web. 6 Apr. 2010.

67. Article in a newspaper on the Web

List the name of the newspaper in italics, followed by a period and the
publisher's name. Follow the publisher's name with a comma. The first date
is the date of publication; the second is the date of access.

Brown, Patricia Leigh. "Australia in Sonoma." *New York Times*. New
York Times, 5 July 2008. Web. 3 Aug. 2010.

68. Article in a popular magazine on the Web

Brown, Patricia Leigh. "The Wild Horse Is Us." *Newsweek*.
Newsweek, 1 July 2008. Web. 12 Dec. 2010.

BOOKS, ARCHIVES, AND GOVERNMENT PUBLICATIONS ON THE WEB

69. Book on the Web

If the book was printed and then scanned, give the print publication information. Then give the name of the database or Web site in italics, the medium of publication (*Web*), and the date of access (day, month, and year).

> Prebish, Charles S., and Kenneth K. Tanaka. *The Faces of Buddhism in America*. Berkeley: U of California P, 2003. *eScholarship Editions*. Web. 2 May 2010.

70. Document within an archive on the Web

Give the print information, then the title of the scholarly project or archive in italics, the medium of publication (*Web*), and the date of access (day, month, and year).

> "New York Quiet." *Franklin Repository* 5 Aug. 1863, 1. *Valley of the Shadow*. Web. 23 Feb. 2010.

71. Government publication

If you cannot locate the author of the document, give the name of the government and the agency that published it.

> United States. Dept. of Health and Human Services. *Salmonellosis Outbreak in Certain Types of Tomatoes*. US Dept. of Health and Human Services, 5 July 2008. Web. 30 Nov. 2010.

UNEDITED ONLINE SOURCES

72. Wiki entry

Wiki content is written collaboratively, thus no author is listed. Because the content on a wiki changes frequently, wikis are not considered reliable scholarly sources.

> "Snowboard." *Wikipedia*. Wikimedia Foundation, 2010. Web. 30 Jan. 2010.

73. E-mail and text messaging

Give the name of the writer, the subject line, a description of the message, the date, and the medium of delivery (*E-mail, Text message*).

Ballmer, Steve. "A New Era of Business Productivity and Innovation."
Message to Microsoft Executive E-mail. 30 Nov. 2006. E-mail.

74. Posting to a discussion list

Give the name of the writer, the subject line, the name of the list in italics, the publisher, the date of the posting, the medium (*Web*), and the date of access.

Dobrin, Sid. "Re: ecocomposition?" *Writing Program Administration*.
Arizona State U, 19 Dec. 2008. Web. 5 Jan. 2009.

75. Course home page

Sparks, Julie. "English Composition 1B." Course home page. San
Jose State U, Fall 2008. Web. 17 Sept. 2008.

76. Personal home page

List *Home page* without quotation marks in place of the title.

Graff, Harvey J. Home page. Dept. of English, Ohio State U, n.d.
Web. 15 Nov. 2008.

77. Blog entry

If there is no sponsor or publisher for the blog, use *N.p.*

Arrington, Michael. "Think Before You Voicemail." *TechCrunch*.
N.p., 5 July 2008. Web. 10 Sept. 2010.

17i Visual Sources

78. Cartoon or comic strip

Trudeau, G. B. "Doonesbury." Comic strip. *Washington Post* 21 Apr.
2008. C15. Print.

79. Advertisement

Begin with the name of the advertiser or product, then the word *Advertisement*.

Nike. Advertisement. ABC. 8 Oct. 2010. Television.

80. Map, graph, or chart

Specify *Map, Graph,* or *Chart* after the title.

Greenland. Map. Vancouver: International Travel Maps, 2004. Print.

81. Painting, sculpture, or photograph

Give the artist's name if available, the title of the work in italics, its date of creation, the medium of composition, the name of the institution that houses the work and the city, or the name of the collection.

Manet, Edouard. *Olympia.* 1863. Oil on canvas. Musée d'Orsay, Paris.

VISUAL SOURCES ON THE WEB

82. Video on the Web

Video on the Web often lacks a creator and a date. Begin the entry with a title if you cannot find a creator. Use *n.d.* if you cannot find a date.

Wesch, Michael. *A Vision of Students Today. YouTube.* YouTube,
2007. Web. 28 May 2010.

83. Work of art on the Web

Include the artist, title of the work in italics, and the date. For works found on the Web, omit the medium but include the location or museum, then add the name of the Web site, the medium (*Web*), and the date of access.

Mapplethorpe, Robert. *Self Portrait.* 1972. Palm Springs Art Museum.
Robert Mapplethorpe Foundation. n.d. Web. 3 Nov. 2010.

84. Map on the Web

"Lansing, Michigan." Map. *Google Maps.* Google, 2008. Web. 19 Nov. 2010.

85. Cartoon or comic strip on the Web

> Tomorrow, Tom. "Modern World." Comic strip. *Huffington Post.*
> HuffingtonPost.com, 2 Jan. 2009. Web. 20 Jan. 2009.

17j Multimedia Sources

86. Sound recording

> McCoury, Del, perf. "1952 Vincent Black Lightning." By Richard
> Thompson. *Del and the Boys.* Ceili, 2001. CD.

87. Podcast

> Sussingham, Robin. "All Things Autumn." No. 2. *HighLifeUtah.*
> N.p., 20 Nov. 2006. Web. 28 Feb. 2011.

88. Film

Begin with the title in italics. List the director, the distributor, the date, and the medium. Other data, such as the names of the screenwriters and performers, is optional.

> *Wanted.* Dir. Timur Bekmambetov. Perf. James McAvoy, Angelina
> Jolie, and Morgan Freeman. Universal, 2008. Film.

89. DVD

> *No Country for Old Men.* Dir. Joel Coen and Ethan Coen. Perf.
> Tommy Lee Jones, Javier Bardem, and Josh Brolin.
> Paramount, 2007. DVD.

90. Television or radio program

> "Kaisha." *The Sopranos.* Perf. James Gandolfini, Lorraine Bracco,
> and Edie Falco. HBO. 4 June 2006. Television.

91. Telephone interview

> Minnelli, Liza. Telephone interview. 5 Mar. 2008.

92. Speech, debate, mediated discussion, or public talk

> Clinton, Hillary Rodham. "Remarks on Internet Freedom."
> Newseum. Washington. 21 Jan. 2010. Address.

17k Sample Research Paper with MLA Documentation

FORMATTING A RESEARCH PAPER IN MLA STYLE

MLA offers these general guidelines for formatting a research paper.

- **Use white, 8½-by-11-inch paper.** Don't use colored or lined paper.
- **Double-space everything—the title, headings, body of the paper, quotations, and works-cited list.** Set the line spacing on your word processor for double spacing and leave it there.
- **Put your last name and the page number at the top of every page, aligned with the right margin, ½ inch from the top of the page.** Your word processor has a header command that will automatically put a header with the page number on every page.
- **Specify 1-inch margins.** One-inch margins are the default setting for most word processors.
- **Do not justify (make even) the right margin.** Justifying the right margin throws off the spacing between words and makes your paper harder to read. Use the left-align setting instead.
- **Indent the first line of each paragraph ½ inch (5 spaces).** Set the paragraph indent command or the tab on the ruler of your word processor at ½ inch.
- **Use the same readable typeface throughout your paper.** Use a standard typeface such as Times New Roman, 12 point.
- **Use block format for quotations longer than four lines.** See pages 167–168.
- **MLA does not require a title page.** Unless your instructor asks for a separate title page, put 1 inch from the top of the page your name, your instructor's name, the course, and the date on separate lines. Center your title on the next line. Do not underline your title or put it inside quotation marks.

MLA style does not require a title page. Check with your instructor to find out whether you need one.

Gabriella Lopez

Professor Kimbro

English 1102

6 May 2010

Include your last name and page number as page header, beginning with the first page, 1/2" from the top.

Establishing a Campus Garden

Center the title. Do not underline the title, put it inside quotation marks, or type it in all capital letters.

When high school seniors begin to look at colleges and universities, they consider many factors: location, academics, and the quality of campus life, including food service. Now prospective students are also considering sustainability. According to a 2006 article in *USA Today*, students are increasingly interested in schools with "green" practices, which offer local, sustainable, and organic options in their food service (Horovitz). In 2009, the *Princeton Review* found that 66% of high school-age college applicants and parents surveyed "would find information about a college's dedication to the environment useful in their college selection process" (Klinck).

Do not include a page number for items without pagination, such as Web sites.

Specify 1" margins all around. Double-space everything.

Higher education is responding. Colleges and universities lead other institutions and industries with 3,850 LEED (Leadership in Energy and Environmental Design) certified buildings (Klinck), and show commitment to recycling and waste-reduction programs. Furthermore, schools are increasingly devoting at least a portion of food budgets to buying from local farms and producers (Pino). And this trend should only grow: the 2009-2014 Strategic Plan of the National Association of College and University Food Service (NACUFS) calls for the organization to become an integral player in sustainability policy-making and programming for higher education by advocating for and

Lopez 2

providing education on sustainable food service policies and
practices. Some schools, most notably Yale University, have even
established farms and gardens on or near campus that serve as
living classrooms for environmental studies and provide food for
students as well as the community (Samadzadeh).

"Going green" is not easy, nor is it inexpensive. For those
reasons, many schools, including our own, are finding it difficult
to move beyond campus-wide recycling programs to other
initiatives such as increasing the amount of local organic foods in
the dining halls. The fact that many colleges contract with
outside food service vendors makes this goal even more difficult.
An alternative approach, however, can provide both fresh, healthy
food and hands-on experience in environmental stewardship.
Establishing a small organic campus garden is a low-cost, high-
yield way to support our school's mission, our students, the local
community, and the global environment.

Our school in particular has a stated commitment to
creating a campus in which students feel safe and sustained in
an environment that is, according to the Web page, "contingent
on the every-day learning process." One of the immediate
benefits to establishing a campus organic garden is promoting
a healthy relationship to food. According to a survey of 2,200
American college students, a significant number of women and
a smaller group of men have "major concerns about eating and
food with respect to both weight and health" (Rozin, Bauer,
and Catanese 132). The negative feelings about food that result
from these concerns can lead to eating disorders, primarily in

---

Indent each paragraph five spaces (1/2" on the ruler in your word processor).

Lopez's thesis appears here, at the end of her third paragraph.

Give page numbers for paraphrases as well as direct quotations.

Lopez 3

young women (Rozin, Bauer, and Catanese 140). In short, Americans have become neurotic about eating. Michael Pollan attributes this anxiety to "nutritionism": the belief, fueled by food scientists and the food industry, that nutrients and the energy (or calorie) count is more important than actual food, and since nutrients exist at the molecular level, we believe we need to eat "scientifically," under the direction of the experts (8). This promotion of discrete nutrients over whole food has led to the industrialization of food production—more processed foods, more artificial grains, more chemicals to raise animals and vegetables in vast "monocultures," more sugars and fats, and less variety in our diet that has been reduced to a glut of wheat, corn, and soy (Pollan 10). Thus, not only is our industrialized diet making us physically sick; in fact, it is also making us emotionally unhealthy. Pollan observes that food concerns much more than nutrition: "Food is all about pleasure, about community, about family and spirituality, about our relationship to the natural world, and about expressing our identity"(8).

> Use a signal phrase to include the author's name before a quotation from a source.

Colleges are becoming increasingly aware of the relationships among individual, social, and environmental health, and that projects like campus farms and gardens serve not only students, but also the local population, and even the planet (Pino). The Dartmouth Organic Farm Web site points to these connections:

> Lopez introduces the block quotation, naming the source in the text.

> The very nature of an agricultural enterprise lies
> in the intersection of culture and the environment, to
> identify and respond to the needs of a society while

Lopez 4

Quotations of
more than four
lines should be
indented 1" or ten
spaces. Do not
use quotation
marks.

recognizing the limits and demands of the immediate,

local ecosystem. A farm is one of the last

institutionalized vestiges of our direct connection to

the natural world that surrounds and supports us.

There is evidence to support these claims. A study in the United

Kingdom found that people with the highest levels of

"ecoliteracy" (accumulated ecological knowledge) acquired that

knowledge through direct experience and talking with others

rather than from schooling and television (Pilgrim, Smith, and

Pretty).

One of the missions of our school, as stated on our Web

site, is "the development of men and women dedicated to

the service of others." Establishing a campus organic farm

that could immediately serve as a model of sound nutritional

and environmental practices, and perhaps one day provide

food for local relief organizations, certainly supports this

mission.

Another benefit to establishing a campus organic garden is

that it would provide educational opportunities to students who

are interested in the growing field of sustainability. As concern

about the environment grows, colleges and universities are

beginning to incorporate sustainability into their programs.

Environmental studies classes and majors are growing and

diversifying. Students can now get MBAs in sustainable-business

practices and train to build and operate wind turbines, among

other things (Berman). In the area of public policy, a major in

this field is also becoming more valuable. The *New York*

Lopez 5

Sources not identified with an author are referenced by a shortened title.

Times Magazine notes this cultural trend: "Time was, environmental-studies majors ran campus recycling programs. Now they run national campaigns" ("Learn").

Because our school is much smaller and has fewer resources than Yale or most of the other schools with well-known and successful sustainable food projects including Dartmouth, Rutgers, Dickinson, Boston College, Colby, Columbia, Wisconsin-Madison, Iowa State, UCSD (University of California, San Diego), UCLA, and the University of Nebraska, establishing a farm or a large garden seems improbable. I propose that we establish a campus garden following the very simple principles of organic "square foot" gardening. Square-foot gardening is raised bed gardening that takes place in 6- to 12-inch-deep frames that have been segmented into a grid (see fig. 1). The size of each square in the grid depends on what plants are planted there; certain plants require larger and deeper grids (Bartholomew 15-16). The main benefit of square-foot gardening is that one can grow the same amount of

Position figures close to the text where they are mentioned. Include a figure number followed by a caption.

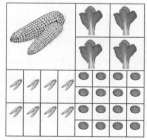

Fig. 1. The grid in a square-foot gardening plot is divided according to the mature size of each plant.

Because Lopez illustrates the point with a figure she created, no source information is needed.

Lopez 6

produce in a 140-square-foot grid that is typically grown in the average 700-square-foot, single-row garden (Bartholomew 42). Thus, a garden—or multiple gardens, placed strategically according to the sunlight needs of the plants—can be fitted into small spaces around campus.

Another great benefit to the square-foot garden is that the smaller beds are easily adapted to grow seasonal crops, making it easier to recognize and explore the foods within our foodshed, or regional food chain, as the locavore movement encourages ("Why"). The smaller size of the beds also means that crops and harvests can be staggered. Regular row planting replicates the same kinds of yields as industrial farming, meaning that an entire row of the same item is harvested all at once, which can lead to waste. Staggering crops ensures that only what is needed is grown and harvested (Bartholomew 18), and staggering maximizes use of the space. In short, square-foot gardening is ideal for a small group of beginning gardeners (Bartholomew 13). In addition, it is easy to modify as need and skill level dictates, as amateur gardeners show in their YouTube videos (see, for example, mokahdeelyte).

Even though our campus organic garden will not be built on the same scale as at the larger schools, much can still be learned from them, especially regarding how they gain support and how they maintain interest in their project. The key to both Yale's Sustainable Food Project and Dartmouth's Organic Farm is activist students. Unlike student activists of the past, however, today's students are working with school administrators to make change

Lopez mentions a YouTube video and parenthetical reference leads to entry in Works Cited list.

Lopez 7

possible. And school administrators are seeing the surge in green

activism on campus as something that could appeal to prospective

freshmen and alumni alike (Lewington). Establishing a core group

of students responsible for shepherding the project is essential;

these students can then start finding allies on campus. Other

successful activist student groups are a good possibility, as are

like-minded faculty, and food service administration and staff.

Once support is gained from students, faculty, staff, and

administration, the logistics of building the gardens can get

under way. Little space and few resources and tools are

necessary for square-foot gardening but supplies such as

building materials, ingredients for the soil mixture, and seeds

will still have to be gathered. Compost for the soil mixture can

be made from existing kitchen waste. Seeds, peat moss,

vermiculite, and small tools are not expensive and can be

bought with donated funds. Partnering with a community

organic gardening organization or individuals in the community

may not only yield donated or discounted supplies, but also

training for student volunteers and a tie to the local

community, which can help maintain support for the project in

the long term.

Maintaining interest is important to keeping support,

getting volunteer labor, and allowing for future growth. Holding

events is one way to keep the excitement going. Yale's Sustainable

Food Project offers cooking classes, uses a pizza oven installed

on the farm to bake pizzas every Friday to thank volunteers,

and even hosts an annual pig roast to celebrate the end of

Cite publications within the text by the name of the author (or authors).

Lopez uses sources to show how her proposal has worked for other campuses.

classes (Samadzadeh). Events of this scale are probably not an option for a smaller garden, but working with food service to create theme menus, such as Colby's "Garlic Fest," can attract attention (Jacobs). In addition, highlighting the farm or garden during student orientation and during parent weekends not only helps garner financial support but also attracts new volunteers.

As sustainability becomes increasingly important in society, colleges and universities have increased responsibility not only to be models of sustainable practices, but also to train students for jobs in an economy and environment informed by sustainability. The Sustainable Endowments Institute urges, "Colleges and universities, as leaders of innovation in our society, have the potential to demonstrate sustainable principles in their campus operations and endowment policies. Their examples can provide a road map for others to follow" ("Frequently"). For our college to remain competitive with other schools, we need to increase our commitment to these important ideas. Establishing a campus garden should be the first step.

The conclusion uses a quotation that appeals to readers' values and repeats call to action.

Lopez 9

Works Cited

"About the Student Sustainable Farm at Rutgers." *Student
    Sustainable Farm at Rutgers*. Rutgers U, n.d. Web. 2 Apr.
    2010.

Bartholomew, Mel. *All New Square Foot Gardening: Grow More in
    Less Space*. Franklin: Cool Spring P, 2006. Print.

Berman, Jillian. "Sustainability Could Secure a Good Future: College
    Students Flock to 'Green' Degrees, Careers." *USA Today* 3 Apr.
    2009, final ed.: 7D. *LexisNexis Academic*. Web. 6 Apr. 2010.

"Dartmouth Organic Farm." *Dartmouth Outdoor Club*. Dartmouth
    Coll., n.d. Web. 5 Apr. 2010.

"Frequently Asked Questions." *The College Sustainability Report
    Card*. Sustainable Endowments Institute, n.d. Web. 2 Apr.
    2010.

Horovitz, Bruce. "More University Students Call for Organic,
    'Sustainable' Food." *USA Today*. USA Today, 26 Sept. 2006.
    Web. 2 Apr. 2010.

Jacobs, Ruth. "Organic Garden Gives Back." *Colby
    Magazine* 99.1 (2010): n. pag. Web. 2 Apr. 2010.

Klinck, Betty. "Find a Green College: Check! Princeton Review
    Helps Applicants Who Seek Sustainability." *USA Today* 20 Apr.
    2010, final ed.: 7D. *LexisNexis Academic*. Web. 20 Apr. 2010.

"Learn," *New York Times Magazine* 20 Apr. 2008: 61. *LexisNexis Ac-
    ademic*. Web. 2 Apr. 2010.

Lewington, Jennifer. "Lean Green Campus Machines: Students Are
    at the Forefront of a Grassroots Environmental Revolution As
    They Coax—and Sometimes Embarrass—Administrators into
    Walking the Walk with Them." *Globe and Mail* [Toronto] 23
    Oct. 2008: 14. *LexisNexis Academic*. Web. 8 Apr. 2010.

Center "Works Cited" on a new page.

Double-space all entries. Indent all but the first line in each entry 1/2".

If the date of publication is not available, use the abbreviation *n.d.*

Alphabetize entries by the last names of the authors or by the first important word in the title if no author is listed.

When the city of publication is not included in the name of a newspaper, add the city name in brackets after the name of the newspaper.

Lopez 10

List the title of videos or films in italics if the work is independent. Include in quotation marks if it is part of a larger work.

mokahdeelyte. *Square Foot Gardening Modified Tutorial*. *YouTube*. YouTube, 17 May 2008. Web. 3 Apr. 2010.

NACUFS. "Strategic Plan, 2009-2014." *NACUFS*. Natl. Assn. of Coll. and Univ. Food Services, n.d. Web. 5 Apr. 2010.

Pilgrim, Sarah, David Smith, and Jules Pretty. "A Cross-Regional Assessment of the Factors Affecting Ecoliteracy: Implications for Policy and Practice." *Ecological Applications* 17.6 (2007): 1742-51. Print.   *Journal article*

Pino, Carl. "Sustainability on the Menu: College Cafeterias Are Buying Local and Going Organic." *E-Magazine.com*. E-The Environmental Magazine, Mar./Apr. 2008. Web. 3 Apr. 2010.

Pollan, Michael. *In Defense of Food: An Eater's Manifesto*. New York: Penguin, 2008. Print.   *Book*

Rozin, Paul, Rebecca Bauer, and Dana Catanese. "Food and Life, Pleasure and Worry, among American College Students: Gender Differences and Regional Similarities." *Journal of Personality and Social Psychology* 85.1 (2003): 132-41. *PsycARTICLES*. Web. 6 Apr. 2010.   *Journal article from a database*

Samadzadeh, Nozlee. "Farm Update: The Third Annual Jack Hitt Annual Last Day of Classes Pig Roast." *Yale Sustainable Food Project Student Blog*. Yale Sustainable Food Project, 3 May 2010. Web. 5 Apr. 2010.   *Blog entry*

"Why Eat Locally?" *Locavore*. Locavores, n.d. Web. 6 Apr. 2010.

Go through your text and make sure all the sources you have used are in the list of works cited.

FORMATTING THE WORKS CITED IN MLA STYLE

- **Begin the works-cited list on a new page.** Insert a page break with your word processor before you start the works-cited page.
- **Center "Works Cited" on the first line at the top of the page.**
- **Double-space all entries.**
- **Alphabetize each entry by the last name of the author or, if no author is listed, by the first content word in the title (ignore *a, an, the*).**
- **Indent all but the first line in each entry $1/2$ inch.**
- **Italicize the titles of books and periodicals.**
- **If an author has more than one entry, list the entries in alphabetical order by title. Use three hyphens in place of the author's name for the second and subsequent entries.**

    Murphy, Dervla. *Cameroon with Egbert*. Woodstock: Overlook, 1990.
    Print.

    ---. *Full Tilt: Ireland to India with a Bicycle*. London: Murray, 1965.
    Print.

- **Go through your paper to check that each source you have used is in the works-cited list.**

18 | APA Documentation

Social sciences disciplines—including government, linguistics, psychology, sociology, and education—frequently use the American Psychological Association (APA) documentation style. If you have questions that the examples in this chapter do not address, consult the *Publication Manual of the American Psychological Association*, sixth edition (2010).

18a In-text Citations in APA Style

APA style emphasizes the date of publication. When you cite an author's name in the body of your paper, always follow it with the date of publication. Notice too that APA style includes the abbreviation for page (p.) in front of the page number. A comma separates each element of the citation.

> Zukin (2004) observes that teens today begin to shop for themselves at age 13 or 14, "the same age when lower-class children, in the past, became apprentices or went to work in factories" (p. 50).

If the author's name is not mentioned in the sentence, the reference looks like this:

> One sociologist notes that teens today begin to shop for themselves at age 13 or 14, "the same age when lower-class children, in the past, became apprentices or went to work in factories" (Zukin, 2004, p. 50).

The corresponding entry in the references list would be

> Zukin, S. (2004). *Point of purchase: How shopping changed American culture*. New York, NY: Routledge.

Quotations 40 words or longer

Orlean (2001) has attempted to explain the popularity of the painter
Thomas Kinkade:

> People like to own things they think are valuable. . . . The high
> price of limited editions is part of their appeal; it implies that
> they are choice and exclusive, and that only a certain class of
> people will be able to afford them. (p. 128)

The sentence introducing the
quotation names the author.

Note that the period appears
before the parentheses in an indented "block" quote.

The date appears in parentheses immediately following the
author's name.

Index of in-text citations

Sample in-text citations

1. **Author named in your text**

The influential sociologist Daniel Bell (1973) noted a shift in the
United States to the "postindustrial society" (p. 3).

2. **Author not named in your text**

In 1997, the Gallup poll reported that 55% of adults in the United States think secondhand smoke is "very harmful," compared to only 36% in 1994 (Saad, 1997, p. 4).

3. **Work by a single author**

(Bell, 1973, p. 3)

4. **Work by two authors**
List both authors' last names, joined with an ampersand.

(Suzuki & Irabu, 2002, p. 404)

5. **Work by three to five authors**
The authors' last names follow the order of the title page.

(Francisco, Vaughn, & Romano, 2006, p. 7)

Subsequent references can use the first name and *et al.*

(Francisco et al., 2006, p. 17)

6. **Work by six or more authors**
Use the first author's last name and *et al.* for all in-text references.

(Swallit et al., 2007, p. 49)

7. **Work by a group or organization**
Identify the group in the text and place the page number in parentheses.

The National Organization for Women (2001) observed that this "generational shift in attitudes towards marriage and childrearing" will have profound consequences (p. 325).

8. Work by an unknown author

Use a shortened version of the title (or the full title if it is short) in place of the author's name. Capitalize all key words in the title. If it is an article title, place it inside quotation marks.

("Derailing the Peace Process," 2003, p. 44)

9. Two works by one author published in the same year

Assign the dates letters (*a*, *b*, etc.) according to their alphabetical arrangement in the references list.

The majority of books written about coauthorship focus on partners of the same sex (Laird, 2007a, p. 351).

10. Parts of an electronic source

If an online or other electronic source does not provide page numbers, use the paragraph number preceded by the abbreviation *para.*

(Robinson, 2007, para. 7)

11. Two or more sources within the same sentence

Place each citation directly after the statement it supports.

Some surveys report an increase in homelessness rates (Alford, 2004) while others chart a slight decrease (Rice, 2006a) . . .

If you need to cite two or more works within the same parentheses, list them in the order in which they appear in the references list.

(Alford, 2004; Rice, 2006a)

12. Work quoted in another source

Saunders and Kellman's study (as cited in Rice, 2006a)

18b Illustrated Samples and Index of References Entries in APA Style

Periodical Sources

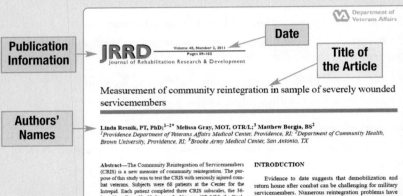

Publication Information

Date

Title of the Article

Authors' Names

VA Department of Veterans Affairs

JRRD
Volume 48, Number 2, 2011
Pages 89–102
Journal of Rehabilitation Research & Development

Measurement of community reintegration in sample of severely wounded servicemembers

Linda Resnik, PT, PhD;[1–2*] Melissa Gray, MOT, OTR/L;[3] Matthew Borgia, BS[2]
[1]Providence Department of Veterans Affairs Medical Center, Providence, RI; [2]Department of Community Health, Brown University, Providence, RI; [3]Brooke Army Medical Center, San Antonio, TX

Abstract—The Community Reintegration of Servicemembers (CRIS) is a new measure of community reintegration. The purpose of this study was to test the CRIS with seriously injured combat veterans. Subjects were 68 patients at the Center for the Intrepid. Each patient completed three CRIS subscales, the 36-Item Short Form Health Survey for Veterans (SF-36V), the Quality of Life Scale (QOLS), and two Craig Handicap Assessment and Reporting Technique subscales at visit 1 and the 3-month follow-up. Of the patients, 11 also completed the measures within 2 weeks of visit 1. We abstracted diagnoses and activities of daily living from the medical record. We evaluated test-retest reliability using intraclass correlation coefficients (ICCs). We evaluated concurrent validity with Pearson product moment correlations. We used multivariate analyses of variance to compare scores for subjects with and without posttraumatic stress disorder (PTSD), traumatic brain injury (TBI), and depression. Responsiveness analyses evaluated floor and ceiling effects, percent achieving minimal detectable change (MDC), effect size (ES), and the standardized response mean (SRM). CRIS subscale ICCs were 0.90 to 0.91. All subscales were moderately or strongly correlated with QOLS and SF-36V subscales. CRIS subscale scores were lower in PTSD and TBI groups ($p < 0.05$). CRIS Extent of Participation and Satisfaction with Participation subscales were lower for subjects with depression ($p < 0.05$). Of the sample, 17.4% to 23.2% had change greater than MDC. The ES ranged from 0.227 to 0.273 (SRM = 0.277–0.370), showing a small effect between visit 1 and the 3-month follow-up. Results suggest that the CRIS is a psychometrically sound choice for community reintegration measurement in severely wounded servicemembers.

Key words: community reintegration, disability, measurement, military healthcare, outcomes assessment, participation, psychometric testing, reliability, traumatic brain injury, veterans.

INTRODUCTION

Evidence to date suggests that demobilization and return home after combat can be challenging for military servicemembers. Numerous reintegration problems have been reported among veterans from the gulf war and more recent conflicts in Iraq and Afghanistan, including marital difficulties, financial difficulties, problems with alcohol or substance abuse, medical problems, behavioral problems such as depression or anxiety [1], homelessness [2], and motor vehicle accidents [3]. Readjustment to

Abbreviations: ADL = activity of daily living, ANOVA = analysis of variance, BAMC = Brooke Army Medical Center, CFI = Center for the Intrepid, CHART = Craig Handicap Assessment and Reporting Technique, CRIS = Community Reintegration of Servicemembers, ES = effect size, ICC = intraclass correlation coefficient, ICF = International Classification of Function, IED = improvised explosive device, MANOVA = multivariate analysis of variance, MDC = minimal detectable change, OEF = Operation Enduring Freedom, OIF = Operation Iraqi Freedom, PF-10 = 10-Item Physical Functioning Subscale, PTSD = posttraumatic stress disorder, QOLS = Quality of Life Scale, SD = standard deviation, SF-36V = 36-Item Short Form Health Survey for Veterans, SRM = standardized response mean, TBI = traumatic brain injury, VA = Department of Veterans Affairs.
*Address all correspondence to Linda Resnik, PT, PhD; Providence VA Medical Center, 830 Chalkstone Ave, Providence, RI 02908; 401-273-7100, ext 2368; fax: 401-863-3489. Email: Linda_Resnik@brown.edu
DOI:10.1682/JRRD.2010.04.0070

DOI

Resnik, L., Gray, M., & Borgia, M. (2011). "Measurement of community reintegration in sample of severely wounded servicemembers." *Journal of Rehabilitation Research and Development 48*, 89–102. doi: 10.1682/JRRD.2010.04.0070

Elements of the citation

Author's Name

The author's last name comes first, followed by the author's initials.

Join two authors' names with a comma and an ampersand.

Date of Publication

Give the year the work was published in parentheses.

Newspapers and popular magazines are referenced by the year, month, and day of publication.

Title of Article

- Do not use quotation marks. If there is a book title in the article title, italicize it.
- Titles of articles in APA style follow standard sentence capitalization.

Publication Information

Name of journal

- Italicize the journal name.
- Put a comma after the journal name.

Volume, issue, and page numbers

- Italicize the volume number.
- If each issue of the journal begins on page 1, give the issue number in parentheses, followed by a comma.
- If the article has been assigned a DOI (Digital Object Identifier), list it after the page numbers but without a period at the end.

Find the right example for your model (you may need to refer to more than one model)

What type of article do you have?

A scholarly journal article or abstract?

- For an article in a journal with continuous pagination, go to page 187, #17.
- For an article in a journal paginated by issue, go to page 187, #18.

A newspaper article?

- For a newspaper article, go to page 188, #20.

How many authors are listed?

- One, two, or more authors: go to page 187, #13–15.
- Unknown author: go to page 187, #16.

Books and Nonperiodical Sources

FIVE MINDS FOR THE

Title of the Book

FUTURE

Author's Name → Howard Gardner

HARVARD BUSINESS SCHOOL PRESS
BOSTON, MASSACHUSETTS

Publisher and Place of Publication

Gardner, H. (2007). *Five minds for the future*. Boston, MA: Harvard
Business School Press.

Elements of the citation

Author's or Editor's Name

The author's last name comes first, followed by a comma and the author's initials.

If an editor, put the abbreviation *Ed.* in parentheses after the name. **Kavanagh, P. (Ed.).**

Year of Publication

- Give the year the work was copyrighted in parentheses.

- If no year of publication is given, write n.d. ("no date") in parentheses.

Book Title

- Italicize the title.

- Titles of books in APA style follow standard sentence capitalization: Capitalize only the first word, proper nouns, and the first word after a colon.

Publication Information

Place of publication

- For all books, list the city with a two-letter state abbreviation (or full country name) after the city name.

- If more than one city is given on the title page, list only the first.

Publisher's name

Do not shorten or abbreviate words like *University* and *Press*. Omit words such as *Co.*, *Inc.*, and *Publishers*.

Find the right example for your model (you may need to refer to more than one model)

How many authors are listed?

One, two, or more authors: go to pages 188–189, #21–24.

Do you have only a part of a book?

- For a chapter in an edited collection, go to page 189, #25.
- For an article in a reference work, go to page 189, #26.

Online Sources

Journal Title

Title of the Article

Author

Date

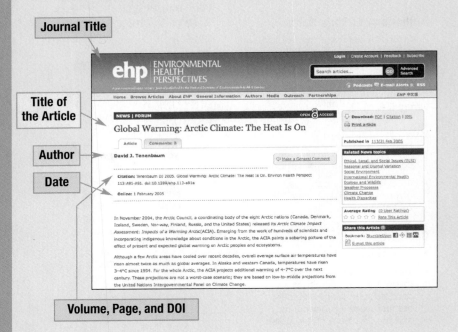

Volume, Page, and DOI

Tennenbaum, D. J. (2005). Global warming: Arctic climate:
    The heat is on. *Environmental Health Perspectives, 113,*
    A91. doi:10.1289/ehp.113–a91a

Elements of the citation

Author's Name or Organization

- Authorship is sometimes hard to discern for online sources. if you do have an author or creator to cite, follow the rules for periodicals and books.

- If the only authority you find is a group or organization, list its name as the author.

Dates

Give the date the site was produced or last revised (sometimes the copyright date) after the author.

Title of Page or Article

- Web sites are often made up of many separate pages or articles. Each page or article on a Web site may or may not have a title.

URL

- Copy the address exactly as it appears in your browser window. You can even copy and paste the address into your text for greater accuracy.

- Break a URL at the end of a line *before* a mark of punctuation. Do not insert a hyphen.

- If the article has a DOI (Digital Object Identifier), give the DOI after the title. Do not list the URL.

Find the right example for your model (you may need to refer to more than one model)

What kind of publication do you have?

- For a publication in a database, go to page 189, #28
- For an article with a DOI assigned, go to page 190, #33
- For an article with no DOI assigned, go to page 191, #34
- For an article in a newspaper or magazine, go to page 191, #35–36
- For a government publication, go to page 190, #32

Do you have a source that is posted by an individual?

- For a blog, go to page 191, #37
- For a post to a discussion list, go to page 191, #38
- For e-mail or text messaging, go to page 191, #40

Index of References Entries

18c Periodical Sources in the APA-style References List

13. **Article by one author**

> Kellogg, R. T. (2001). Competition for working memory among writing processes. *American Journal of Psychology, 114*, 175–192.

14. **Article by two authors**

> McClelland, D., & Eismann, K. (1998).

15. **Article by three or more authors**

List last names and initials for up to seven authors, with an ampersand between the last two names. For works with eight or more authors, list the first six names, then an ellipsis, then the last author's name.

> Andis, S., Franks, D., Gee, G., Ng, K., Orr, V., Ray, B., . . . Tate, L.

16. **Article by an unknown author**

> The green gene revolution [Editorial]. (2004, February). *Scientific American, 291*, 8.

17. **Article in a journal with continuous pagination**

Include only the volume number and the year, not the issue number.

> Engen, R., & Steen, S. (2000). The power to punish: Discretion and sentencing reform in the war on drugs. *American Journal of Sociology, 105*, 1357–1395.

18. **Article in a journal paginated by issue**

If each issue of the journal begins on page 1, give the issue number in parentheses (not italicized) after the volume number.

> Bunyan, T. (2010). Just over the horizon—the surveillance society and the state in the EU. *Race and Class, 51*(3), 1–12.

19. **Monthly publications**

> Barth, A. (2010, March). Brain science gets squishy. *Discover*,
>   11–12.

20. **Newspaper article**

> Olsen, E. (2010, June 22). A campaign for M&Ms with a salty cen-
>   ter? Sweet. *The New York Times*, p. B6.

18d Books in the APA-style References List

21. **Book by one author**

> Ball, E. (2000). *Slaves in the family*. New York, NY: Ballantine
>   Books.

If an editor, put the abbreviation *Ed.* in parentheses after the name.

> Rasgon, N. L. (Ed.). (2006). *The effects of estrogen on brain func-
>   tion*. Baltimore, MD: Johns Hopkins University Press.

22. **Two or more books by the same author**

Arrange according to the date, with the earliest publication first.

> Jules, R. (2003). *Internal memos and other classified documents*.
>   London, England: Hutchinson.

> Jules, R. (2004). *Derelict cabinet*. London, England: Corgi-
>   Transworld.

23. **Book by two authors**

> Hardt, M., & Negri, A. (2000). *Empire*. Cambridge, MA: Harvard
>   University Press.

24. Book by three or more authors

List last names and initials for up to seven authors, with an ampersand between the last two names. For works with eight or more authors, list the first six names, then an ellipsis, then the last author's name.

> Anders, K., Child, H., Davis, K., Logan, O., Orr, J., Ray, B., . . .
> Wood, G.

25. Chapter in an edited collection

> Boyaton, D. (2010). Behaviorism and its effect upon learning in
> schools. In G. Goodman (Ed.), *The educational psychology*
> *reader: The art and science of how people learn* (pp. 49–66).
> New York, NY: Peter Lang.

26. Article in a reference work

> Viscosity. (2001). In *The Columbia encyclopedia* (6th ed.). New
> York, NY: Columbia University Press.

27. Religious or classical texts

Reference entries are not required for major classical works or the Bible, but in the first in-text citation, identify the edition used.

> John 3.16 (Modern Phrased Version)

18e Online Sources in the APA-style References List

28. Document from a database

APA no longer requires listing the names of well-known databases. Include the name of the database only for hard-to-find books and other items.

> Holloway, J. D. (2004). Protecting practitioners' autonomy. *Moni-*
> *tor on Psychology, 35*(1), 30.

29. Abstract retrieved from a database

Putsis, W. P., & Bayus, B. L. (2001). An empirical analysis of firms' product line decisions. *Journal of Marketing Research, 37*(8), 110–118. Abstract retrieved from PsycINFO database.

30. Online publication by a known author

Carr, A. (2003, May 22). *AAUW applauds Senate support of title IX resolution*. Retrieved from http://www.aauw.org/about /newsroom/press_releases/030522.cfm

31. Online publication by a group or organization

Girls Incorporated. (2003). *Girls' bill of rights*. Retrieved from http://www.girlsinc.org/gc/page.php?id=9

32. Online government publication

U.S. Public Health Service. Office of the Surgeon General. (2001, March 11). *Women and smoking*. Retrieved from http://www .surgeongeneral.gov/library/womenandtobacco/

In-text

(U.S. Public Health Service [USPHS], 2001)

33. Online article with DOI assigned

There is no need to list the database, the retrieval date, or the URL if the DOI is listed.

Erdfelder, E. (2008). Experimental psychology: Good news. *Experimental Psychology, 55*(1), 1–2. doi:0.1027 /1618–3169.55.1.1

34. Online article with no DOI assigned

Brown, B. (2004). The order of service: the practical management of customer interaction. *Sociological Research Online, 9*(4). Retrieved from http://www.socresonline.org.uk/9/4/brown.html

35. Article in an online newspaper

Erard, M. (2001, November 16). A colossal wreck. *Austin Chronicle*. Retrieved from http://www.austinchronicle.com

36. Article in an online magazine

Resinkoff, N. (2010, June 22). Media ignores Gulf tragedy: Focuses on campaign narrative. *Salon*. Retrieved from http://www.salon.com

37. Blog entry

Spinuzzi, C. (2010, January 7). In the pipeline [Web log post]. Retrieved from http://spinuzzi.blogspot.com/search?updated-max=2010-01-25T12%3A35%3A00-06%3A00

38. Message posted to a newsgroup, online forum, or discussion group

Tjelmeland, A. (2010, January 26). Zacate Creek [Electronic mailing list message]. Retrieved from http://server1.birdingonthe.net/mailinglists/TEXS.html#1264558433

39. Wiki

Mount Everest [Wikipedia entry]. (n.d.). Retrieved November 12, 2010, from http://en.wikipedia.org/wiki/Mt._Everest

40. E-mail

E-mail sent from one individual to another should be cited as a personal communication. Personal communication is cited in text but not included in the reference list.

(D. Jenkins, personal communication, July 28, 2010)

18f **Visual and Multimedia Sources in the APA-style References List**

41. Television program

Ball, A. (Writer), & Winant, S. (Director). (2008). The first taste [Television series episode]. In A. Ball (Producer), *True Blood*. New York, NY: HBO.

42. Film, Video, or DVD

Stroller, N. (Writer and Director). (2010). *Get him to the Greek* [Motion picture]. United States: Universal Studios.

43. Musical recording

Waits, T. (1980). Ruby's arms. On *Heartattack and vine* [CD]. New York, NY: Elektra Entertainment.

44. Graphic, audio, or video file

Aretha Franklin: A life of soul. (2004, January 24). *NPR Online*. Retrieved from http://www.npr.org/features/feature .php?wfId=1472614

45. Photograph or work of art

American Heart Association. (2009). Hands-only CPR graphic [Photograph]. Retrieved from http://handsonlycpr.org/assets /files/Hands-only%20me.pdf

18g   Sample Pages from a Research Paper with APA Documentation

Type the running head (the shortened title) for publication in all caps, flush left at the top.

Running head: SURVEILLANOMICS   1

Surveillanomics: The Need for

Governmental Regulation of Video Surveillance

John M. Jones

The University of Texas at Austin

APA style uses a title page with a page number at the top right.

Center the title, name of author(s), and name of school.

Continue to use the running head with the page number in the top right.

The abstract appears on a separate page with the title *Abstract.* An abstract may not exceed 150 words.

SURVEILLANOMICS   2

Abstract

Because recent technological advances have made it possible to use surveillance video to gather information about private citizens, and because unregulated data-mining has made this information economically valuable, the collection and use of video surveillance data should be regulated by the government. This regulation, based on the model introduced by Taylor (2002), should mandate that all video surveillance must be in accordance with the law, have a legitimate objective, and be necessary for the maintenance of a free society. These guidelines would ensure that surveillance data could not be used for purposes other than those for which it was collected, and would make the primary concerns in debates over the use of surveillance democratic, not economic as they are now.

Do not indent the first line of the abstract.

Double-space the abstract.

Surveillanomics: The Need for Governmental

Regulation of Video Surveillance

On September 5, 2005, the operators of the social networking site Facebook gave the service a facelift. One of the innovations they introduced was the "news feed" feature, which "automatically alerted users when their friends made changes to their online pro-files," like changing personal details or adding new "friends" (Meredith, 2006). This service, which was automatically installed for all accounts, outraged users, 700,000 of whom formed the group "Students Against Facebook News Feeds." Before Facebook altered its implementation of this feature, the members of this group were preparing to protest the changes at the company's headquarters.

At first, this negative reaction by users took the company completely by surprise. As Schneier (2006) puts it, in their eyes, all they had done "was take available data and aggregate it in a novel way for what [they] perceived was [their] customers' benefit"; however, users realized that this change "made an enormous difference" in the way that their information could be aggregated, accessed, and distributed. In other words, although Facebook news feeds did nothing more than take information that was already publicly available and repackage it in a new form, this new information source was seen by users as a massive invasion of their privacy.

In light of this reaction, it is interesting to note that right now companies referred to as "data brokers" are creating

Give the full title at the beginning of the body of the report.

Specify 1" margins.

Indent each paragraph 1/2" on the ruler in the word processing program. Include the date in parentheses when you mention authors in the text.

SURVEILLANOMICS   10

Center *References*.   References

Koskela, H. (2000). 'The gaze without eyes': Video-

Alphabetize entries
by last name of the
author.

surveillance and the changing nature of urban space. *Progress
in Human Geography, 24*(2), 243–265.

Koskela, H. (2003). 'Cam era'—the contemporary urban panopticon.
Surveillance & Society, 1(3), 292–313. Retrieved from http://
www.surveillance-and-society.org

Double-space all
entries.

Lee, J. (2005, May 22). Caught on tape, then just caught: Private
cameras transform police work. *The New York Times*. Retrieved
from http://www.nytimes.com

Indent all but the
first line of each
entry five spaces.

Meredith, P. (2006, September 22). Facebook and the politics
of privacy. *Mother Jones*. Retrieved from http://www
.motherjones.com

Mieszkowski, K. (2003, September 25). We are all paparazzi now. *Salon*. Retrieved from http://archive.salon.com/tech/feature
/2003/09/25/webcams/index.html

Nieto, M., Johnston-Dodds, K., & Simmons, C. W. (2002). *Public
and private applications of video surveillance and biometric
technologies*. Sacramento, CA: California Research Bureau,

Go through your
text and make
sure that every-
thing you have
cited, except for
personal com-
munication, is
in the list of
references.

California State Library. Retrieved from http:// www.library
.ca.gov/CRB/02/06/02-006.pdf

O'Harrow, R. (2005). *No place to hide*. New York, NY: Free Press.

Schneier, B. (2006, September 21). Lessons from the Facebook
riots. *Wired News*. Retrieved from http:// www.wired.com
/news/columns/0,71815-0.html

19 | CMS Documentation

Writers who publish in business, social sciences, fine arts, and humanities outside the discipline of English often use *The Chicago Manual of Style* (CMS) method of documentation. CMS guidelines allow writers a clear way of using footnotes and endnotes (rather than MLA and APA in-text citations) for citing the sources of quotations, summaries, and paraphrases. If you have questions after consulting this chapter, you can consult *The Chicago Manual of Style*, sixteenth edition (Chicago: University of Chicago Press, 2010), or visit the Web site (www.chicagomanualofstyle.org).

19a The Elements of CMS Documentation

CMS describes two systems of documentation, one similar to APA and the other a style that uses footnotes or endnotes, which is the focus of this chapter. In the footnote style CMS uses a superscript number directly after any quotation, paraphrase, or summary. Notes are numbered consecutively throughout the essay, article, or chapter.

> In *Southern Honor: Ethics and Behavior in the Old South*, Wyatt-Brown argues that "paradox, irony, and guilt have been three current words used by historians to describe white Southern life before the Civil War."[1]

Note

> 1. Bertram Wyatt-Brown, *Southern Honor: Ethics and Behavior in the Old South* (Oxford: Oxford University Press, 1983), 3.

Bibliography

> Wyatt-Brown, Bertram. *Southern Honor: Ethics and Behavior in the Old South*. Oxford: Oxford University Press, 1983.

Footnote and endnote placement

Footnotes appear at the bottom of the page on which each citation appears. Begin your footnote four lines from the last line of text on the page. Double-space footnotes and endnotes.

Endnotes are compiled at the end of the text on a separate page titled *Notes*. Center the title at the top of the page and list your endnotes in the order they appear within the text. The entire endnote section should be double-spaced—both within and between each entry.

CMS Bibliography

Because footnotes and endnotes in CMS format contain complete citation information, a separate list of references is often optional. This list of references can be called the *Bibliography*, or if it has only works referenced in your text, *Works Cited, Literature Cited*, or *References*.

Index of CMS Documentation

19b Books and Nonperiodical Sources in CMS Style

Note

1. Nell Irvin Painter, *Creating Black Americans: African-American History and Its Meanings, 1619 to the Present* (New York: Oxford University Press, 2006), 5.

Bibliography

Painter, Nell Irvin. *Creating Black Americans: African-American History and Its Meanings, 1619 to the Present.* New York: Oxford University Press, 2006.

Author's or Editor's Name

In a note, the author's name is given in normal order.

In the bibliography, give the author's last name first. If an editor, put ed. after the name.

Book Title

Use the exact title, as it appears on the title page (not the cover).

Italicize the title.

Capitalize all nouns, verbs, adjectives, adverbs, and pronouns, and the first word of the title and subtitle.

Publication Information

In a note, the place of publication, publisher, and year of publication are in parentheses.

Place of publication
- Add the state's postal abbreviation or country when the city is not well known or ambiguous (Cambridge, MA, or Cambridge, UK).
- If more than one city is given on the title page, use the first.

Publisher's name
- You may use acceptable abbreviations (e.g., Co. for Company).

Year of publication
- If no year of publication is given, write n.d. ("no date") in place of the date.

Sample citations for books and nonperiodical sources

1. Book by one author

In a note the author's name is given in normal order.

1. Thomas Friedman, *The World Is Flat: A Brief History of the Twenty-first Century* (New York: Farrar, Straus, and Giroux, 2005), 9.

In subsequent references, cite the author's last name only:

2. Friedman, 10.

If the reference is to the same work as the preceding note, you can use the abbreviation *Ibid.*:

3. Ibid., 10.

In the bibliography, give the author's name in reverse order.

Friedman, Thomas. *The World Is Flat: A Brief History of the Twenty-first Century*. New York: Farrar, Straus, and Giroux, 2005.

For edited books, put *ed.* after the name.

Chen, Kuan-Hsing, ed. *Trajectories: Inter-Asia Cultural Studies*. London: Routledge, 1998.

2. Book by multiple authors

For books with two or three authors, in a note, put all authors' names in normal order. (For subsequent references, give only the authors' last names.)

4. Taylor Hauser and June Kashpaw, *January Blues* (Foster City, CA: IDG Books, 2003), 32.

In the bibliography, give second and third names in normal order.

Hauser, Taylor, and June Kashpaw. *January Blues*. Foster City, CA: IDG Books, 2003.

When there are more than three authors, give the name of the first author listed, followed by *et al* in a note. List all of the authors in the bibliography.

3. Book by a group or organization
Note

> 7. World Health Organization, *Advancing Safe Motherhood through Human Rights* (Geneva, Switzerland: World Health Organization, 2001), 18.

Bibliography

> World Health Organization. *Advancing Safe Motherhood through Human Rights*. Geneva, Switzerland: World Health Organization, 2001.

4. A selection in an anthology or a chapter in an edited collection
Note

> 2. Renato Constantino, "Globalization and the South," in *Trajectories: Inter-Asia Cultural Studies*, ed. Kuan-Hsing Chen (London: Routledge, 1998), 57–64.

Bibliography

> Constantino, Renato. "Globalization and the South." In *Trajectories: Inter-Asia Cultural Studies*, edited by Kuan-Hsing Chen, 57–64. London: Routledge, 1998.

5. **Book with an editor**

Note

> 1. Thomas Hardy, *Jude the Obscure*, ed. Norman Page (New York: Norton, 1999), 35.

Bibliography

> Hardy, Thomas. *Jude the Obscure*. Edited by Norman Page. New York: Norton, 1999.

6. **Government document**

Note

> 5. House Committee on Armed Services, *Comptroller General's Assessment of the Iraqi Government's Record of Performance* (Washington, DC: Government Printing Office, 2008), 40.

Bibliography

> House Committee on Armed Services. *Comptroller General's Assessment of the Iraqi Government's Record of Performance*. Washington, DC: Government Printing Office, 2008.

7. **Religious texts**

Citations from religious texts appear in the notes but not in the bibliography. Give the version in parentheses in the first citation only.

Note

> 4. John 3:16 (King James Version).

19c Periodical Sources in CMS Style

Note

1. Michael Hutt, "A Nepalese Triangle: Monarchists, Maoists, and Political Parties," *Asian Affairs* 38 (2007): 11–22.

Bibliography

Hutt, Michael. "A Nepalese Triangle: Monarchists, Maoists, and Political Parties." *Asian Affairs* 38 (2007): 11–22.

Author's or Editor's Name

In a note, the author's name is given in normal order.

In a bibliography, give the author's last name first.

Title of Article

- Put the title in quotation marks. If there is a title of a book within the title, italicize it.
- Capitalize nouns, verbs, adjectives, adverbs, and pronouns, and the first word of the title and subtitle.

Publication Information

Name of journal

- Italicize the name of the journal.
- Journal titles are normally not abbreviated in the arts and humanities unless the title of the journal is an abbreviation (*PMLA, ELH*).

Volume, issue, and page numbers

- Place the volume number after the journal title without intervening punctuation.
- For journals that are paginated from issue to issue within a volume, do not list the issue number.

Date

- The date or year of publication is given in parentheses after the volume number, or issue number, if provided.

Sample citations for periodical sources

8. Article by one author
Note

> 1. Sumit Guha, "Speaking Historically: The Changing Voices of Historical Narration in Western India, 1400–1900," *American Historical Review* 109 (2004): 1084–98.

Bibliography

> Guha, Sumit. "Speaking Historically: The Changing Voices of Historical Narration in Western India, 1400–1900," *American Historical Review* 109 (2004): 1084–98.

9. Article by two or three authors
Note

> 3. Pamela R. Matthews and Mary Ann O'Farrell, "Introduction: Whose Body?" *South Central Review* 18, no. 3–4 (Fall–Winter 2001): 1–5.

Bibliography

> Matthews, Pamela R., and Mary Ann O'Farrell. "Introduction: Whose Body?" *South Central Review* 18, no. 3–4 (Fall–Winter 2001): 1–5.

10. Article by more than three authors
Note

Give the name of the first listed author, followed by *et al*.

> 5. Michael J. Thompson et al., "The Internal Rotation of the Sun," *Annual Review of Astronomy and Astrophysics* 41 (2003): 602.

Bibliography

> Thompson, Michael J., Jorgen Christensen-Dalsgaard, Mark S. Miesch, and Juri Toomre. "The Internal Rotation of the Sun." *Annual Review of Astronomy and Astrophysics* 41 (2003): 599–643.

11. **Journals paginated by volume**
    Note

> 4. Susan Welsh, "Resistance Theory and Illegitimate Reproduction," *College Composition and Communication* 52 (2001): 553–73.

Bibliography

> Welsh, Susan. "Resistance Theory and Illegitimate Reproduction." *College Composition and Communication* 52 (2001): 553–73.

12. **Journals paginated by issue**
    Note

> 5. Tzvetan Todorov, "The New World Disorder," *South Central Review* 19, no. 2 (2002): 28–32.

Bibliography

> Todorov, Tzvetan. "The New World Disorder." *South Central Review* 19, no. 2 (2002): 28–32.

13. **Weekly and biweekly magazines**
    Note

> 5. Malcolm Gladwell, "Pandora's Briefcase," *New Yorker*, May 10, 2010, 72–78.

Bibliography

> Gladwell, Malcolm. "Pandora's Briefcase." *New Yorker*, May 10, 2010, 72–78.

14. **Newspaper article**
    Note

> 1. Melena Ryzik, "Off the Beaten Beat," *New York Times*, May 11, 2007, late edition, sec. E.

19d Online Sources in CMS Style

15. Document or page from a Web site

To cite original content from within a Web site, include as many descriptive elements as you can: author of the page, title of the page, title and owner of the Web site, and the URL. Include the date accessed only if the site is time-sensitive or is frequently updated. If you cannot locate an individual author, the owner of the site can stand in for the author.

Note

11. National Organization for Women, "NOW History," accessed October 8, 2010, http://www.now.org/history/history.html.

Bibliography

National Organization for Women. "NOW History." Accessed October 8, 2010. http://www.now.org.history/history.html.

16. Online book

Note

12. Angelina Grimké, *Appeal to the Christian Women of the South* (New York: New York Anti-Slavery Society, 1836), accessed November 2, 2010, http://history.furman.edu/~benson/docs /grimke2.htm.

Bibliography

Grimké, Angelina. *Appeal to the Christian Women of the South*. New York: New York Anti-Slavery Society, 1836. Accessed November 2, 2010. http://history.furman.edu/~benson/docs/grimke2.htm.

17. Online article

Note

13. Margaret Cohen, "Literary Studies on the Terraqueous Globe," *PMLA* 125, no. 3 (2010): 657–62, doi:10.1632/pmla.2010.125.3.657.

Bibliography

Cohen, Margaret. "Literary Studies on the Terraqueous Globe." *PMLA* 125, no. 3 (2010): 657–62. doi:10.1632/pmla.2010.125.3.657.

18. **Posting to a discussion list or group**

Note

16. Jason Marcel, post to U.S. Politics Online Today in Politics Forum, April 4, 2004, http://www.uspoliticsonline.com/forums /forumdisplay.php?f=24.

19. **E-mail**

Because personal e-mails are not available to the public, they are not usually listed in the bibliography.

Note

11. Erik Lynn Williams, "Social Anxiety Disorder," e-mail to author, August 12, 2007.

19e　Sample Pages with CMS Documentation

Laker 1

Jason Laker

American History 102

January 28, 2011

The Electoral College: Does It Have a Future?

Until the presidential election of 2000, few Americans thought much about the Electoral College. It was something they had learned about in civics class and had then forgotten about as other, more pressing bits of information required their

Laker 2

attention. In November 2000, however, the Electoral College took center stage and sparked an argument that continues today: Should the Electoral College be abolished?

The founders of the new nation established the Electoral College as a compromise between elections by Congress and those by popular vote.[1] The College consists of a group of electors who meet to vote for the president and vice president of the United States. The electors are nominated by political parties within each state and the number each state gets relates to the state's congressional delegation. The process and the ideas behind it sound simple, but the actual workings of the Electoral College remain a mystery to many Americans.

The complicated nature of the Electoral College is one of the reasons why some people want to see it abolished. One voter writes in a letter to the editor of the *New York Times* that the elimination of the Electoral College is necessary "to demystify our voting system in the eyes of foreigners and our own citizenry."[2] Other detractors claim that it just does not work, and they cite the presidential elections of 1824, 1876, 1888, and, of course, 2000 as representative of the failures of the College. Those who defend the Electoral College, however, claim that the failures of these elections had little to do with the Electoral College itself.[3]

According to Gary Gregg, director of the McConnell Center for Political Leadership, a new study shows that much of what Americans think we know about the Electoral College is wrong. Consequently, we should actively question the wisdom of those who want to see it abolished.[4]

Laker 6

NOTES

    1. Lawrence D. Longley and Neal R. Peirce, *The Electoral College Primer 2000* (New Haven: Yale University Press, 1999).

    2. William C. McIntyre, "Revisiting the Electoral College," *New York Times*, November 17, 2001, late edition, sec. A.

    3. Avagara, *EC: The Electoral College Webzine*, accessed January 21, 2011, http://www.avagara.com/e_c/.

    4. Gary Gregg, "Keep the College," *National Review Online*, November 7, 2001, accessed January 19, 2011, http://www.lexisnexis.com/universe/.

Laker 7

BIBLIOGRAPHY

Avagara. *EC: The Electoral College Webzine*. Accessed January 21, 2011.
    http://www.avagara.com/e_c/.

Gregg, Gary. "Keep the College." *National Review Online*. November 7, 2001.
    Accessed January 19, 2011. http://www.lexisnexis.com/ universe/.

Longley, Lawrence D., and Neal R. Peirce. *The Electoral College Primer 2000*.
    New Haven: Yale University Press, 1999.

McIntyre, William C. "Revisiting the Electoral College." *New York Times*.
    November 17, 2001.

20 | CSE Documentation

Within the disciplines of the natural and applied sciences, citation styles are highly specialized. Many disciplines follow the guidelines of particular journals or style manuals within their individual fields. Widely followed by writers in the sciences is the comprehensive guide published by the Council of Science Editors: *Scientific Style and Format: The CSE Manual for Authors, Editors, and Publishers*, seventh edition (2006).

The preferred documentation system in CSE places references in the body of the text marked by a superscript number preceded by a space and placed inside punctuation. For example:

> Cold fingers and toes are common circulatory problems found in most heavy cigarette smokers [1].

This number corresponds to a numbered entry on the CSE source list, titled *References*.

The CSE References page lists all sources cited in the paper. To create a CSE References page, follow these guidelines:

1. Title your page "References," and center this title at the top of the page.
2. Double-space the entire References page, both within and between citations.
3. List citations in the order in which they appear in the body of the paper. Begin each citation with its citation number, followed by a period, flush left.
4. Authors are listed by last name, followed by initials. Capitalize only first words and proper nouns in cited titles. Book titles are not underlined, and article titles are not placed between quotation marks. Names of journals should be abbreviated where possible.
5. Cite publication year, and volume or page numbers if applicable.

20a In-text References in CSE Style

CSE documentation of sources does not require the names of authors in the text but only a number that refers to the References list at the end.

> In 1997, the Gallup poll reported that 55% of adults in the United States think secondhand smoke is "very harmful," compared to only 36% in 1994 [1].

The superscript [1] refers to the first entry on the References list, where readers will find a complete citation for this source.

What if you need more than one citation in a passage?

If the numbers are consecutive, separate with a hyphen. If nonconsecutive, use only a comma.

> The previous work [1,3,5–8,11]

Index of CSE Documentation

20b Books and Nonperiodical Sources in CSE-style References

1. Nance JJ. What goes up: the global assault on our atmosphere. New York: W Morrow; 1991.

Author's or Editor's Name

The author's last name comes first, followed by the initials of the author's first name and middle name (if provided). If an editor, put the word *editor* after the name.

Book Title

- Do not italicize or under-line titles.
- Capitalize only the first word and proper nouns.

Publication Information

Year of publication

- The year comes after the other publication information. It follows a semicolon.
- If it is a multivolume edited work published over a period of more than one year, give the span of years.

Page numbers

- When citing part of a book, give the page range for the selection: *p. 60–90*.

Sample references

1. **Book by a single author/editor**

2. Minger TJ, editor. Greenhouse glasnost: the crisis of global warming. New York (NY): Ecco; 1990.

2. **Book by two or more authors/editors**

3. O'Day DH, Horgen PA, editors. Sexual interactions in eukaryotic microbes. New York (NY): Academic Press; 1981.

3. Book by a group or organization

> 4. IAEA. Manual on radiation haematology. Vienna (Austria): IAEA; 1971.

4. Two or more books by the same author

Number the references according to the order in which they appear in the text.

> 5. Gould SJ. The structure of evolutionary theory. Cambridge (MA): Harvard University Press; 2002.

> 8. Gould SJ. Wonderful life: the Burgess Shale and the nature of history. New York (NY): Norton; 1989.

5. A selection in an anthology or a chapter in an edited collection

> 7. Kraft K, Baines DM. Computer classrooms and third grade development. In: Green MD, editor. Computers and early development. New York (NY): Academic; 1997. p. 168–179.

6. Technical and research reports

> 9. Austin A, Baldwin R, editors. Faculty collaboration: enhancing the quality of scholarship and teaching. ASCHE-ERIC Higher Education Report 7. Washington (DC): George Washington University; 1991.

20c Periodical Sources in CSE-style References

1. Bohannon J. Climate change: IPCC report lays out options for taming greenhouse gases. Science. 2007;316(5826): 812–814.

Author's Name

The author's last name comes first, followed by the initials of the author's first name and middle name (if provided).

Title of Article

- Do not place titles inside quotation marks.
- Capitalize only the first word and proper nouns.

Publication Information

Name of journal

- Do not abbreviate single-word titles. Abbreviate multiple-word titles according to the National Information Standards Organization (NISO) list of serials.

- Capitalize each word of the journal title, even if abbreviated.

Date of publication, volume, and issue numbers

- Include the issue number inside parentheses if it is present in the document. Leave no spaces between these items.

---

7. **Article by one author**

> 1. Board J. Reduced lodging for soybeans in low plant population is related to light quality. Crop Science. 2001;41:379–387.

8. **Article by two or more authors/editors**

> 2. Simms K, Denison D. Observed interactions between wild and domesticated mixed-breed canines. J Mamm. 1997;70:341–342.

9. Article by a group or organization

> 4. Center for Science in the Public Interest. Meat labeling: help!
> Nutrition Action Health Letter: 2. 2001 Apr 1.

10. Journals paginated by issue

Use the month or season of publication (and day, if given) for journals paginated by issue. Include the issue number in parentheses after the volume number.

> 8. Barlow JP. Africa rising: everything you know about Africa is
> wrong. Wired. 1998 Jan:142–158.

20d Online Sources in CSE-style References

11. Online journal articles

> 2. Schunck CH, Shin Y, Schirotzek A, Zwierlein MW, Ketterle A.
> Pairing without superfluidity: the ground state of an
> imbalanced fermi mixture. Science [Internet]. 2007 [cited 2007
> Jun 15]; 316(5826):867–870. Available from: http://www.
> sciencemag.org/cgi/content/full/3165826/867/DC1

12. Scientific databases on the Internet

> 3. Comprehensive Large Array-data Stewardship System [Internet].
> 2007. Release 4.2. Silver Spring (MD): National Environmental
> Satellite, Data, and Information Service (US). [updated 2007
> May 2; cited 2007 May 14]. Available from: http://www.class.
> noaa.gov/saa/products/welcome

PART 5 Effective Style and Language

21 | Write with Power

In photographs
You imagine actions when subjects are captured in motion.

In writing
Your readers expect actions to be expressed in verbs:
gallop, canter, trot, run, sprint, dash, bound, thunder, tear away.

In photographs

Viewers interpret the most prominent person or thing as the subject—what the photograph is about.

In writing

Readers interpret the first person or thing they meet in a sentence as what the sentence is about (the jockey, the horse). They expect that person or thing to perform the action expressed in the verb.

21a Recognize Active and Passive Voice

In the **active voice** the subject of the sentence is the actor. In the **passive voice** the subject is being acted upon.

Active   **Leonardo da Vinci** painted *Mona Lisa* between 1503 and 1506.

Passive   *Mona Lisa* was painted by Leonardo da Vinci between 1503 and 1506.

To write with power, use the active voice. Observe the difference:

Passive　The pear tree in the front yard **was demolished** by the unexpected storm.

Active　The unexpected storm **demolished** the pear tree in the front yard.

21b　Use Action Verbs

Where are the action words in the following sentences?

> Red hair flying, professional snowboarder and skateboarder Shaun White became a two-time Olympic gold medalist with a record score of 48.4 at the 2010 Winter Olympics. White was a skier before he was five, but became a snowboarder at age six, and by age seven he had become a professional, receiving corporate sponsorships. At age nine, White became friends with professional skateboarder Tony Hawk, who became White's mentor in becoming a professional skateboarder. White is known for accomplishing several "firsts" in snowboarding, including being the first to land back-to-back double corks and to master a trick called a Cab 7 Melon Grab. He is also the holder of record for the highest score in the men's halfpipe at the winter Olympics.

No action words here! The passage describes a series of actions, yet most of the verbs are *is*, *was*, and *became*. Think about what the actions are and choose powerful verbs that express those actions.

> Red hair flying, professional snowboarder and skateboarder Shaun White scored a 48.4 during the 2010 Winter Olympics and won his second gold medal. White skied before he was five, but switched to snowboarding at age six, and by age seven received corporate sponsorships. At age nine, White befriended professional skateboarder Tony Hawk, who mentored White and helped him become a professional skateboarder. White has accomplished several "firsts" in snowboarding, including landing

back-to-back double corks and mastering a trick called a Cab 7 Melon Grab. He also **holds** the record for the highest score in the men's halfpipe at the Winter Olympics.

Many sentences contain words that express action, but those words are nouns instead of verbs. Often the nouns can be changed into verbs. For example:

The arson unit conducted an investigation of **investigated** the mysterious fire.

The committee had a debate over **debated** how best to spend the surplus funds.

Notice that changing nouns into verbs also eliminates unnecessary words.

21c Find Agents

The **agent** is the person or thing that does the action. Powerful writing puts the agents in sentences.

Focus on people

Read the following sentence aloud:

The use of a MIDI keyboard for playing the song will facilitate capturing it in digital form on a laptop for the subsequent purpose of uploading it to a Web site.

It sounds dead, doesn't it? Putting people into the sentence makes it come alive:

By playing the song on a MIDI keyboard, **we** can record the digitized sound on **our** laptop and then upload it to **our** Web site.

Including people makes your writing more emphatic. Most readers relate better to people than to abstractions. Putting people in your sentences also introduces active verbs because people do things.

Identify characters

If people are not your subject, then keep the focus on other types of characters.

> **Without characters** The celebration of Martin Luther King Day had to be postponed because of inclement weather.

> **With characters** A severe ice storm forced the city to postpone the Martin Luther King Day celebration.

21d Vary Your Sentences

Read the following passage.

> On the first day Garth, Jim, and I paddled fourteen miles down Johnstone Strait. The next day we headed down the strait about five more miles to Robson Bight. It is a famous scratching place for orcas. The Bight is a small bay. We paddled out into the strait so we could see the entire Bight. There were no orcas inside. By this time we were getting tired. We were hungry. The clouds assumed a wintry dark thickness. The wind was kicking up against us. Our heads were down going into the cold spray.

The subject matter is interesting, but the writing isn't. The passage is a series of short sentences, one after the other. When you have too many short sentences one after the other, try combining a few of them.

The result of combining some (but not all) short sentences is a paragraph whose sentences match the interest of the subject.

> On the first day Garth, Jim, and I paddled fourteen miles down Johnstone Strait. The next day we headed down the strait about five more miles to Robson Bight, a small bay known as a famous scratching place for orcas. We paddled out into the strait so we could see the entire Bight, but there were no orcas inside. By this time we were tired and hungry, the clouds had assumed a wintry dark thickness, and the wind was kicking up against us—our heads dropped going into the cold spray.

22 | Write Concisely

22a Eliminate Unnecessary Words

Clutter creeps into our lives every day. Clutter also creeps into writing through unnecessary words, inflated constructions, and excessive jargon.

In regards to the Web site, the content is pretty successful in consideration of the topic. The site is fairly good writing-wise and is very unique in telling you how to adjust the rear derailleur one step at a time.

The words in red are clutter. Get rid of the clutter. You can say the same thing with half the words and gain more impact as a result.

The well-written Web site on bicycle repair provides step-by-step instructions on adjusting your rear derailleur.

Redundancy

Some words act as modifiers, but when you look closely at them, they repeat the meaning of the word they pretend to modify. Have you heard a store advertise "Come in for a *free gift*?" Aren't gifts free by definition? Likewise, you may have heard expressions such as *red in color, small in size, round in shape,* or *honest truth.* Imagine *red* not referring to color or *round* not referring to shape.

22b Reduce Wordy Phrases

Many inexperienced writers use phrases like "It is my opinion that" or "I think that" to begin sentences. These phrases are deadly to read. If you find them in your prose, cut them. Unless a writer is citing a source, we assume that the ideas are the writer's.

Coaches are among the worst at using many words for what could be said in a few:

> After much deliberation about Brown's future in football with regard to possible permanent injuries, I came to the conclusion that it would be in his best interest not to continue his pursuit of playing football again.

The coach might have said simply:

> Because Brown risks permanent injury if he plays football again, I decided to release him from the team.

Perhaps the coach wanted to sound impressive, authoritative, or thoughtful. But the result is the opposite. Speakers and writers who impress us are those who use words efficiently.

COMMON ERRORS

Empty intensifiers

Intensifiers modify verbs, adjectives, and other adverbs, and they are often overused. One of the most overused intensifiers is *very*. Take the following sentence as an example:

Empty intensifier   Her clothing style was very unique.

If something is unique, it is one of a kind. The word *very* doesn't make something more than unique.

Improved   Her clothing style was unique.

Or

Improved   Her clothing style was strange.

COMMON ERRORS

Very and *totally* are but two of a list of empty intensifiers that can usually be eliminated with no loss of meaning. Other empty intensifiers include *absolutely, awfully, definitely, incredibly, particularly,* and *really.*

Remember: When you use *very, totally,* or another intensifier before an adjective or adverb, always ask yourself whether there is a more accurate adjective or adverb you could use instead to express the same thought.

WORDY PHRASES

Certain stock phrases plague writing in the workplace, in the media, and in academia. Many can be replaced by one or two words with no loss in meaning.

Wordy	Concise
at this point in time	now
due to the fact that	because
for the purpose of	for
have the ability to	can
in spite of the fact that	although
in the event that	if

22c Simplify Tangled Sentences

Long sentences can be graceful and forceful. Such sentences, however, often require several revisions before they achieve elegance. Too often long sentences reflect wandering thoughts that the writer did not bother to go back and sort out. Two of the most important strategies for untangling long sentences are described in Chapter 21: using active verbs (Section 21b) and naming your agents (Section 21c). Here are some other strategies.

Revise expletives

Expletives are empty words that can occupy the subject position in a sentence. The most frequently used expletives are *there is, there are,* and *it is.*

Wordy   There were several important differences between the positions raised by the candidates in the debate.

To simplify the sentence, find the agent and make it the subject.

Revised   The two candidates raised several important differences between their positions in the debate.

A few kinds of sentences—for example, *It is raining*—do require you to use an expletive. In most cases, however, expletives add unnecessary words, and sentences will read better without them.

Use positive constructions

Sentences become wordy and hard to read when they include two or more negatives, such as the words *no, not,* and *nor,* plus the prefix *un-* or *mis-.* For example:

Difficult   A not uncommon complaint among employers of new college graduates is that they cannot communicate effectively in writing.

Revised   Employers frequently complain that new college graduates cannot write effectively.

Even simpler   Employers value the rare college graduate who can write well.

Phrasing sentences positively usually makes them more economical. Moreover, it makes your style more forceful and direct.

Simplify sentence structure

Long sentences can be hard to read, not because they are long but because they are convoluted and hide the relationships among ideas. Take the following sentence as an example.

Some historians are arguing that World War II actually ended with German reunification in 1990 instead of when the Japanese surrendered in 1945, after which time the Cold War got in the way of formal legal settlements among the involved nations and Germany was divided between the Western powers and the Soviet Union meaning that no comprehensive peace treaty was signed.

This sentence is hard to read. To rewrite sentences like this one, find the main ideas, and then determine the relationships among them.

After examining the sentence, you decide there are two key ideas:

1 Some historians argue that World War II actually ended in 1990 with German reunification, not when the Japanese surrendered in 1945.
2 The Cold War and the division of Germany between the Western powers and the Soviet Union hindered formal legal settlements among the involved nations.

Next ask what the relationship is between the two ideas. When you identify the key ideas, the relationship is often obvious; in this case (2) is the cause of (1). Thus the word you want to connect the two ideas is *because*.

Because the Cold War and the division of Germany between the Western powers and the Soviet Union hindered formal legal settlements among the involved nations, some historians argue that World War II actually ended in 1990 with German reunification rather than with the Japanese surrender in 1945.

The revised sentence is both clearer and more concise, reducing the number of words from sixty-one to forty-seven.

23 | Write with Emphasis

Photographs and writing gain energy when key ideas are emphasized.

In visuals

Photographers create emphasis by composing the image to direct the attention of the viewer. Putting people and objects in the foreground and making them stand out against the background gives them emphasis.

In writing

Writers have many tools for creating emphasis. Writers can design a page to gain emphasis by using headings, white space, type size, color, and boldfacing. Just as important, learning the craft of structuring sentences will empower you to give your writing emphasis.

23a Manage Emphasis Within Sentences

Put your main ideas in main clauses

Placing more important information in **main clauses** and less important information in subordinate clauses emphasizes what is important.

In the following paragraph all the sentences are main clauses:

> Lotteries were common in the United States before and after the American Revolution. They eventually ran into trouble. They were run by private companies. Sometimes the companies took off with the money. They didn't pay the winners.

This paragraph is grammatically correct, but it does not help the reader understand which pieces of information the author wants to emphasize. Combining the simple sentences into main and subordinate clauses and phrases can significantly improve the paragraph.

First, identify the main ideas:

> Lotteries were common in the United States before and after the American Revolution. They eventually ran into trouble.

These ideas can be combined into one sentence:

> Lotteries were common in the United States before and after the American Revolution, but they eventually ran into trouble.

Now think about the relationship of the three remaining sentences to the main ideas. Those sentences explain why lotteries ran into trouble; thus the relationship is *because*.

> Lotteries were common in the United States before and after the American Revolution, but they eventually ran into trouble because they were run by private companies that sometimes took off with the money instead of paying the winners.

Put key ideas at the beginning and end of sentences

Read these sentences aloud:

> 1 The Cottingley Fairies, a series of five photographs taken in 1917 by Elsie Wright and Frances Griffiths, depicts the girls interacting with what seem to be fairies.

2 A series of photographs showing two girls interacting with what seem to be fairies, known as the Cottingley Fairies, was taken by Elsie Wright and Frances Griffiths in 1917.

3 The series of photos Elsie Wright and Frances Griffiths took in 1917 showing them interacting with what seem to be fairies is called the Cottingley Fairies.

Most readers put the primary emphasis on words at the beginning and end of a sentence. The front of a sentence usually gives what is known: the topic. At the back is the new information about the topic. Subordinate information is in the middle. If a paragraph is about the Cottingley Fairies, we would not expect the writer to choose sentence 2 over 1 or 3. In sentence 2, the reference to the Cottingley Fairies is buried in the middle.

23b Forge Links Across Sentences

When your writing maintains a focus of attention across sentences, the reader can distinguish the important ideas and how they relate to each other. To achieve this coherence, you need to control which ideas occupy the positions of greatest emphasis. The words you repeat from sentence to sentence act as links.

Link sentences from front to front

In front-to-front linkage, the subject of the sentence remains the focus from one sentence to the next. In the following sequence, sentences 1 through 5 are all about Arthur Wright. The subject of each sentence refers to the first sentence with the pronouns *he* and *his*.

1 Arthur Wright was one of the first electrical engineers in England.

2 He loaned his camera to his daughter Elsie, who took the fairy pictures in the yard behind their house.

3 His opinion was that the pictures were fake.

4 However, his wife, Polly, was convinced that they were real.

5 Nevertheless, he banned Elsie from ever using his camera again.

Each sentence adds more information about the repeated topic, Arthur Wright.

Link sentences from back to front

In back-to-front linkage, the new information at the end of the sentence is used as the topic of the next sentence. Back-to-front linkage allows new material to be introduced and commented on.

1 By summer of 1919, the girls and their photographs had become so well known that author Sir Arthur Conan Doyle even wrote an article for a leading magazine claiming that the photos and the fairies were real.

2 Not everyone believed that the Cottingley Fairies were authentic, however, and other public figures wrote the papers calling the photographs a hoax.

3 The hoax continued until the 1980s, when both Elsie and Frances finally admitted that all but one of the pictures were fake.

Back-to-front linkage is useful when ideas need to be advanced quickly, as when you are telling stories. Rarely, however, will you use either front-to-front linkage or back-to-front linkage continuously throughout a piece of writing. Use front-to-front linkage to add more information and back-to-front linkage to move the topic along.

Check the links between your sentences to find any gaps that will cause your readers to stumble.

23c Use Parallel Structure with Parallel Ideas

What if Patrick Henry had written "Give me liberty or I prefer not to live"? Would we remember those words today? We remember the words he did use: "Give me liberty or give me death." Writers who use parallel structure often create memorable sentences.

Use parallelism with *and, or, nor, but*

When you join elements with coordinating conjunctions (*and, or, nor, yet, so, but,* and *for*), normally you should use parallel grammatical structure for those elements.

Awkward

In today's global economy, the method of production and where factories are located has become relatively unimportant in comparison with the creation of new concepts and marketing those concepts.

Parallel

> In today's global economy, how goods are made and where they are produced has become relatively unimportant in comparison with creating new concepts and marketing those concepts.

Use parallelism with *either/or, not only/but*

Make identical in structure the parts of sentences linked by correlative conjunctions: *either . . . or, neither . . . nor, not only . . . but also, whether . . . or.*

Awkward

> Purchasing the undeveloped land **not only** gives us a new park **but also** it is something that our children will benefit from in the future.

Parallel

> Purchasing the undeveloped land **not only** will give our city a new park **but also** will leave our children a lasting inheritance.

The more structural elements you match, the stronger the effect that parallelism will achieve.

COMMON ERRORS

Faulty parallel structure

When writers neglect to use parallel structure, the result can be jarring. Reading your writing aloud will help you catch problems in parallelism. Read this sentence aloud:

Not parallel   At our club meeting we identified problems in finding new members, publicizing our activities, and maintenance of our Web site.

The end of the sentence does not sound right because the parallel structure is broken. We expect to find another verb + *ing* following *finding*

COMMON ERRORS

and *publicizing*. Instead, we run into *maintenance*, a noun. The problem is easy to fix: Change the noun to the *-ing* verb form.

Parallel   At our club meeting we identified problems in finding new members, publicizing our activities, and **maintaining** our Web site.

Remember: Use parallel structure for parallel ideas.

 24 | # Find the Right Words

24a Be Aware of Levels of Formality

While you may get plenty of practice in informal writing—e-mails and notes to friends and family members—mastering formal writing is essential in academic and professional settings. How formal or informal should your writing be? That depends on your audience and the writing task at hand.

DECIDE HOW FORMAL YOUR WRITING SHOULD BE

- Who is your audience?
- What is the occasion?
- What level of formality is your audience accustomed to in similar situations?
- What impression of yourself do you want to give?

Colloquialisms

Colloquialisms are words or expressions that are used informally, often in conversation but less often in writing.

> I'm not happy with my grades, but that's the way the cookie crumbles.

> Liz is always running off at the mouth about something.

> I enjoyed the restaurant, but it was nothing to write home about.

In academic and professional writing, colloquialisms often suggest a flippant attitude, carelessness, or even thoughtlessness. Sometimes colloquialisms can be used for ironic or humorous effect, but as a general rule, if you want to be taken seriously, avoid using them.

Avoiding colloquialisms does not mean, however, that you should use big words when small ones will do as well, or that you should use ten words instead of two. Formality does not mean being pretentious or wordy.

Wordy

> In this writer's opinion, one could argue that the beaches on the west coast of Florida are far superior to their counterparts on the east coast.

Better

> Florida's west coast beaches are better than those on the east coast.

Slang

The most conspicuous kind of language that is usually avoided in formal writing is slang. The next time a friend talks to you, listen closely to the words he or she uses. Chances are you will notice several words that you probably would not use in a college writing assignment. Slang words are created by and for a particular group—even if that group is just you and your friend.

> The party was bumpin with all my peeps.

> Joey's new ride is totally pimped out.

Slang is used to indicate membership in a particular group. But because slang excludes readers who are not members of the group, it is best avoided in academic writing.

24b Be Aware of Denotation and Connotation

Words have both literal meanings, called **denotations**, and associated meanings, called **connotations**. The contrast is evident in words that mean roughly the same thing but have different connotations. For example, some people are set in their opinions, a quality that can be described positively as *persistent, firm,* and *steadfast* or negatively as *stubborn, bull-headed,* and *close-minded.*

24c Use Specific Language

Be precise

Effective writing conveys information clearly and precisely. Words such as *situation, sort, thing, aspect,* and *kind* often signal undeveloped or even lazy thinking.

Vague	The violence aspect determines how video games are rated.
Better	The level of violence determines how video games are rated.

When citing numbers or quantities, be as exact as possible. A precise number, if known, is always better than slippery words like *several* or *many,* which some writers use to cloak the fact that they don't know the quantity in question.

Use a dictionary

There is no greater tool for writers than the dictionary. Always have a dictionary handy when you write—either a book or an online version—and get into the habit of using it. In addition to checking spelling, you can find additional meanings of a word that perhaps you had not considered, and you can find the etymology—the origins of a word. In many cases knowing the etymology of a word can help you use it to better effect. For example, if you want to argue that universities as institutions have succeeded because they bring people together in contexts that prepare them for their lives after college, you might point out the etymology of *university. University* can be traced back to the late Latin word *universitas,* which means "society or guild," thus emphasizing the idea of a community of learning.

24d Write to Be Inclusive

While the conventions of language change continually, three guidelines for inclusive language toward all groups remain constant:

- Do not point out people's differences unless those differences are relevant to your argument.
- Call people whatever they prefer to be called.
- When given a choice of terms, choose the more accurate one. (*Vietnamese,* for example, is preferable to *Asian.*)

Be inclusive about gender

Don't use masculine nouns and pronouns to refer to both men and women. *He, his, him, man,* and *mankind* are outmoded and inaccurate terms for both genders. Eliminate gender bias by using the following tips:

- Don't say *boy* when you can say *child.*
- Use *men and women* or *people* instead of *man.*
- Use *humanity* or *humankind* in place of *mankind.*

Eliminating *he, his,* and *him* when referring to both men and women is more complicated. Many readers consider *he/she* to be an awkward alternative. Try one of the following instead:

- Make the noun and its corresponding pronoun plural. The pronoun will change from *he, him,* or *his* to *they, them,* or *theirs.*

Biased Masculine Pronouns

An undercover agent won't reveal his identity, even to other agents, if he thinks doing so will jeopardize the case.

Better

Undercover agents won't reveal their identities, even to other agents, if they think doing so will jeopardize the case.

- Replace the pronoun with an article (*the, a,* or *an*)

Biased Masculine Pronoun

> Each prospective driving instructor must pass a state test before receiving his license.

Better

> Each prospective driving instructor must pass a state test before receiving a license.

Be inclusive about race and ethnicity

Use the terms for racial and ethnic groups that the groups use for themselves. Use *black* to write about members of the Black Coaches' Association and *African American* to write about members of the Society for African American Brotherhood.

If you are still in doubt, err on the side of specificity. For instance, while *Latino(a)*, *Hispanic*, and *Chicano(a)* are all frequently accepted terms for many people, choosing a term that identifies a specific country or region (*Mexican* or *Puerto Rican*) would be more accurate. When discussing an American's heritage, often the best term to use is the country of origin plus the word *American*, as in *Swedish American* or *Mexican American* (note that these terms are not hyphenated). Currently *black* and *African American* are acceptable.

Some people prefer *Native American* over *American Indian*, but both terms are used. In Canada the preferred name for indigenous peoples is *First Peoples* (or *Inuit* for those who live in the far north). *First Peoples* is increasingly used by indigenous peoples in the United States in solidarity with their Canadian relatives. If you are writing about specific people, use the name of the specific American or Canadian Indian group (*Cree*, *Hopi*, *Mi'kmaq*, *Ute*).

Be inclusive about people with disabilities

The *Publication Manual of the American Psychological Association* (6th ed.) offers some good advice about putting people first, not their disabilities (76). Write *people who are deaf* instead of *the deaf* and *a student who is quadriplegic* instead of *a quadriplegic student*. Don't reduce people to their deficiencies.

Be inclusive about people of different ages

Avoid bias by choosing accurate terms to describe age. If possible, use the person's age. *Eighty-two-year-old Adele Schumacher* is better than *elderly Adele Schumacher.*

24e Recognize International Varieties of English

English today comes in various shapes and forms. Many applied linguists now speak of "World Englishes" in the plural, to highlight the diversity of the English language as it is used worldwide.

English has long been established as the dominant language in Australia, Canada, New Zealand, the United Kingdom, and the United States, although many people in those countries also use other languages at home and in their communities. Englishes used in these countries share many characteristics, but there also are some differences in sentence structures, vocabulary, spelling, and punctuation. For example:

British English	The outdoor concert was rained off.
U.S. English	The outdoor concert was rained out.
British English	What's the price of petrol (petroleum) these days?
U.S. English	What's the price of gas (gasoline) these days?

Newer varieties of English have emerged outside traditionally English-speaking countries. Many former British and U.S. colonies—Hong Kong, India, Malaysia, Nigeria, Papua New Guinea, the Philippines, Singapore, and others—continue to use a local variety of English for both public and private communication. Englishes used in many of these countries are based primarily on the British variety, but they also include many features that reflect the local context.

Indian English	Open the air conditioner.
U.S. English	Turn on the air conditioner.
Singaporean English	I was arrowed to lead the discussion.
U.S. English	I was selected to lead the discussion.

Remember that correctness differs from one variation of English to another.

PART 6 Understanding Grammar

25 | Fragments, Run-ons, and Comma Splices

25a Fragments

Fragments are incomplete sentences. They are punctuated to look like sentences, but they lack a key element—often a subject or a verb—or else they are subordinate clauses or phrases. Consider this example of a full sentence followed by a fragment:

> The university's enrollment rose unexpectedly during the fall semester. Because the percentage of students who accepted offers of admission was much higher than in previous years and fewer students than usual dropped out or transferred.

When a sentence starts with *because,* we expect to find a main clause later. Instead, the *because* clause refers back to the previous sentence. The writer no doubt knew that the fragment gave the reasons why enrollment rose, but a reader must stop to determine the connection.

In formal writing you should avoid fragments. Readers expect words punctuated as a sentence to be a complete sentence. They expect writers to complete their thoughts rather than force readers to guess the missing element.

Basic strategies for turning fragments into sentences

Incorporate the fragment into an adjoining sentence.

In many cases you can incorporate the fragment into an adjoining sentence.

I was hooked on the ~~game. Playing~~ *game, playing* day and night.

Add the missing element.

If you cannot incorporate a fragment into another sentence, add the missing element.

When aiming for the highest returns, ~~and also~~ *investors should think* ~~thinking~~ about the possible losses.

COMMON ERRORS

e Edit Help

Recognizing fragments

If you can spot fragments, you can fix them. Grammar checkers can find some of them, but they miss many fragments and may identify other sentences wrongly as fragments. Ask these questions when you are checking for sentence fragments.

- **Does the sentence have a subject?** Except for commands, sentences need subjects:

  Incorrect   Jane spent every cent of credit she had available. And then applied for more cards.

- **Does the sentence have a complete verb?** Sentences require complete verbs. Verbs that end in *-ing* must have an auxiliary verb to be complete.

  Incorrect   Ralph keeps changing majors. He trying to figure out what he really wants to do after college.

- **If the sentence begins with a subordinate clause, is there a main clause in the same sentence?**

  Incorrect   Even though Seattle is cloudy much of the year, no American city is more beautiful when the sun shines. Which is one reason people continue to move there.

Remember:
1. A sentence must have a subject and a complete verb.
2. A subordinate clause cannot stand alone as a sentence.

25b Run-on Sentences

While fragments are incomplete sentences, run-ons (also called "fused sentences") jam together two or more sentences, failing to separate them with appropriate punctuation.

Fixing run-on sentences

Take three steps to fix run-on sentences: (1) identify the problem, (2) determine where the run-on sentence needs to be divided, and (3) choose the punctuation that best indicates the relationship between the main clauses.

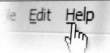

COMMON ERRORS

Recognizing run-on sentences

When you read this sentence, you realize something is wrong.

Incorrect   I do not recall what kind of printer it was all I remember is that it could sort, staple, and print a packet at the same time.

The problem is that two main clauses are not separated by punctuation. The reader must look carefully to determine where one main clause stops and the next one begins.

> I do not recall what kind of printer it was | all I remember is that it could sort, staple, and print a packet at the same time.

A period should be placed after *was,* and the next sentence should begin with a capital letter:

Correct   I do not recall what kind of printer it was. All I remember is that it could sort, staple, and print a packet at the same time.

Run-on sentences are major errors.

Remember: Two main clauses must be separated by correct punctuation.

1. Identify the problem.

When you read your writing aloud, run-on sentences will often trip you up, just as they confuse readers. If you find two main clauses with no punctuation separating them, you have a run-on sentence. You can also search for subject and verb pairs to check for run-ons.

> ┌──── SUBJ ────┐ ┌── VERB ──┐
> **Internet businesses are** not **bound** to specific locations or old
> ┌S┐ ┌V┐
> ways of running a business **they are** more flexible in allowing
> employees to telecommute and to determine the hours they work.

2. Determine where the run-on sentence needs to be divided.

> Internet businesses are not bound to specific locations or old ways of running a business | they are more flexible in allowing employees to telecommute and to determine the hours they work.

3. Determine the relationship between the main clauses.

You will revise a run-on more effectively if you first determine the relationship between the main clauses and understand the effect or point you are trying to make. There are several punctuation strategies for fixing run-ons.

- **Insert a period.** This is the simplest way to fix a run-on sentence.

> Internet businesses are not bound to specific locations or old ways of running a business. They are more flexible in allowing employees to telecommute and to determine the hours they work.

However, if you want to indicate more clearly a closer relationship between the two main clauses, you may want to choose one of the following strategies.

- **Insert a semicolon (and possibly a transitional word specifying the relationship between the two main clauses).**

> Internet businesses are not bound to specific locations or old ways of running a business; therefore, they are more flexible in allowing employees to telecommute and to determine the hours they work.

- **Insert a comma and a coordinating conjunction** (*and, but, or, nor, for, so, yet*).

> Internet businesses are not bound to specific locations or old ways of running a business, so they are more flexible in allowing employees to telecommute and to determine the hours they work.

- **Make one of the clauses subordinate.**

> Because Internet businesses are not bound to specific locations or old ways of running a business, they are more flexible in allowing employees to telecommute and to determine the hours they work.

25c　Comma Splices

Comma splices occur when two or more sentences are incorrectly joined by a comma: A comma should not be used to link two clauses that could stand on their own. In this example, the comma following "classes" should be a period.

> Most of us were taking the same classes, if someone had a
> question, we would all help out.

Such sentences include a punctuation mark—a comma—separating two main clauses. However, a comma is not a strong enough punctuation mark to separate two main clauses.

COMMON ERRORS

Recognizing comma splices

When you edit your writing, look carefully at sentences that contain commas. Does the sentence contain two main clauses? If so, are the main clauses joined by a comma and a coordinating conjunction (*and, but, for, or, not, so, yet*)?

Incorrect　The concept of "nature" depends on the concept of
　　　　　　human "culture," the problem is that "culture" is itself
　　　　　　shaped by "nature." [Two main clauses joined by only a
　　　　　　comma]

Correct　Even though the concept of "nature" depends on the
　　　　　　concept of human "culture," "culture" is itself shaped by
　　　　　　"nature." [Subordinate clause plus a main clause]

Correct　The concept of "nature" depends on the concept of hu-
　　　　　　man "culture," but "culture" is itself shaped by "nature."
　　　　　　[Two main clauses joined by a comma and a coordinating
　　　　　　conjunction]

The word *however* produces some of the most common comma splice errors. When *however* begins a main clause, it should be preceded by a semicolon or a period, not a comma.

COMMON ERRORS

Incorrect   The White House press secretary repeatedly vowed the Administration was not choosing a side between the two countries embroiled in conflict, however the developing foreign policy suggested otherwise.

Correct   The White House press secretary repeatedly vowed the Administration was not choosing a side between the two countries embroiled in conflict; however, the developing foreign policy suggested otherwise. [Two main clauses joined by a semicolon]

Remember: Do not use a comma as a period.

Fixing comma splices

You have several options for fixing comma splices. Select the one that best fits where the sentence is located and the effect you are trying to achieve.

1. Change the comma to a period.

Most comma splices can be fixed by changing the comma to a period.

It didn't matter that I worked in a windowless room for 40 hours a ~~week, on~~ *week. On* the Web I was exploring and learning more about distant people and places than I ever had before.

2. Change the comma to a semicolon.

A semicolon indicates a close connection between two main clauses.

It didn't matter that I worked in a windowless room for 40 hours a ~~week,~~ *week;* on the Web I was exploring and learning more about distant people and places than I ever had before.

3. Insert a coordinating conjunction.

Other comma splices can be repaired by inserting a coordinating conjunction (*and, but, or, nor, so, yet, for*) to indicate the relationship of the two

main clauses. The coordinating conjunction must be preceded by a comma.

> Digital technologies have intensified a global culture that affects us daily in large and small ways, **yet** their impact remains poorly understood.

4. Make one of the main clauses a subordinate clause.

If a comma splice includes one main clause that is subordinate to the other, rewrite the sentence using a subordinating conjunction (such as *after, although, because, if*).

> *Because community*
> ~~Community~~ is the vision of a great society trimmed down to the size of a small town, it is a powerful metaphor for real estate developers who sell a mini-utopia along with a house or condo.

5. Make one of the main clauses a phrase.

You can also rewrite one of the main clauses as a phrase.

> Community—**the vision of a great society trimmed down to the size of a small town**—is a powerful metaphor for real estate developers who sell a mini-utopia along with a house or condo.

26 | Subject-Verb Agreement

26a Agreement in the Present Tense

When your verb is in the present tense, agreement in number is straightforward: The subject takes the base form of the verb in all but the third person singular. For example, the verb *walk,* in the present tense, agrees in number with most subjects in its base form:

First person singular   I walk

Second person singular   You walk

First person plural	We walk
Second person plural	You walk
Third person plural	They walk

Third person singular subjects are the exception to this rule. When your subject is in the third person singular (*he, it, Fido, Lucy, Mr. Jones*), you need to add *s* or *es* to the base form of the verb.

| Third person singular (add *s*) | He walks. It walks. Fido walks. |
| Third person singular (add *es*) | Lucy goes. Mr. Jones goes. |

26b Singular and Plural Subjects

Follow these rules when you have trouble determining whether to use a singular or plural verb form.

Subjects joined by *and*

When two subjects are joined by *and,* treat them as a compound (plural) subject.

Mary and Jane are leaving for New York in the morning.

Some compound subjects work together as a single noun and are treated as singular. Although they appear to be compound and therefore plural, these subjects take the singular form of the verb:

Rock and roll remains the devil's music, even in the twenty-first century.

When two nouns linked by *and* are modified by *every* or *each,* these two nouns are likewise treated as one singular subject:

Each night and day brings no new news of you.

An exception to this rule arises when the word *each* follows a compound subject. In these cases, usage varies depending on the number of the direct object.

The army and the navy each have their own airplanes.

The owl and the pussycat each has a personal claim to fame.

Subjects joined by *or, either . . . or,* or *neither . . . nor*

When a subject is joined by *or, either . . . or,* or *neither . . . nor,* make sure the verb agrees with the subject closest to the verb.

Is it **the sky or the mountains** that **are** blue?

Is it **the mountains or the sky** that **surrounds** us?

Neither the animals nor the zookeeper **knows** how to relock the gate.

Either a coyote or several dogs **were** howling last night.

Subjects along with another noun

Verbs agree with the subject of a sentence, even when a subject is linked to another noun with a phrase like *as well as, along with,* or *alongside.* These modifying phrases are usually set off from the main subject with commas.

Chicken, alongside various steamed vegetables, **is** my favorite meal.

Besides B. B. King, **John Lee Hooker and Muddy Waters** **are** my favorite blues artists of all time.

COMMON ERRORS

e Edit Help

Subjects separated from verbs

The most common agreement errors occur when words come between the subject and verb. These intervening words do not affect subject-verb agreement. To ensure that you use the correct verb form, identify the subject and the verb. Ignore any phrases that come between them.

Incorrect **Students** at inner-city Washington High **reads** more than suburban students.

Correct **Students** at inner-city Washington High **read** more than suburban students.

Students is plural and *read* is plural; subject and verb agree.

Incorrect **The whale shark,** the largest of all sharks, **feed** on plankton.

Correct **The whale shark,** the largest of all sharks, **feeds** on plankton.

COMMON ERRORS

The plural noun *sharks* that appears between the subject *the whale shark* and the verb *feeds* does not change the number of the subject. The subject is singular and the verb is singular. Subject and verb agree.

Remember: When you check for subject-verb agreement, identify the subject and the verb. Ignore any words that come between them.

26c Indefinite Pronouns as Subjects

The choice of a singular or plural pronoun is determined by the **antecedent**—the noun that pronoun refers to. Indefinite pronouns, such as *some, few, all, someone, everyone,* and *each,* often do not refer to identifiable subjects; hence they have no antecedents. Most indefinite pronouns are singular and agree with the singular forms of verbs. Some, like *both* and *many,* are always plural and agree with the plural forms of verbs. Other indefinite pronouns are variable and can agree with either singular or plural verb forms, depending on the context of the sentence.

COMMON ERRORS

Agreement errors using *each*

When a pronoun is singular, its verb must be singular. A common stumbling block to this rule is the pronoun *each. Each* is always treated as a singular pronoun in college writing. When *each* stands alone, the choice is easy to make:

Incorrect	Each are an outstanding student.
Correct	Each is an outstanding student.

But when *each* is modified by a phrase that includes a plural noun, the choice of a singular verb form becomes less obvious:

Incorrect	**Each** of the girls are fit.
Correct	**Each** of the girls is fit.
Incorrect	**Each** of our dogs get a present.
Correct	**Each** of our dogs gets a present.

Remember: *Each* is always singular.

26d Collective Nouns as Subjects

Collective nouns refer to groups (*audience, class, committee, crowd, family, government, group, jury, public, team*). When members of a group are considered as a unit, use singular verbs and singular pronouns.

> The **crowd** is unusually quiet at the moment, but it will get noisy soon.

When members of a group are considered as individuals, use plural verbs and plural pronouns.

> The **faculty** have their differing opinions on how to address the problems caused by reduced state support.

Sometimes collective nouns can be singular in one context and plural in another. Writers must decide which verb form to use based on sentence context.

> The **number** of people who live downtown is increasing.

> A **number** of people are moving downtown from the suburbs.

26e Inverted Word Order

Writers use inverted word order most often in forming questions. The statement *Cats are friendly* becomes a question when you invert the subject and the verb: *Are cats friendly?* Writers also use inverted word order for added emphasis or for style considerations.

Do not be confused by inverted word order. Locate the subject of your sentence, and then make sure your verb agrees with that subject.

26f Amounts, Numbers, and Pairs

Subjects that describe amounts of money, time, distance, or measurement are singular and require singular verbs.

> **Three days** is never long enough to unwind.

Some subjects, such as courses of study, academic specializations, illnesses, and even some nations, are treated as singular subjects even though their names end in *-s* or *-es*. For example, *economics, news, ethics, measles,* and *the United States* all end in *-s* but are all singular subjects.

> **Economics is** a rich field of study.

Other subjects require a plural verb form even though they refer to single items such as *jeans, slacks, glasses, scissors,* and *tweezers.* These items are all treated as pairs.

> My **glasses are** scratched.

27 | Verbs

27a Basic Verb Forms

Almost all verbs in English have five possible forms. The exception is the verb *be.* Regular verbs follow this basic pattern:

Base form	Third-person singular	Past tense	Past participle	Present participle
jump	jumps	jumped	jumped	jumping
like	likes	liked	liked	liking
talk	talks	talked	talked	talking
wish	wishes	wished	wished	wishing

Base form

The base form of the verb is the one you find listed in the dictionary. This form indicates an action or condition in the present.

> I **like** New York in June.

Third person singular

Third person singular subjects include *he, she, it,* and the nouns they replace, as well as other pronouns, including *someone, anybody,* and *everything.* Present tense verbs in the third person singular end with *s* or *es*.

> Ms. Nessan **speaks** in riddles.

Past tense

The past tense describes an action or condition that occurred in the past. For most verbs, the past tense is formed by adding *d* or *ed* to the base form of the verb.

> She **inhaled** the night air.

Many verbs, however, have irregular past tense forms. (See Section 27b.)

Past participle

The past participle is used with *have* to form verbs in the perfect tense, with *be* to form verbs in the passive voice (see Section 21a), and to form adjectives derived from verbs.

Past perfect	They **had** gone to the grocery store prematurely.
Passive	The book **was** written thirty years before it **was** published.
Adjective	In the eighties, teased hair was all the rage.

COMMON ERRORS
e <u>Edit</u> Help

Missing verb endings

Verb endings are not always pronounced in speech, especially in some dialects of English. It's also easy to omit these endings when you are writing quickly. Spelling checkers will not mark these errors, so you have to find them while proofreading.

Incorrect	Jeremy feel as if he's catching a cold.
Correct	Jeremy feels as if he's catching a cold.
Incorrect	Sheila hope she would get the day off.
Correct	Sheila hoped she would get the day off.

Remember: Check verbs carefully for missing *s* or *es* endings in the present tense and missing *d* or *ed* endings in the past tense.

Present participle

The present participle functions in one of three ways. Used with an auxiliary verb, it can describe a continuing action. The present participle can also function as a noun, known as a **gerund**, or as an adjective. The present participle is formed by adding *ing* to the base form of a verb.

Present participle	Wild elks **are** competing for limited food resources.
Gerund	Sailing around the Cape of Good Hope is rumored to bring good luck.
Adjective	We looked for shells in the ebbing tide.

27b Irregular Verbs

A verb is **regular** when its past and past participle forms are created by adding *ed* or *d* to the base form. If this rule does not apply, the verb is considered an **irregular** verb. Here are selected common irregular verbs and their basic forms.

Common irregular verbs

Base form	Past tense	Past participle
be (is, am, are)	was, were	been
become	became	become
bring	brought	brought
come	came	come
do	did	done
get	got	got or gotten
have	had	had
go	went	gone
know	knew	known
see	saw	seen

COMMON ERRORS

e Edit Help

Past tense forms of irregular verbs

The past tense and past participle forms of irregular verbs are often confused. The most frequent error is using a past tense form instead of the past participle with *had*.

	PAST TENSE
Incorrect	She had never **rode** a horse before.

	PAST PARTICIPLE
Correct	She had never **ridden** a horse before.

	PAST TENSE
Incorrect	He had **saw** many alligators in Louisiana.

	PAST PARTICIPLE
Correct	He had **seen** many alligators in Louisiana.

Remember: Change any past tense verbs preceded by *had* to past participles.

27c Transitive and Intransitive Verbs

Lay/lie, set/sit, and *raise/rise*

Do your house keys lay or lie on the kitchen table? Does a book set or sit on the shelf? *Raise/rise, lay/lie,* and *set/sit* are transitive/intransitive verb pairs that writers frequently confuse. **Transitive verbs** take direct objects— nouns that receive the action of the verb. **Intransitive verbs** act in sentences that lack direct objects.

The following charts list the trickiest pairs of transitive and intransitive verbs and the correct forms for each verb tense. Pay special attention to *lay* and *lie,* which are irregular.

	lay (put something down)	**lie (recline)**
Present	lay, lays	lie, lies
Present participle	laying	lying
Past	laid	lay
Past participle	laid	lain

Transitive   When you complete your test, please lay your pencil [direct object, the thing being laid down] on the desk.

Intransitive   The *Titanic* lies upright in two pieces at a depth of 13,000 feet.

	raise (elevate something)	**rise (get up)**
Present	raise, raises	rise, rises
Present participle	raising	rising
Past	raised	rose
Past participle	raised	risen

Transitive   We raise our glasses [direct object, the things being raised] to toast Uncle Han.

Intransitive   The sun rises over the bay.

	set (place something)	**sit (take a seat)**
Present	set, sets	sit, sits
Present participle	setting	sitting
Past	set	sat
Past participle	set	sat

Transitive   Every morning Stanley sets two dollars [direct object, the amount being set] on the table to tip the waiter.

Intransitive   I sit in the front seat if it's available.

28 Pronouns

28a Pronoun Case

Subjective pronouns function as the subjects of sentences. **Objective pronouns** function as direct or indirect objects. **Possessive pronouns** indicate ownership.

Subjective pronouns	Objective pronouns	Possessive pronouns
I	me	my, mine
we	us	our, ours
you	you	your, yours
he	him	his
she	her	her, hers
it	it	its
they	them	their, theirs
who	whom	whose

Pronouns in compound phrases

Picking the right pronoun can sometimes be confusing when the pronoun appears in a compound phrase.

> If we work together, you and **me** can get the job done quickly.

> If we work together, you and **I** can get the job done quickly.

Which is correct—*me* or *I*? Removing the other pronoun usually makes the choice clear.

Incorrect	Me can get the job done quickly.
Correct	I can get the job done quickly.

We and *us* before nouns

Another pair of pronouns that can cause difficulty is *we* and *us* before nouns.

> **Us** friends must stick together.

> **We** friends must stick together.

Which is correct—*us* or *we*? Removing the noun indicates the correct choice.

| Incorrect | **Us** must stick together. |
| Correct | **We** must stick together. |

Who versus *whom*

Choosing between *who* and *whom* is often difficult, even for experienced writers. The distinction between *who* and *whom* is disappearing from spoken language. *Who* is more often used in spoken language, even when *whom* is correct.

COMMON ERRORS  e Edit Help

Who or *whom*

In writing, the distinction between *who* and *whom* is still often observed. *Who* and *whom* follow the same rules as other pronouns: *Who* is the subject pronoun; *whom* is the object pronoun. If you are dealing with an object, *whom* is the correct choice.

| Incorrect | **Who** did you send the letter to? |
| | **Who** did you give the present to? |

| Correct | To **whom** did you send the letter? |
| | **Whom** did you give the present to? |

Who is always the right choice for the subject pronoun.

| Correct | **Who** gave you the present? |
| | **Who** brought the cookies? |

(Continued on next page)

COMMON ERRORS *(Continued)*

If you are uncertain of which one to use, try substituting *she* and *her* or *he* and *him*.

Incorrect	You sent the letter to she **[who]**?
Correct	You sent the letter to her **[whom]**?
Incorrect	Him **[Whom]** gave you the present?
Correct	He **[Who]** gave you the present?

Remember: *Who* = subject
                Whom = object

Whoever versus *whomever*

With the rule regarding *who* and *whom* in mind, you can distinguish between *whoever* and *whomever*. Which is correct?

> Her warmth touched **whoever** she met.

> Her warmth touched **whomever** she met.

In this sentence the pronoun functions as the direct object in its own clause: she met whomever. Thus *whomever* is the correct choice.

Pronouns in comparisons

When you write a sentence using a comparison that includes *than* or *as* followed by a pronoun, usually you will have to think about which pronoun is correct. Which of the following is correct?

> Vimala is a faster swimmer than **him**.

> Vimala is a faster swimmer than **he**.

The test that will give you the correct answer is to add the verb that finishes the sentence—in this case, *is*.

Incorrect	Vimala is a faster swimmer than him is.
Correct	Vimala is a faster swimmer than he is.

Adding the verb makes the correct choice evident.

Possessive pronouns

Possessive pronouns are confusing at times because possessive nouns are formed with apostrophes, but possessive pronouns do not require apostrophes. Pronouns that use apostrophes are always **contractions**.

It's	=	It is
Who's	=	Who is
They're	=	They are

The test for whether to use an apostrophe is to determine if the pronoun is possessive or a contraction. The most confusing pair is *its* and *it's*.

Incorrect	Its a sure thing she will be elected. [Contraction needed]
Correct	It's a sure thing she will be elected. [**It is** a sure thing.]
Incorrect	The dog lost it's collar. [Possessive needed]
Correct	The dog lost its collar.

Possessive pronouns before -*ing* verbs

Pronouns that modify an -*ing* verb (called a *gerund*) or an -*ing* verb phrase (*gerund phrase*) should appear in the possessive.

Incorrect	The odds of you making the team are excellent.
Correct	The odds of your making the team are excellent.

28b Pronoun Agreement

Because pronouns usually replace or refer to other nouns, they must match those nouns in number and gender. The noun that the pronoun replaces is called its **antecedent**. If pronoun and antecedent match, they are in **agreement**. When a pronoun is close to the antecedent, usually there is no problem.

> **Maria** forgot her coat.

> The band **members** collected their uniforms.

Pronoun agreement errors often happen when pronouns and the nouns they replace are separated by several words.

Incorrect

> The **players**, exhausted from the double-overtime game, picked up **his** sweats and walked toward the locker rooms.

Correct

> The **players**, exhausted from the double-overtime game, picked up **their** sweats and walked toward the locker rooms.

Careful writers make sure that pronouns match their antecedents.

COMMON ERRORS

Indefinite pronouns

Indefinite pronouns (such as *anybody, anything, each, either, everybody, everything, neither, none, somebody, something*) refer to unspecified people or things. Most take singular pronouns.

Incorrect	Everybody can choose **their** roommates.
Correct	Everybody can choose **his or her** roommate.
Correct alternative	All students can choose **their** roommates.

A few indefinite pronouns (*all, any, either, more, most, neither, none, some*) can take either singular or plural pronouns.

Correct	**Some** of the shipment was damaged when **it** became overheated.
Correct	**All** thought **they** should have a good seat at the concert.

A few pronouns are always plural (*few, many, several*).

Correct	**Several** want refunds.

Remember: Words that begin with *any, some,* and *every* are usually singular.

Collective nouns

Collective nouns (such as *audience, class, committee, crowd, family, herd, jury, team*) can be singular or plural depending on whether the emphasis is on the group or on its individual members.

Correct   The **committee** was unanimous in **its** decision.

Correct   The **committee** put **their** opinions ahead of the goals of the unit.

COMMON ERRORS   *e* Edit Help

Pronoun agreement with compound antecedents
Antecedents joined by *and* take plural pronouns.

Correct   *Moncef and Driss* practiced **their** music.

Exception: When compound antecedents are preceded by *each* or *every,* use a singular pronoun.

Correct   **Every male cardinal and warbler** arrives before the female to define **its** territory.

When compound antecedents are connected by *or* or *nor,* the pronoun agrees with the antecedent closer to it.

Incorrect   **Either the Ross twins or Angela** should bring **their** CDs.

Correct   **Either the Ross twins or Angela** should bring **her** CDs.

Better   **Either Angela or the Ross twins** should bring **their** CDs.

When you put the plural *twins* last, the correct choice becomes the plural pronoun *their.*

Remember:
1. Use plural pronouns for antecedents joined by *and.*
2. Use singular pronouns for antecedents preceded by *each* or *every.*
3. Use a pronoun that agrees with the nearest antecedent when compound antecedents are joined by *or* or *nor.*

28c Avoid Sexist Pronouns

English does not have a neutral singular pronoun for a group of mixed genders or a person of unknown gender. Referring to a group of mixed genders using male pronouns is unacceptable to many people. Unless the school in the following example is all male, many readers would object to the use of *his*.

> **Sexist**   **Each student** must select **his** courses using the online registration system.

One strategy is to use *her or his* or *his or her* instead of *his*.

> **Correct**   **Each student** must select **his or her** courses using the online registration system.

Often you can avoid using *his or her* by changing the noun to the plural form.

> **Better**   **All students** must select **their** courses using the online registration system.

In some cases, however, using *his or her* is necessary.

28d Vague Reference

Pronouns can sometimes refer to more than one noun, thus confusing readers.

> The **coach** rushed past the injured **player** to yell at the **referee**. **She** was hit in the face by a stray elbow.

You have to guess which person *she* refers to—the coach, the player, or the referee. Sometimes you cannot even guess the antecedent of a pronoun.

> The new subdivision destroyed the last remaining habitat for wildlife within the city limits. **They** have ruined our city with their unchecked greed.

Whom does *they* refer to? the mayor and city council? the developers? the people who live in the subdivision? or all of the above?

Pronouns should never leave the reader guessing about antecedents. If different nouns can be confused as the antecedent, then the ambiguity should be clarified.

Vague   Mafalda's pet boa constrictor crawled across Tonya's foot. She was mortified.

Better   When Mafalda's pet boa constrictor crawled across Tonya's foot, Mafalda was mortified.

COMMON ERRORS

e Edit Help

Vague use of *this*

Always use a noun immediately after *this, that, these, those,* and *some.*

Vague   Enrique asked Meg to remove the viruses on his computer. This was a bad idea.

Was it a bad idea for Enrique to ask Meg because she was insulted? Because she didn't know how? Because removing viruses would destroy some of Enrique's files?

Better   Enrique asked Meg to remove the viruses on his computer. This imposition on Meg's time was a bad idea.

Remember: Ask yourself "this *what?*" and add the noun that *this* refers to.

29 | Shifts

29a Shifts in Tense

Appropriate shifts in verb tense

Changes in verb tense are sometimes necessary to indicate a shift in time.

Past to future   Because Oda **won** [PAST TENSE] the lottery, she **will quit** [FUTURE TENSE] her job at the hospital as soon as her supervisor **finds** [PRESENT TENSE] a qualified replacement.

Inappropriate shifts in verb tense

Be careful to avoid confusing your reader with shifts in verb tense.

Incorrect   While Brazil **looks** [PRESENT TENSE] to ecotourism to fund rain forest preservation, other South American nations **relied** [PAST TENSE] on foreign aid and conservation efforts.

The shift from present tense (*looks*) to past tense (*relied*) is confusing. Correct the mistake by putting both verbs in the present tense.

Correct   While Brazil **looks** [PRESENT TENSE] to ecotourism to fund rain forest preservation, other South American nations **rely** [PRESENT TENSE] on foreign aid and conservation efforts.

COMMON ERRORS

e Edit Help

Unnecessary tense shift
Notice the tense shift in the following example.

Incorrect

In May of 2000 the "I Love You" virus **crippled** [PAST TENSE] the computer systems of major American companies and **irritated** [PAST TENSE] millions of private computer users. As the virus **generates** [PRESENT TENSE] millions of e-mails and **erases** [PRESENT TENSE] millions of computer files, companies such as Ford and Time Warner **are** [PRESENT TENSE] forced to shut down their clogged e-mail systems.

The second sentence shifts unnecessarily to the present tense, confusing the reader. Did the "I Love You" virus have its heyday several years ago, or is it still wreaking havoc now? Changing the verbs in the second sentence to the past tense eliminates the confusion.

Correct

In May of 2000 the "I Love You" virus **crippled** [PAST TENSE] the computer systems of major American companies and **irritated** [PAST TENSE] millions of private computer users. As the virus **generated** [PAST TENSE] millions of e-mails and **erased** [PAST TENSE] millions of computer files, companies such as Ford and Time Warner **were** [PAST TENSE] forced to shut down their clogged e-mail systems.

Remember: Shift verb tense only when you are referring to different time periods.

29b ## Shifts in Mood

Verbs can be categorized into three moods—indicative, imperative, and subjunctive—defined by the functions they serve.

Indicative verbs state facts, opinions, and questions.

Fact   Many same-sex couples in the United States are
              fighting for the right to marry.

Imperative verbs make commands, give advice, and make requests.

Command   Tell me why you support same-sex marriage.

Subjunctive verbs express wishes, unlikely or untrue situations, hypothetical situations, requests with *that* clauses, and suggestions.

Unlikely or   If heterosexual marriage were as sacred as some
untrue   pundits would have us believe, there would be no
situation   divorce.

Be careful not to shift from one mood to another in mid-sentence.

Incorrect   If the government **were** to shift funding priorities away
                from earthquake research, scientists lose even more
                time in understanding how to predict earthquakes.

The sudden shift from subjunctive to indicative mood in this sentence is confusing. Are the scientists losing time now, or is losing time a likely result of a government funding shift? Revise the sentence to keep both verbs in the subjunctive.

Correct   If the government **were** to shift funding priorities away
                from earthquake research, scientists would lose even
                more time in understanding how to predict earthquakes.

29c Shifts in Voice

Watch for unintended shifts from active (*I ate the cookies*) to passive voice (*the cookies were eaten*).

Incorrect   The sudden storm toppled several trees, and numerous
                windows were shattered.

The unexpected shift from active voice (*toppled*) to passive (*were shattered*) forces readers to wonder whether it was the sudden storm, or something else, that broke the windows.

Correct   The sudden storm toppled several trees and shattered
                numerous windows.

Revising the sentence to eliminate the shift to passive voice (see Section 21a) also creates a parallel structure (see 23c).

29d Shifts in Person and Number

Sudden shifts from third person (*he, she, it, one*) to first (*I, we*) or second (*you*) are confusing to readers and often indicate a writer's uncertainty about how to address a reader. We often make such shifts in spoken English, but in formal writing shifts in person need to be recognized and corrected.

Incorrect   When **one** is reading a magazine, **you** often see several different type fonts used on a single page.

The shift from third person to second person in this sentence is confusing.

Correct   When reading a magazine, **you** often see several different type fonts used on a single page.

Similarly, shifts from singular to plural subjects (see Section 26b) within a single sentence confuse readers.

Incorrect   Administrators often make more money than **professors**, but only **a professor** has frequent contact with students.

Correct   Administrators often make more money than **professors**, but only **professors** have frequent contact with students.

The revised sentence eliminates a distracting and unnecessary shift from plural to singular.

30 | Modifiers

30a Choose the Correct Modifier

Modifiers come in two varieties: adjectives and adverbs. The same words can function as adjectives or adverbs, depending on what they modify.

Adjectives modify

nouns—*iced* tea, *power* forward
pronouns—He is *brash*.

Adverbs modify

verbs—*barely* reach, drive *carefully*
adjectives—*truly* brave activist, *shockingly* red lipstick
other adverbs—*not* soon forget, *very* well
clauses—*Honestly,* I find ballet boring.

Adjectives answer the questions *Which one? How many?* and *What kind?* Adverbs answer the questions *How often? To what extent? When? Where? How?* and *Why?*

Use the correct forms of comparatives and superlatives

Comparative modifiers weigh one thing against another. They either end in *er* or are preceded by *more.*

> Road bikes are faster on pavement than mountain bikes.

> The more courageous juggler tossed flaming torches.

Superlative modifiers compare three or more items. They either end in *est* or are preceded by *most.*

> April is the hottest month in New Delhi.

> Wounded animals are the most ferocious.

Some frequently used comparatives and superlatives are irregular. The following list can help you become familiar with them.

Adjective	Comparative	Superlative
good	better	best
bad	worse	worst
little (amount)	less	least
many, much	more	most

Adverb	Comparative	Superlative
well	better	best
badly	worse	worst

Do not use both a suffix (*er* or *est*) and *more* or *most*.

Incorrect	The service at Jane's Restaurant is more slower than the service at Alphonso's.
Correct	The service at Jane's Restaurant is slower than the service at Alphonso's.

Absolute modifiers are words that represent an unvarying condition and thus aren't subject to the degrees that comparative and superlative constructions convey. Common absolute modifiers include *complete, ultimate,* and *unique. Unique,* for example, means "one of a kind." There's nothing else like it. Thus something cannot be *very unique* or *totally unique.* It is either unique or it isn't. Absolute modifiers should not be modified by comparatives (*more* + modifier or modifier + *er*) or superlatives (*most* + modifier or modifier + *est*).

Double negatives

In English, as in mathematics, two negatives equal a positive. Avoid using two negative words in one sentence, or you'll end up saying the opposite of what you mean. The following are negative words that you should avoid doubling up:

barely	nobody	nothing
hardly	none	scarcely
neither	no one	

Incorrect, double negative	Barely no one noticed that the pop star lip-synched during the whole performance.
Correct, single negative	Barely anyone noticed that the pop star lip-synched during the whole performance.
Incorrect, double negative	When the pastor asked if anyone had objections to the marriage, nobody said nothing.
Correct, single negative	When the pastor asked if anyone had objections to the marriage, nobody said anything.

30b Place Adjectives Carefully

As a general rule, the closer you place a modifier to the word it modifies, the less the chance you will confuse your reader.

> **Confusing** Watching from the ground below, the kettle of broad-wing hawks circled high above the observers.

Is the kettle of hawks watching from the ground below? You can fix the problem by putting the modified subject immediately after the modifier or placing the modifier next to the modified subject.

> **Better** The kettle of broadwing hawks circled high above the **observers** who were watching from the ground below.

> **Better** Watching from the ground below, the **observers** saw a kettle of broadwing hawks circle high above them.

30c Place Adverbs Carefully

Single-word adverbs and adverbial clauses and phrases can usually sit comfortably either before or after the words they modify.

> Dimitri quietly **walked** down the hall.

> Dimitri **walked** quietly down the hall.

Conjunctive adverbs—*also, however, instead, likewise, then, therefore, thus,* and others—are adverbs that show how ideas relate to one another. They prepare a reader for contrasts, exceptions, additions, conclusions, and other shifts in an argument. Conjunctive adverbs can usually fit well into more than one place in the sentence. In the following example, *however* could fit in three different places.

Between two main clauses

> Professional football players earn exorbitant salaries; however, they pay for their wealth with lifetimes of chronic pain and debilitating injuries.

Within second main clause

Professional football players earn exorbitant salaries; they pay for their wealth, however, with lifetimes of chronic pain and debilitating injuries.

At end of second main clause

Professional football players earn exorbitant salaries; they pay for their wealth with lifetimes of chronic pain and debilitating injuries however.

Subordinating conjunctions—words such as *after, although, because, if, since, than, that, though, when,* and *where*—often begin **adverb clauses**. Notice that we can place adverb clauses with subordinating conjunctions either before or after the word(s) being modified:

After someone in the audience yelled, he **forgot** the lyrics.

He **forgot** the lyrics after someone in the audience yelled.

COMMON ERRORS

e Edit Help

Placement of limiting modifiers

Words such as *almost, even, hardly, just, merely, nearly, not, only,* and *simply* are called limiting modifiers. Although people often play fast and loose with their placement in everyday speech, limiting modifiers should always go immediately before the word or words they modify in your writing. Like other limiting modifiers, *only* should be placed immediately before the word it modifies.

Incorrect	The Gross National Product **only** gives one indicator of economic growth.
Correct	The Gross National Product gives **only** one indicator of economic growth.

The word *only* modifies *one* in this sentence, not *Gross National Product*.

Remember: Place limiting modifiers immediately before the word(s) they modify.

30d   Hyphens with Compound Modifiers

When to hyphenate

Hyphenate a compound modifier that precedes a noun.
When a compound modifier precedes a noun, you should usually hyphenate the modifier. A **compound modifier** consists of words that join together as a unit to modify a noun.

     middle-class values   self-fulfilling prophecy

Hyphenate a phrase when it is used as a modifier that precedes a noun.

     all-you-can-eat buffet   step-by-step instructions

Hyphenate the prefixes *pro-, anti-, post-, pre-, neo-,* and *mid-* before proper nouns.

     neo-Nazi racism   mid-Atlantic states

Hyphenate a compound modifier with a number when it precedes a noun.

     eighteenth-century drama   one-way street

When not to hyphenate

Do not hyphenate a compound modifier that follows a noun.

     The instructor's approach is student centered.

Do not hyphenate compound modifiers when the first word is *very* or ends in *ly*.

     newly recorded data   very cold day

30e   Revise Dangling Modifiers

Some modifiers are ambiguous because they could apply to more than one word or clause. Dangling modifiers are ambiguous for the opposite reason; they don't have a word to modify. In such cases the modifier is usually an introductory clause or phrase. What is being modified should immediately follow the phrase, but in the following sentence it is absent.

> After bowling a perfect game, Surfside Lanes hung Marco's photo on the wall.

You can eliminate a dangling modifier in two ways:

1. Insert the noun or pronoun being modified immediately after the introductory modifying phrase.

   > After bowling a perfect game, Marco was honored by having his photo hung on the wall at Surfside Lanes.

2. Rewrite the introductory phrase as an introductory clause to include the noun or pronoun.

   > After Marco bowled a perfect game, Surfside Lanes hung his photo on the wall.

COMMON ERRORS
e Edit Help

Dangling modifiers

A dangling modifier does not seem to modify anything in a sentence; it dangles, unconnected to the word or words it presumably is intended to modify. Frequently, it produces funny results:

Incorrect   When still a girl, my father joined the army.

It sounds like *father* was once a girl. The problem is that the subject, *I*, is missing:

Correct   When I was still a girl, my father joined the army.

Remember: Modifiers should be clearly connected to the words they modify, especially at the beginning of sentences.

31 Grammar for Multilingual Writers

31a Nouns

Perhaps the most troublesome conventions for nonnative speakers are those that guide usage of the common articles *the, a,* and *an.* To understand how articles work in English, you must first understand how the language uses **nouns**.

Kinds of nouns

There are two basic kinds of nouns. A **proper noun** begins with a capital letter and names a unique person, place, or thing: *Theodore Roosevelt, Russia, Eiffel Tower.*

The other basic kind of noun is called a **common noun**. Common nouns do not name a unique person, place, or thing: *man, country, tower.*

Count and noncount nouns

Common nouns can be classified as either *count* or *noncount.* **Count nouns** can be made plural, usually by adding *-s* (*finger, fingers*) or by using their plural forms (*person, people; datum, data*). **Noncount nouns** cannot be counted directly and cannot take the plural form (*information,* but not *informations; garbage,* but not *garbages*). Some nouns can be either count or noncount, depending on how they are used. *Hair* can refer to either a strand of hair, where it serves as a count noun, or a mass of hair, where it becomes a noncount noun.

COMMON ESL ERRORS

Edit Help

Singular and plural forms of count nouns

Count nouns are simpler to quantify than noncount nouns. But remember that English requires you to state both singular and plural forms of nouns explicitly. Look at the following sentences.

Incorrect   The three bicyclist shaved their leg before the big race.

Correct   The three bicyclists shaved their legs before the big race.

Remember: English requires you to use plural forms of count nouns even if a plural number is otherwise indicated.

31b Articles

Articles indicate that a noun is about to appear, and they clarify what the noun refers to. There are only two kinds of articles in English, definite and indefinite:

1. **the:** *The* is a **definite article**, meaning that it refers to (1) a specific object already known to the reader, (2) one about to be made known to the reader, or (3) a unique object.
2. **a, an:** The **indefinite articles** *a* and *an* refer to an object whose specific identity is not known to the reader. The only difference between *a* and *an* is that *a* is used before a consonant sound (*man, friend, yellow*), while *an* is used before a vowel sound (*animal, enemy, orange*).

COMMON ESL ERRORS
e Edit Help

Articles with count and noncount nouns

Knowing how to distinguish between count and noncount nouns can help you decide which article to use. Noncount nouns are never used with the indefinite articles *a* or *an*.

Incorrect   Maria jumped into a water.

Correct   Maria jumped into the water.

No articles are used with noncount and plural count nouns when you wish to state something that has a general application.

Incorrect   The water is a precious natural resource.

Correct   Water is a precious natural resource.

Remember:
1. Noncount nouns are never used with *a* and *an*.
2. Noncount and plural nouns used to make general statements do not take articles.

31c Verbs

The verb system in English can be divided between simple verbs like *run, speak,* and *look,* and verb phrases like *may have run, have spoken,* and *will be looking.* In these examples, the words that appear before the main verbs—*may, have, will,* and *be*—are called **auxiliary verbs** (also called **helping verbs**).

Indicating tense and voice with *be* verbs

Like the other auxiliary verbs *have* and *do, be* changes form to signal tense. In addition to *be* itself, the **be verbs** are *is, am, are, was, were,* and *been.* To show ongoing action, *be* verbs are followed by the present participle, which is a verb with an *-ing* ending:

Incorrect	I am think of all the things I'd rather be do.
Correct	I am thinking of all the things I'd rather be doing.

To show that an action is being done to, rather than by, the subject, follow *be* verbs with the past participle (a verb usually ending in *-ed, -en,* or *-t*):

Incorrect	The movie was direct by John Woo.
Correct	The movie was directed by John Woo.

Modal auxiliary verbs

Modal auxiliary verbs *will, would, can, could, may, might, shall, must,* and *should* express conditions like possibility, permission, speculation, expectation, obligation, and necessity. Unlike the auxiliary verbs *be, have,* and *do,* modal verbs do not change form based on the grammatical subject of the sentence (*I, you, she, he, it, we, they*).

Two basic rules apply to all uses of modal verbs. First, modal verbs are always followed by the simple form of the verb. The simple form is the verb by itself, in the present tense, such as *have* but not *had, having,* or *to have.*

Incorrect	She should studies harder to pass the exam.
Correct	She should study harder to pass the exam.

The second rule is that you should not use modals consecutively.

Incorrect	If you work harder at writing, you might could improve.
Correct	If you work harder at writing, you might improve.

Phrasal verbs

The liveliest and most colorful feature of the English language, its numerous idiomatic verbal phrases, gives many multilingual speakers the greatest difficulty.

Phrasal verbs consist of a verb and one or two **particles**: either a preposition, an adverb, or both. The verb and particles combine to form a phrase with a particular meaning that is often quite distinct from the meaning of the verb itself. Consider the following sentence.

I need to go over the chapter once more before the test.

Here, the meaning of *go over*—a verb and a preposition that, taken together, suggest casual study—is only weakly related to the meaning of either *go* or *over* by itself. English has hundreds of such idiomatic constructions, and the best way to familiarize yourself with them is to listen to and read as much informal English as you can.

Like regular verbs, phrasal verbs can be either transitive (they take a direct object) or intransitive. In the preceding example, *go over* is transitive. *Quiet down*—as in *Please quiet down*—is intransitive. Some phrases, like *wake up*, can be both: *Wake up!* is intransitive, while *Jenny, wake up the children* is transitive.

In some transitive phrasal verbs, the particles can be separated from the verb without affecting the meaning: *I made up a song* is equivalent to *I made a song up*. In others, the particles cannot be separated from the verb.

Incorrect	You shouldn't **play** with love **around**.
Correct	You shouldn't **play around** with love.

Unfortunately, there are no shortcuts for learning which verbal phrases are separable and which are not. As you become increasingly familiar with English, you will grow more confident in your ability to use phrasal verbs.

PART 7 Understanding Punctuation and Mechanics

32 | Commas

32a Commas with Introductory Elements

Introductory elements usually need to be set off by commas. Introductory words or phrases signal a shift in ideas or a particular arrangement of ideas; they help direct the reader's attention to the writer's most important points.

When a conjunctive adverb (see Section 27c) or introductory phrase begins a sentence, the comma follows.

> Therefore, the suspect could not have been at the scene of the crime.
> Above all, remember to let water drip from the faucets if the temperature drops below freezing.

When a conjunctive adverb comes in the middle of a sentence, set it off with commas preceding and following.

> If you really want to prevent your pipes from freezing, however, you should insulate them before the winter comes.

Occasionally the conjunctive adverb or phrase blends into a sentence so smoothly that a pause would sound awkward.

Awkward   Even if you take every precaution, the pipes in your home may freeze, nevertheless.

Better   Even if you take every precaution, the pipes in your home may freeze nevertheless.

COMMON ERRORS

e _Edit_ _Help_

Commas with long introductory modifiers

Long subordinate clauses or phrases that begin sentences should be followed by a comma. The following sentence lacks the needed comma.

Incorrect Because teens and younger adults are so comfortable with and reliant on cell phone devices texting while driving does not immediately seem like an irresponsible and possibly deadly act.

When you read this sentence, you likely had to go back to sort it out. The words *cell phone devices* and *texting* tend to run together. When the comma is added, the sentence is easier to understand because the reader knows where the subordinate clause ends and where the main clause begins:

Correct Because teens and younger adults are so comfortable with and reliant on cell phone devices, texting while driving does not immediately seem like an irresponsible and possibly deadly act.

How long is a long introductory modifier? Short introductory adverbial phrases and clauses of five words or fewer can get by without the comma if the omission does not mislead the reader. Using the comma is still correct after short introductory adverbial phrases and clauses:

Correct In the long run stocks have always done better than bonds.

Correct In the long run, stocks have always done better than bonds.

Remember: Put commas after long introductory modifiers.

32b Commas with Compound Clauses

Two main clauses joined by a coordinating conjunction (*and, or, so, yet, but, nor, for*) form a compound sentence. Writers sometimes get confused about when to insert a comma before a coordinating conjunction.

Use a comma and a coordinating conjunction to separate main clauses

Main clauses carry enough grammatical weight to be punctuated as sentences. When two main clauses are joined by a coordinating conjunction, place a comma before the coordinating conjunction in order to distinguish them.

> Sandy borrowed Martin's netbook on Tuesday, **and** she returned it on Friday.

Very short main clauses joined by a coordinating conjunction do not need commas.

> She called and she called, but no one answered.

Do not use a comma to separate two verbs with the same subject

> **Incorrect** Sandy borrowed Martin's video camera on Tuesday, and returned it on Friday.

Sandy is the subject of both *borrowed* and *returned*. This sentence has only one main clause; it should not be punctuated as a compound sentence.

> **Correct** Sandy borrowed Martin's video camera on Tuesday and returned it on Friday.

Do not use a comma to separate a main clause from a restrictive clause or phrase

When clauses and phrases that follow the main clause are essential to the meaning of a sentence, they should not be set off with a comma.

> **Incorrect** Sandy plans to borrow Felicia's DVD collection, while Felicia is on vacation.

> **Correct** Sandy plans to borrow Felicia's DVD collection while Felicia is on vacation.

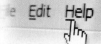

COMMON ERRORS

Commas in compound sentences

The easiest way to distinguish between compound sentences and sentences with phrases that follow the main clause is to isolate the part that comes after the conjunction. If the part that follows the conjunction can stand on its own as a complete sentence, insert a comma. If it cannot, omit the comma.

> **Main clause plus phrases**
>
> Mario thinks he lost his passport while riding the bus or by absentmindedly leaving it on the counter when he checked into the hostel.

Look at what comes after the coordinating conjunction *or:*

> by absentmindedly leaving it on the counter when he checked into the hostel

This group of words is not a main clause and cannot stand on its own as a complete sentence. Do not set it off with a comma.

> **Main clauses joined with a conjunction**
>
> On Saturday Mario went to the American consulate to get a new passport, but the officer told him that replacement passports could not be issued on weekends.

Read the clause after the coordinating conjunction *but:*

> the officer told him that replacement passports could not be issued on weekends

This group of words can stand on its own as a complete sentence. Thus, it is a main clause; place a comma before *but.*

Remember:

1. Place a comma before the coordinating conjunction (*and, but, for, or, nor, so, yet*) when there are two main clauses.
2. Do not use a comma before the coordinating conjunction when there is only one main clause.

COMMON ERRORS

Do not use a comma to set off a *because* clause that follows a main clause

Writers frequently place unnecessary commas before *because* and similar subordinate conjunctions that follow a main clause. *Because* is not a coordinating conjunction; thus it should not be set off by a comma unless the comma improves readability.

Incorrect	I struggled to complete my term papers last year, because I worked at two jobs.
Correct	I struggled to complete my term papers last year because I worked at two jobs.

But do use a comma after an introductory *because* clause.

Incorrect	Because Danny left his red jersey at home Coach Russell benched him.
Correct	Because Danny left his red jersey at home, Coach Russell benched him.

Remember: Use a comma after a *because* clause that begins a sentence. Do not use a comma to set off a *because* clause that follows a main clause.

32c Commas with Nonrestrictive Modifiers

Imagine that you are sending a friend a group photo that includes your aunt. Which sentence is correct?

> In the back row the woman wearing the pink hat is my aunt.

> In the back row the woman, wearing the pink hat, is my aunt.

Both sentences can be correct depending on what is in the photo. If there are three women standing in the back row and only one is wearing a pink hat, this piece of information is necessary for identifying your aunt. In this case the sentence without commas is correct because it identifies your aunt as the woman wearing the pink hat. Such necessary modifiers are **restric-tive** and do not require commas.

If only one woman is standing in the back row, *wearing the pink hat* is extra information and not necessary to identify your aunt. The modifier in this case is **nonrestrictive** and is set off by commas.

Distinguish restrictive and nonrestrictive modifiers

You can distinguish between restrictive and nonrestrictive modifiers by deleting the modifier and then deciding whether the essential meaning of the sentence is changed. For example, delete the modifier *still stained by its bloody Tianamen Square crackdown* from the following sentence:

> Some members of the Olympic Site Selection Committee wanted to prevent China, still stained by its bloody Tianamen Square crackdown, from hosting the 2008 games.

The result leaves the meaning of the main clause unchanged.

> Some members of the Olympic Site Selection Committee wanted to prevent China from hosting the 2008 games.

The modifier is nonrestrictive and should be set off by commas.

Pay special attention to appositives

Clauses and phrases can be restrictive or nonrestrictive, depending on the context. Often the difference is obvious, but some modifiers require close consideration, especially appositives. An **appositive** is a noun or noun phrase that identifies or adds information to the noun preceding it.

Consider the following pair.

1 Apple's tablet computer the iPad introduced a class of devices between smartphones and laptops.

2 Apple's tablet computer, the iPad, introduced a class of devices between smartphones and laptops.

Which is correct? The appositive *the iPad* is not essential to the meaning of the sentence and simply offers additional information. Sentence 2 is correct.

Use commas to mark off parenthetical expressions

A **parenthetical expression** provides information or commentary that usually is not essential to the sentence's meaning.

Incorrect	My mother much to my surprise didn't say anything when she saw my pierced nose.
Correct	My mother, much to my surprise, didn't say anything when she saw my pierced nose.

32d Commas with Items in a Series

In a series of three or more items, place a comma after each item except the last one. The comma between the last two items goes before the conjunction (*and, or*).

> Health officials in Trenton, Manhattan, and the Bronx have all reported new cases of the West Nile virus.

32e Commas with Coordinate Adjectives

Coordinate adjectives are two or more adjectives that modify the same noun independently. Coordinate adjectives that are not linked by *and* must be separated by a comma.

> After the financial crisis of 2007–2010, the creators of credit-default swaps and other risky investments are no longer the fresh-faced, giddy kids of Wall Street.

You can recognize coordinate adjectives by reversing their order; if their meaning remains the same, the adjectives are coordinate and must be linked by *and* or separated by a comma.

Commas are not used between **cumulative adjectives**. Cumulative adjectives are two or more adjectives that work together to modify a noun: *deep blue sea, inexpensive mountain bike*. If reversing their order changes the description of the noun (or violates the order of English, such as *mountain inexpensive bike*), the adjectives are cumulative and should not be separated by a comma.

The following example doesn't require a comma in the cumulative adjective series *massive Corinthian.*

> Visitors to Rome's Pantheon pass between the massive Corinthian columns flanking the front door.

We know they are cumulative because reversing their order to read *Corinthian massive* would alter the way they modify *columns*—in this case, so much so that they no longer make sense.

32f Commas with Quotations

Properly punctuating quotations with commas can be tricky unless you know a few rules about when and where to use commas.

When to use commas with quotations

Commas set off signal phrases that attribute quotations to a speaker or writer, such as *he argues, they said,* and *she writes.*

> "When you come to a fork in the road," said Yogi Berra, "take it!"

If the signal phrase follows a quotation that is a complete sentence, replace the period that would normally come at the end of the quotation with a comma.

Incorrect	"Simplicity of language is not only reputable but perhaps even sacred." writes Kurt Vonnegut.
Correct	"Simplicity of language is not only reputable but perhaps even sacred," writes Kurt Vonnegut.

When not to use commas with quotations

Do not replace a question mark or exclamation point with a comma.

Incorrect	"Who's on first," Costello asked Abbott.
Correct	"Who's on first?" Costello asked Abbott.

Not all phrases that mention the author's name are signal phrases. When quoting a term or using a quotation within a subordinate clause, do not set off the quotation with commas.

> "Stonewall" Jackson gained his nickname at the First Battle of Bull Run when General Barnard Bee shouted to his men that Jackson was "standing like a stone wall."

32g Commas with Dates, Numbers, Titles, and Addresses

Some of the easiest comma rules to remember are the ones we use every day in dates, numbers, personal titles, place names, direct address, and brief interjections.

Commas with dates

Use commas to separate the day of the week from the month and to set off a year from the rest of the sentence.

> Monday, November 14, 2011

> On July 27, 2012, the opening ceremony of the World Scout Jamboree will be televised.

Do not use a comma when the month immediately precedes the year.

> April 2013

Commas with numbers

Commas mark off thousands, millions, billions, and so on.

> 16,500,000

However, do not use commas in street addresses or page numbers.

> page 1542

> 7602 Elm Street

Commas with personal titles

When a title follows a person's name, set the title off with commas.

Gregory House, MD

Commas with place names

Place a comma between street addresses, city names, state names, and countries but not before zip codes.

Write to the president at 1600 Pennsylvania Avenue, Washington, DC 20500.

Commas in direct address

When addressing someone directly, set off that person's name in commas.

I was happy to get your letter yesterday, Jamie.

Commas with brief interjections

Use commas to set off brief interjections like *yes* and *no*, as well as short questions that fall at the ends of sentences.

Have another piece of pie, won't you?

32h Commas to Avoid Confusion

Certain sentences can be confusing if you do not indicate where readers should pause within the sentence. Use a comma to guide a reader through these usually compact constructions.

Unclear   With supplies low prices of gasoline and fuel oil will increase.

This sentence could be read as meaning *With supplies, low prices will increase.*

Clear   With supplies low, prices of gasoline and fuel oil will increase.

32i Unnecessary Commas

Do not place a comma between a subject and the main verb.

Incorrect	American children of immigrant parents, often do not speak their parents' native language.
Correct	American children of immigrant parents often do not speak their parents' native language.

However, you do use commas to set off modifying phrases that separate subjects from verbs.

Correct	Steven Pinker, author of *The Language Instinct,* argues that the ability to speak and understand language is an evolutionary adaptive trait.

Do not use a comma with a coordinating conjunction unless it joins two main clauses. (See the Common Errors box on page 281.)

Incorrect	Susana thought finishing her first novel was hard, but soon learned that getting a publisher to buy it was much harder.
Correct	Susana thought finishing her first novel was hard but soon learned that getting a publisher to buy it was much harder.
Correct	Susana thought finishing her first novel was hard, but she soon learned that getting a publisher to buy it was much harder.

Do not use a comma after a subordinating conjunction such as *although, despite,* or *while.*

Incorrect	Although, soccer is gaining popularity in the States, it will never be as popular as football or baseball.
Correct	Although soccer is gaining popularity in the States, it will never be as popular as football or baseball.

Some writers mistakenly use a comma with *than* to try to heighten the contrast in a comparison.

Incorrect	Any teacher will tell you that acquiring critical thinking skills is more important, than simply memorizing information.
Correct	Any teacher will tell you that acquiring critical thinking skills is more important than simply memorizing information.

A common mistake is to place a comma after *such as* or *like* before introducing a list.

Incorrect	Many hourly workers, such as, waiters, dishwashers, and cashiers, do not receive health benefits from their employers.
Correct	Many hourly workers, such as waiters, dishwashers, and cashiers, do not receive health benefits from their employers.

33 | Semicolons and Colons

33a Semicolons with Closely Related Main Clauses

Why use semicolons? Sometimes we want to join two main clauses to form a complete sentence in order to indicate a relationship and avoid wordiness. We can connect them with a comma and a coordinating conjunction like *or, but,* or *and*. To create variation in sentence style and show a closer relationship, we can omit the comma and coordinating conjunction and insert a semicolon between the two clauses.

Semicolons can join only clauses that are grammatically equal. In other words, they join main clauses only to other main clauses, not to phrases or subordinate clauses. Look at the following examples:

Incorrect
┌────────────────MAIN CLAUSE────────────────┐
Gloria's new weightlifting program will help her recover
                                ┌───────PHRASE───────┐
from knee surgery; doing a series of squats and presses
with a physical therapist.

Correct
┌────────────────MAIN CLAUSE────────────────┐
Gloria's new weightlifting program will help her recover
                             ┌────MAIN CLAUSE────┐
from knee surgery; a physical therapist leads her
through a series of squats and presses.

COMMON ERRORS   e <u>E</u>dit   Help

Semicolons with transitional words and phrases

Closely related main clauses sometimes use a conjunctive adverb (such as *however, therefore, moreover, furthermore, thus, meanwhile, nonetheless, otherwise*) or a transitional phrase (*in fact, for example, that is, for instance, in addition, in other words, on the other hand, even so*) to indicate the relationship between them. When the second clause begins with a conjunctive adverb or a transitional phrase, a semicolon is needed to join the two clauses. This sentence pattern is frequently used; therefore, it pays to learn how to punctuate it correctly.

Incorrect
(comma splice)
No one doubts that exercise burns calories, however, few people can lose weight by exercise alone.

Correct
No one doubts that exercise burns calories; however, few people can lose weight by exercise alone.

Remember: Two main clauses joined by a conjunctive adverb or a transitional phrase require a semicolon.

Do not use a semicolon to introduce quotations

Use a comma or colon instead.

| Incorrect | Robert Frost's poem "Mending Wall" contains this line; "Good fences make good neighbors." |
| Correct | Robert Frost's poem "Mending Wall" contains this line: "Good fences make good neighbors." |

Do not use a semicolon to introduce lists

| Incorrect | William Shakespeare wrote four romance plays at the end of his career; *The Tempest, The Winter's Tale, Cymbeline,* and *Pericles.* |
| Correct | William Shakespeare wrote four romance plays at the end of his career: *The Tempest, The Winter's Tale, Cymbeline,* and *Pericles.* |

33b Semicolons Together with Commas

When an item in a series already includes a comma, adding more commas to separate it from the other items will only confuse the reader. Use semicolons instead of commas between items in a series that has internal punctuation.

| Confusing | The church's design competition drew entries from as far away as Gothenberg, Sweden, Caracas, Venezuela, and Athens, Greece. |
| Clearer | The church's design competition drew entries from as far away as Gothenberg, Sweden; Caracas, Venezuela; and Athens, Greece. |

33c Colons in Sentences

Like semicolons, colons can join two closely related main clauses (complete sentences). A colon indicates that what follows will explain or expand on what comes before the colon. Use a colon in cases where the second main clause interprets or sums up the first.

> Anthrozoology, the study of how animals and people relate to one another, sheds light on larger issues in human psychology: people's interactions with animals illustrate concepts of altruism, ethics, and taboo.

You may choose to capitalize the first word of the main clause following the colon or leave it lowercase. Either is correct as long as you are consistent throughout your text.

Colons linking main clauses with appositives

A colon calls attention to an appositive, a noun, or a noun phrase that renames the noun preceding it. If you're not certain whether a colon would be appropriate, put *namely* in its place. If *namely* makes sense when you read the main clause followed by the appositive, you probably need to insert a colon instead of a comma. Remember, the clause that precedes the colon must be a complete sentence.

> I know the perfect person for the job, namely me.

The sentence makes sense with *namely* placed before the appositive. Thus, a colon is appropriate.

> I know the perfect person for the job: me.

Never capitalize a word following a colon unless the word starts a complete sentence or is normally capitalized.

Colons joining main clauses with quotations

Use a colon to link a main clause and a quotation that interprets or sums up the clause. Be careful not to use a colon to link a phrase with a quotation.

Incorrect: phrase–colon–quotation

> President Roosevelt's strategy to change the nation's panicky attitude during the Great Depression: "[T]he only thing we have to fear," he said, "is fear itself."

Correct: main clause–colon–quotation

> President Roosevelt's strategy to end the Great Depression was to change the nation's panicky attitude: "[T]he only thing we have to fear," he said, "is fear itself."

The first example is incorrect because there is no main verb in the first part of the sentence and thus it is a phrase rather than a main clause. The second example adds the verb (*was*), making the first part of the sentence a main clause.

33d Colons with Lists

Use a colon to join a main clause to a list. The main clauses in these cases sometimes include the phrase *the following* or *as follows*. Remember that a colon cannot join a phrase or an incomplete clause to a list.

Incorrect: phrase–colon–list

Three ingredients for soup: chicken stock, peeled shrimp, and chopped tomatoes.

Correct: main clause–colon–list

You can make a tasty soup with just three ingredients: chicken stock, peeled shrimp, and chopped tomatoes.

COMMON ERRORS   e _Edit_ _Help_

Colons misused with lists

Some writers think that anytime they introduce a list, they should insert a colon. Colons are used correctly only when a complete sentence precedes the colon.

Incorrect   Jessica's entire wardrobe for her trip to Cancun included: two swimsuits, one pair of shorts, two T-shirts, a party dress, and a pair of sandals.

Correct   Jessica's entire wardrobe for her trip to Cancun included two swimsuits, one pair of shorts, two T-shirts, a party dress, and a pair of sandals.

Correct   Jessica jotted down what she would need for her trip: two swimsuits, one pair of shorts, two T-shirts, a party dress, and a pair of sandals.

Remember: A colon should be placed only after a clause that can stand by itself as a sentence.

---

34 Dashes and Parentheses

34a Dashes and Parentheses to Set Off Information

Dashes and parentheses call attention to groups of words. In effect, they tell the reader that a group of words is not part of the main clause and should be given special attention. If you want to make an element stand out, especially in the middle of a sentence, use parentheses or dashes instead of commas.

Dashes with final elements

A dash is often used to set off a phrase or subordinate clause at the end of a sentence to offer a significant comment about the main clause. Dashes can also anticipate a shift in tone at the end of a sentence.

> A full-sized SUV can take you wherever you want to go in style— if your idea of style is a gas-guzzling tank.

Parentheses with additional information

Parentheses are more often used for identifying information, afterthoughts or asides, examples, and clarifications. You can place full sentences, fragments, or brief terms within parentheses.

> Some argue that ethanol (the pet solution of politicians for achieving energy independence) costs more energy to manufacture and ship than it produces.

COMMON ERRORS

e Edit Help

Do not use dashes as periods

Do not use dashes to separate two main clauses (clauses that can stand as complete sentences). Use dashes to separate main clauses from subordinate clauses and phrases when you want to emphasize the subordinate clause or phrase.

Incorrect: main clause–dash–main clause

I was one of the few women in my computer science classes—most of the students majoring in computer science at that time were men.

Correct: main clause–dash–phrase

I was one of the few women in computer science—a field then dominated by men.

Remember: Dashes are not periods and should not be used as periods.

34b Dashes and Parentheses versus Commas

Like commas, parentheses and dashes enclose material that adds, explains, or digresses. However, the three punctuation marks are not interchangeable. The mark you choose depends on how much emphasis you want to place on the material. Dashes indicate the most emphasis. Parentheses offer somewhat less, and commas offer less still.

Commas indicate a moderate level of emphasis

Bill covered the new tattoo on his bicep, a pouncing tiger, because he thought it might upset our mother.

Parentheses lend a greater level of emphasis

I'm afraid to go bungee jumping (though my brother tells me it's less frightening than a roller coaster).

Dashes indicate the highest level of emphasis and, sometimes, surprise and drama

> Christina felt as though she had been punched in the gut; she could hardly believe the stranger at her door was really who he claimed to be—the brother she hadn't seen in twenty years.

COMMON ERRORS e **Edit** **Help**

The art of typing a dash

Although dashes and hyphens may look similar, they are actually different marks. The distinction is small but important because dashes and hyphens serve different purposes. A dash is a line much longer than a hyphen. Most word processors will create a dash automatically when you type two hyphens together. Or you can type a special character to make a dash. Your manual will tell you which keys to press to make a dash.

Do not leave a space between a dash or a hyphen and the words that come before and after them. Likewise, if you are using two hyphens to indicate a dash, do not leave a space between the hyphens.

Incorrect A well - timed effort at conserving water may prevent long - term damage to drought - stricken farms -- if it's not already too late.

Correct A well-timed effort at conserving water may prevent long-term damage to drought-stricken farms—if it's not already too late.

Remember: **Do not put spaces before or after hyphens and dashes.**

34c Other Punctuation with Parentheses

Parentheses around letters or numbers that order a series within a sentence make the list easier to read.

> Angela Creider's recipe for becoming a great novelist is to (1) set aside an hour during the morning to write, (2) read what you've written out loud, (3) revise your prose, and (4) repeat every morning for the next thirty years.

Abbreviations made from the first letters of words are often used in place of the unwieldy names of institutions, departments, organizations, or terms. To show readers what the abbreviation stands for, the writer must state the complete name, followed by the abbreviation in parentheses, the first time the organization is mentioned in the text.

> The University of California, Santa Cruz (UCSC) supports its mascot, the banana slug, with pride and a sense of humor. And although the nickname sounds strange to outsiders, UCSC students are even referred to as "the banana slugs."

COMMON ERRORS

e E̲dit Help

Using periods, commas, colons, and semicolons with parentheses

When an entire sentence is enclosed in parentheses, place the period before the closing parenthesis.

Incorrect Our fear of sharks, heightened by movies like *Jaws*, is vastly out of proportion with the minor threat sharks actually pose. (Dying from a dog attack, in fact, is much more likely than dying from a shark attack).

Correct Our fear of sharks, heightened by movies like *Jaws*, is vastly out of proportion with the minor threat sharks actually pose. (Dying from a dog attack, in fact, is much more likely than dying from a shark attack.)

When the material in parentheses is part of the sentence and the parentheses fall at the end of the sentence, place the period outside the closing parenthesis.

(Continued on next page)

COMMON ERRORS *(Continued)*

Incorrect	Reports of sharks attacking people are rare (much rarer than dog attacks.)
Correct	Reports of sharks attacking people are rare (much rarer than dog attacks).

Place commas, colons, and semicolons after the closing parenthesis.

Remember: When an entire sentence is enclosed in parentheses, place the period inside the closing parenthesis; otherwise, put the punctuation outside the closing parenthesis.

---

35 | Apostrophes

35a Possessives

Nouns and indefinite pronouns (for example, *everyone, anyone*) that indicate possession or ownership are marked by attaching an apostrophe and *-s* or an apostrophe only to the end of the word.

Singular nouns and indefinite pronouns

For singular nouns and indefinite pronouns, add an apostrophe plus *-s: -'s*. Even singular nouns that end in *-s* usually follow this principle.

> Iris's coat
>
> everyone's favorite
>
> a woman's choice

There are a few exceptions to adding -'s for singular nouns:

- **Awkward pronunciations** *Herodotus' travels, Jesus' sermons*
- **Official names of certain places, institutions, companies** *Governors Island, Teachers College of Columbia University, Mothers Café, Saks Fifth Avenue, Walgreens Pharmacy.* Note, however, that many companies do include the apostrophe: *Denny's Restaurant, Macy's, McDonald's, Wendy's Old Fashioned Hamburgers.*

Plural nouns

For plural nouns that do not end in -*s*, add an apostrophe plus -*s*: -'s.

media's responsibility

children's section

For plural nouns that end in -*s*, add only an apostrophe at the end.

attorneys' briefs

the Kennedys' legacy

Compound nouns

For compound nouns, add an apostrophe plus -*s* to the last word of the compound noun: -'s.

mayor of Cleveland's speech

Two or more nouns

For joint possession, add an apostrophe plus -*s* to the final noun: -'s.

mother and dad's yard

When people possess or own things separately, add an apostrophe plus -*s* to each noun: -'s.

Roberto's and Edward's views are totally opposed.

COMMON ERRORS

〉e Edit Help

Possessive forms of personal pronouns never take the apostrophe

Incorrect   *her's, it's, our's, your's, their's*

The bird sang in **it's** cage.

Correct   *hers, its, ours, yours, theirs*

The bird sang in **its** cage.

Remember: *It's = It is*

35b Contractions and Omitted Letters

In speech we often leave out sounds and syllables of familiar words. These omissions are noted with apostrophes.

Contractions

Contractions combine two words into one, using the apostrophe to mark what is left out.

I am ⟶ I'm	we are ⟶ we're
I would ⟶ I'd	they are ⟶ they're
you are ⟶ you're	cannot ⟶ can't
you will ⟶ you'll	do not ⟶ don't
he is ⟶ he's	does not ⟶ doesn't
she is ⟶ she's	will not ⟶ won't
it is ⟶ it's	

Omissions

Using apostrophes to signal omitted letters is a way of approximating speech in writing. They can make your writing look informal and slangy, but overuse can quickly become annoying.

rock and roll ⟶ rock 'n' roll
the 1960s ⟶ the '60s
neighborhood ⟶ 'hood

35c Plurals of Letters, Symbols, and Words Referred to as Words

When to use apostrophes to make plurals

The trend is away from using apostrophes to form plurals of letters, symbols, and words referred to as words. In a few cases adding the apostrophe and *s* is still used, as in this old saying:

Mind your p's and q's.

Words used as words are italicized, and their plural is formed by adding an *s* not in italics, not an apostrophe and *s*.

Take a few of the *ands* out of your writing.

Words in quotation marks, however, typically use apostrophe and *s*.

She had too many "probably's" in her letter for me to be confident that the remodeling will be finished on schedule.

When not to use apostrophes to make plurals

Do not use an apostrophe to make family names plural.

Incorrect	You've heard of keeping up with the Jones's.
Correct	You've heard of keeping up with the Joneses.

COMMON ERRORS

Do not use an apostrophe to make a noun plural

Incorrect	The two government's agreed to meet.
Correct	The two governments agreed to meet.
Incorrect	The video game console's of the past were one-dimensional.
Correct	The video game consoles of the past were one-dimensional.

Remember: Add only *-s* = plural
Add apostrophe plus *-s* = possessive

---

36 | Quotation Marks

 Direct Quotations

Use quotation marks to enclose direct quotations

Enclose direct quotations—someone else's words repeated verbatim—in quotation marks.

> Michael Pollan, the author of *Food Rules* and *The Omnivore's Dilemma*, argues that industrial agriculture uses too much fossil fuel to grow food: "We need to reduce the dependence of modern agriculture on oil, an eminently feasible goal—after all, agriculture is the original solar technology."

Do not use quotation marks with indirect quotations

Do not enclose an indirect quotation—a paraphrase of someone else's words—in quotation marks. However, do remember that you need to cite your source not only when you quote directly but also when you paraphrase or borrow ideas.

> Dan Glickman of the MPAA thinks that because parents don't want their children to start smoking, they should be warned when movies contain scenes where characters smoke (98).

Do not use quotation marks with block quotations

When a quotation is long enough to be set off as a block quotation, do not use quotation marks. MLA style defines long quotations as more than four lines of prose or poetry. APA style defines a long quotation as one of more than forty words.

In the following example in MLA format, notice that the long quotation is indented and quotation marks are omitted. Also notice that the parenthetical citation for a long quotation comes after the period.

> Complaints about maintenance in the dorms have been on the rise ever since the physical plant reorganized its crews into teams in August. One student's experience is typical:
>
> > When our ceiling started dripping, my roommate and I went to our resident director right away to file an emergency maintenance request. Apparently the physical plant felt that "emergency" meant they could get around to it in a week or two. By the fourth day without any word from a maintenance person, the ceiling tiles began to fall and puddles began to pool on our carpet. (Trillo)
>
> The physical plant could have avoided expensive ceiling tile and carpet repairs if it had responded to the student's request promptly.

36b Titles of Short Works

While the titles of longer works such as books, magazines, and newspapers are italicized or underlined, titles of shorter works should be set off with quotation marks. Use quotation marks with the following kinds of titles:

Short stories	"Light Is Like Water," by Gabriel García Márquez
Magazine articles	"Race against Death," by Erin West
Newspaper articles	"Cincinnati Mayor Declares Emergency," by Liz Sidoti
Short poems	"We Real Cool," by Gwendolyn Brooks
Essays	"Self-Reliance," by Ralph Waldo Emerson

The exception. Don't put the title of your own paper in quotation marks. If the title of another short work appears within the title of your paper, retain the quotation marks around the short work.

36c Other Uses of Quotation Marks

Quotation marks around a term can indicate that the writer is using the term in a novel way, often with skepticism, irony, or sarcasm. The quotation marks indicate that the writer is questioning the term's conventional definition.

Italics are usually used to indicate that a word is being used as a word, rather than standing for its conventional meaning. However, quotation marks are correct in these cases as well.

> Beginning writers sometimes confuse "their," "they're," and "there."

36d Other Punctuation with Quotation Marks

The rules for placing punctuation with quotation marks fall into three general categories.

Periods and commas with quotation marks

Place periods and commas inside closing quotation marks.

Incorrect	"The smartest people", Dr. Geisler pointed out, "tell themselves the most convincing rationalizations".
Correct	"The smartest people," Dr. Geisler pointed out, "tell themselves the most convincing rationalizations."

Colons and semicolons with quotation marks

Place colons and semicolons outside closing quotation marks.

Incorrect	"From Stettin in the Baltic to Trieste in the Adriatic, an iron curtain has descended across the Continent;" Churchill's statement rang through Cold War politics for the next fifty years.
Correct	"From Stettin in the Baltic to Trieste in the Adriatic, an iron curtain has descended across the Continent"; Churchill's statement rang through Cold War politics for the next fifty years.

Exclamation points, question marks, and dashes with quotation marks

When an exclamation point, question mark, or dash belongs to the original quotation, place it inside the closing quotation mark. When it applies to the entire sentence, place it outside the closing quotation mark.

In the original quotation

"Are we there yet?" came the whine from the back seat.

Applied to the entire sentence

Did the driver in the front seat respond, "Not even close"?

COMMON ERRORS

e _Edit_ Help

Quotations within quotations

Single quotation marks are used to indicate a quotation within a quotation. In the following example single quotation marks clarify who is speaking. The rules for placing punctuation with single quotation marks are the same as the rules for placing punctuation with double quotation marks.

Incorrect   When he showed the report to Paul Probius, Michener reported that Probius "took vigorous exception to the sentence "He wanted to close down the university," insisting that we add the clarifying phrase "as it then existed"" (Michener 145).

Correct   When he showed the report to Paul Probius, Michener reported that Probius "took vigorous exception to the sentence 'He wanted to close down the university,' insisting that we add the clarifying phrase 'as it then existed'" (Michener 145).

Remember: Single quotation marks are used for quotations within quotations.

36e Misuses of Quotation Marks

It's becoming more and more common to see quotation marks used to emphasize a word or phrase. Resist the temptation in your own writing; the usage is incorrect. In fact, because quotation marks indicate that a writer is using a term with skepticism or irony, adding quotation marks for emphasis will highlight unintended connotations of the term.

Incorrect   "fresh" seafood

By using quotation marks here, the writer seems to call into question whether the seafood is really fresh.

Correct	fresh seafood
Incorrect	Enjoy our "live" music every Saturday night.

Again, the quotation marks unintentionally indicate that the writer is skeptical that the music is live.

Correct	Enjoy our live music every Saturday night.

You have better ways of creating emphasis using your word processing program: **boldfacing**, <u>underlining</u>, *italicizing*, and using color.

37 | Other Punctuation Marks

37a Periods

Periods at the ends of sentences

Place a period at the end of a complete sentence that is not a direct question or an exclamatory statement.

Periods with quotation marks and parentheses

When a quotation falls at the end of a sentence, place the period inside the closing quotation marks.

> Although he devoted decades to a wide range of artistic and political projects, Allen Ginsberg is best known as the author of the poem "Howl."

When a parenthetical phrase falls at the end of a sentence, place the period outside the closing parenthesis. When parentheses enclose a whole sentence, place the period inside the closing parenthesis.

Periods with abbreviations

Many abbreviations require periods; however, there are few set rules. The rules for punctuating two types of abbreviations do remain consistent: Postal abbreviations for states and most abbreviations for organizations do not require periods. When an abbreviation with a period falls at the end of a sentence, do not add a second period to conclude the sentence.

 Incorrect Her flight arrives at 6:22 p.m..

 Correct   Her flight arrives at 6:22 p.m.

Periods as decimal points

Decimal points are periods that separate integers from tenths, hundredths, and so on.

 99.98% pure silver   98.6° Fahrenheit
 on sale for $399.97   2.6-liter engine

Since large numbers with long strings of zeros can be difficult to read accurately, writers sometimes clarify them by using words and decimal points. In this way, 16,600,000 can be written as 16.6 million.

37b Question Marks

Question marks with direct questions

Place a question mark at the end of a direct question. A direct question is one that the questioner puts to someone outright. In contrast, an indirect question merely reports the asking of a question. Question marks give readers a cue to read the end of the sentence with rising inflection. Read the following sentences aloud. Hear how your inflection rises in the second sentence to convey the direct question.

 Indirect question
 Desirée asked whether Dan rides his motorcycle without a helmet.

 Direct question
 Desirée asked, "Does Dan ride his motorcycle without a helmet?"

Question marks with quotations

When a quotation falls at the end of a direct question, place the question mark outside the closing quotation mark.

> Did Abraham Lincoln really call Harriet Beecher Stowe "the little lady who started this big war"?

Place the question mark inside the closing quotation when only the quoted material is a direct question.

> Slowly scientists are beginning to answer the question "Is cancer a genetic disease?"

When quoting a direct question in the middle of a sentence, place a question mark inside the closing quotation mark and place a period at the end of the sentence.

> Market researchers estimate that asking Burger World's customers "Do you want fries with that?" was responsible for a 15% boost in french fries sales.

37c Exclamation Points

Exclamation points to convey strong emotion

Exclamation points conclude sentences and, like question marks, tell the reader how a sentence should sound. They indicate strong emotion. Use exclamation points sparingly in formal writing; they are seldom appropriate in academic and professional prose.

Exclamation points with emphatic interjections

Exclamation points can convey a sense of urgency with brief interjections. Interjections can be incorporated into sentences or stand on their own.

> Run! They're about to close the doors to the jetway.

Exclamation points with quotation marks

In quotations, exclamation points follow the same rules as question marks. If a quotation falls at the end of an exclamatory statement, place the exclamation point outside the closing quotation mark.

> The singer forgot the words to "America the Beautiful"!

When quoting an exclamatory statement at the end of a sentence that is not itself exclamatory, place the exclamation point inside the closing quotation mark.

> Jerry thought his car would be washed away in the flood, but Anna jumped into action, declaring, "Not if I can help it!"

37d Brackets

While brackets (sometimes called *square brackets*) look quite similar to parentheses, the two perform different functions. Brackets have a narrow set of uses.

Brackets to provide clarification within quotation marks

Use brackets if you are interjecting a comment of your own or clarifying information within a direct quotation. In the following example the writer quotes a sentence with the pronoun *they*, which refers to a noun in a previous, unquoted sentence. The material in brackets clarifies to whom the pronoun refers.

> The Harris study found that "In the last three years, they [Gonzales Junior High students] averaged 15% higher on their mathematics assessment tests than their peers in Northridge County."

Brackets within parentheses

Since parentheses within parentheses might confuse readers, use brackets to enclose parenthetical information within a parenthetical phrase.

Representative Patel's most controversial legislation (including a version of the hate crimes bill [HR 99-108] the house rejected two years ago) has a slim chance of being enacted this session.

37e Ellipses

Ellipses let a reader know that a portion of a passage is missing. You can use ellipses to keep quotations concise and direct readers' attention to what is important to the point you are making. An ellipsis is a string of three periods with spaces separating the periods.

Ellipses to indicate an omission from a quotation

When you quote only a phrase or a short clause from a sentence, you usually do not need to use an ellipsis.

> Mao Zedong first used "let a hundred flowers blossom" in a Beijing speech in 1957.

Except at the beginning of a quotation, indicate omitted words with an ellipsis.

The original source

> "The female praying mantis, so named for the way it holds its front legs together as if in prayer, tears off her male partner's head during mating. Remarkably, the headless male will continue the act of mating. This brutal dance is a stark example of the innate evolutionary drive to pass genes onto offspring; the male praying mantis seems to live and die only for this moment."

An ellipsis indicates omitted words

> "The female praying mantis . . . tears off her male partner's head during mating."

When the ellipsis is at the end of a sentence, place the period or question mark after the ellipsis and follow with the closing quotation mark.

Words omitted at the end of a sentence

"This brutal dance is a stark example of the innate evolutionary drive to pass genes onto offspring. . . . ."

37f Slashes

Slashes to indicate alternative words

Slashes are used to indicate the concept of *or*. When using slashes for this purpose, do not put a space between the slash and words.

| Incorrect | Maya was such an energetic baby that her exhausted parents wished she had come with an on / off switch. |
| Correct | Maya was such an energetic baby that her exhausted parents wished she had come with an on/off switch. |

Slashes with fractions

Place a slash between the numerator and the denominator in a fraction. Do not put any spaces around the slash.

| Incorrect | 3 / 4 |
| Correct | 3/4 |

38 | Capitalization, Italics, Abbreviations, Numbers

38a Capital Letters

Capitalize the initial letters of proper nouns (nouns that name particular people, places, and things). Capitalize the initial letters of proper adjectives (adjectives based on the names of people, places, and things).

African American bookstore   Avogadro's number   Irish music

Do not capitalize the names of seasons, academic disciplines (unless they are languages), or job titles used without a proper noun.

38b Italics

Italicize the titles of entire works (books, magazines, newspapers, films), but place the titles of parts of those works within quotation marks. Also italicize or underline the names of ships and aircraft.

> I am fond of reading *USA Today* in the morning.

The exceptions.   Do not italicize or underline the names of sacred texts.

Italicize unfamiliar foreign words

Italicize foreign words that are not part of common English usage. Do not italicize words that have become a common word or phrase in the English vocabulary. How do you decide which words are common? If a word appears in a standard English dictionary, it can be considered as adopted into English.

Use italics to clarify your use of a word, letter, or number

In everyday speech, we often use cues—a pause, a louder or different tone—to communicate how we are using a word. In writing, italics help clarify when you use words in a referential manner, or letters and numbers as letters and numbers.

38c Abbreviations

Abbreviations are shortened forms of words. Because abbreviations vary widely, you will need to look in the dictionary to determine how to abbreviate words on a case-by-case basis. Nonetheless, there are a few patterns that abbreviations follow.

Abbreviate titles before and degrees after full names

> Ms. Ella Fitzgerald
> Prof. Vijay Aggarwal

Write out the professional title when it is used with only a last name.

> Professor Chin
>
> Reverend Ames

Conventions for using abbreviations with years and times

BCE (before the common era) and CE (common era) are now preferred for indicating years, replacing BC (before Christ) and AD (*anno Domini* ["the year of our Lord"]). Note that all are now used without periods.

> 479 BCE (or BC)
>
> 1610 CE (or AD, but AD would be placed before the number)

The preferred written conventions for times are a.m. (*ante meridiem*) and p.m. (*post meridiem*).

> 9:03 a.m.
>
> 3:30 p.m.

Latin abbreviations

Some writers sprinkle Latin abbreviations throughout their writing, apparently thinking that they are a mark of learning. Frequently these abbreviations are used inappropriately. If you use Latin abbreviations, make sure you know what they stand for.

> e.g. (*exempli gratia*) for example
>
> et al. (*et alia*) and others
>
> etc. (*et cetera*) and so forth
>
> i.e. (*id est*) that is
>
> N.B. (*nota bene*) note well

In particular, avoid using *etc.* to fill out a list of items. Use of *etc.* announces that you haven't taken the time to finish a thought.

> Lazy   The contents of his grocery cart described his eating habits: a big bag of chips, hot sauce, frozen pizza, etc.

| Better | The contents of his grocery cart described his eating habits: a big bag of chips, a large jar of hot sauce, two frozen pizzas, a twelve-pack of cola, three Mars bars, and a package of Twinkies. |

Conventions for using abbreviations in formal writing

Most abbreviations are inappropriate in formal writing except when the reader would be more familiar with the abbreviation than with the words it represents. When your reader is unlikely to be familiar with an abbreviation, spell out the term, followed by the abbreviation in parentheses, the first time you use it in a paper. The reader will then understand what the abbreviation refers to, and you may use the abbreviation in subsequent sentences.

> The **Office of Civil Rights (OCR)** is the agency that enforces Title IX regulations. In 1979 **OCR** set out three options for schools to comply with Title IX.

38d Acronyms

Acronyms are abbreviations formed from the first letter of each word. Acronyms are pronounced as words.

> **AIDS** for Acquired Immunodeficiency Syndrome
>
> **NASA** for National Air and Space Administration

Initial-letter abbreviations are commonly pronounced as letters.

> **ACLU** for American Civil Liberties Union
>
> **HIV** for human immunodeficiency virus
>
> **rpm** for revolutions per minute

Familiar acronyms and initial-letter abbreviations such as CBS, CIA, FBI, IQ, and UN are rarely spelled out. Unfamiliar acronyms and abbreviations should always be spelled out. Acronyms and abbreviations frequent in particular fields should be spelled out on first use. For example, MMPI (Minnesota Multiphasic Personality Inventory) is a familiar abbreviation in psychology but will be unfamiliar to those outside that discipline.

38e   Numbers

In formal writing spell out any number that can be expressed in one or two words, as well as any number, regardless of length, at the beginning of a sentence. Also, hyphenate two-word numbers from twenty-one to ninety-nine. When a sentence begins with a number that requires more than two words, revise it if possible.

The exceptions.   Most scientific reports and some business writing use numerals consistently. Most styles do not write out in words a year, a date, an address, a page number, the time of day, decimals, sums of money, phone numbers, rates of speed, or the scene and act of a play. Use numerals instead.

> In **2001** only **33%** of respondents said they were satisfied with the City Council's proposals to help the homeless.

> The **17** trials were conducted at temperatures **12-14 °C** with results ranging from **2.43** to **2.89** mg/dl.

When one number modifies another number, write one out and express the other in numeral form.

> In the last year all **four 8th** Street restaurants began to donate their leftovers to the soup kitchen.

> Only after Meryl had run in **12 fifty**-mile ultramarathons did she finally win first place in her age group.

Glossary of Grammatical Terms and Usage

The glossary gives the definitions of grammatical terms and items of usage. The grammatical terms are shown in blue. Some of the explanations of usage that follow are not rules, but guidelines to keep in mind for academic and professional writing. In these formal contexts, the safest course is to avoid words that are described as *nonstandard, informal,* or *colloquial.*

a/an   Use *a* before words that begin with a consonant sound *(a train, a house).* Use *an* before words that begin with a vowel sound *(an airplane, an hour).*

a lot/alot   *A lot* is generally regarded as informal; *alot* is nonstandard.

accept/except   *Accept* is a verb meaning "receive" or "approve." *Except* is sometimes a verb meaning "leave out," but much more often it's used as a conjunction or preposition meaning "other than."

active   A clause with a transitive verb in which the subject is the doer of the action. See also passive.

adjective   A modifier that qualifies or describes the qualities of a noun or pronoun.

adjective clause   A subordinate clause that modifies a noun or pronoun and is usually introduced by a relative pronoun. Sometimes called a *relative clause.*

adverb   A word that modifies a verb, another modifier, or a clause.

adverb clause   A subordinate clause that functions as an adverb by modifying a verb, another modifier, or a clause.

advice/advise   The noun *advice* means a "suggestion"; the verb *advise* means to "recommend" or "give advice."

affect/effect   Usually, *affect* is a verb (to "influence") and *effect* is a noun (a "result"). Less commonly, *affect* is used as a noun and *effect* as a verb.

agreement   The number and person of a subject and verb must match—singular subjects with singular verbs, plural subjects with plural verbs. Likewise, the number and gender of a pronoun and its antecedent must match.

all ready/already   The adjective phrase *all ready* means "completely prepared"; the adverb *already* means "previously."

all right/alright   *All right,* meaning "acceptable," is the correct spelling. *Alright* is nonstandard.

allude/elude   *Allude* means "refer to indirectly." *Elude* means "evade."

allusion/illusion   An *allusion* is an indirect reference; an *illusion* is a false impression.

among/between   *Between* refers to precisely two people or things; *among refers* to three or more.

amount/number   Use *amount* with things that cannot be counted; use *number* with things that can be counted.

an   See **a/an.**

antecedent   The noun (or pronoun) that a pronoun refers to.

anybody/any body; anyone/any one   *Anybody* and *anyone* are indefinite pronouns and have the same meaning. In *any body, body* is a noun modified by *any,* and in *any one, one* is a pronoun or adjective modified by *any.*

anymore/any more   *Anymore* means "now," while *any more* means "no more." Both are used in negative constructions.

anyway/anyways   *Anyway* is correct. *Anyways* is nonstandard.

articles   The words *a, an,* and *the.*

as/as if/as though/like   Use *as* instead of *like* before dependent clauses (which include a subject and verb). Use *like* before a noun or a pronoun.

assure/ensure/insure   *Assure* means "promise," *ensure* means "make certain," and *insure* means to "make certain in either a legal or financial sense."

auxiliary verb   Forms of *be, do,* and *have* combine with verbs to indicate tense and mood. The modal verbs *can, could, may, might, must, shall, should, will,* and *would* are a subset of auxiliaries.

bad/badly   Use *bad* only as an adjective. *Badly* is the adverb.

being as/being that   Both constructions are colloquial and awkward substitutes for *because.* Don't use them in formal writing.

beside/besides   *Beside* means "next to." *Besides* means "in addition to" or "except."

between   See **among/between.**

bring/take   *Bring* describes movement from a more distant location to a nearer one. *Take* describes movement away.

can/may   In formal writing, *can* indicates ability or capacity, while *may* indicates permission.

case   The form of a noun or pronoun that indicates its function. Nouns change case only to show possession: the **dog,** the **dog's** bowl. See pronoun case.

censor/censure   To *censor* is to edit or ban on moral or political grounds. To *censure* is to reprimand publicly.

cite/sight/site   To *cite* is to "mention specifically"; *sight* as a verb means to "observe" and as a noun refers to "vision"; *site* is most commonly used as a noun that means "location," but it is also used as a verb to mean "situate."

clause   A group of words with a subject and a predicate. A main or independent clause can stand as a sentence. A subordinate or dependent clause must be attached to a main clause to form a sentence.

collective noun   A noun that refers to a group or a plurality, such as *team, army,* or *committee.*

comma splice   Two independent clauses joined incorrectly by a comma.

common noun   A noun that names a general group, person, place, or thing. Common nouns are not capitalized unless they begin a sentence.

complement   A word or group of words that completes the predicate. See also **linking verb.**

complement/compliment   To *complement* something is to complete it or make it perfect; to *compliment* is to flatter.

complex sentence   A sentence that contains at least one subordinate clause attached to a main clause.

compound sentence   A sentence that contains at least two main clauses.

compound-complex sentence   A sentence that contains at least two main clauses and one subordinate clause.

conjunction   See **coordinating conjunction** and **subordinating conjunction.**

conjunctive adverb   An adverb that often modifies entire clauses and sentences, such as *also, consequently, however, indeed, instead, moreover, nevertheless, otherwise, similarly,* and *therefore.*

continual/continuous   *Continual* refers to a repeated activity; *continuous* refers to an ongoing, unceasing activity.

coordinate   A relationship of equal importance, in terms of either grammar or meaning.

coordinating conjunction   A word that links two equivalent grammatical elements, such as *and, but, or, yet, nor, for,* and *so.*

could of   Nonstandard. See **have/of.**

count noun   A noun that names things that can be counted, such as *block, cat,* and *toy.*

cumulative adjective   Two or more adjectives not separated by a comma because they do not make sense if the order is changed. For example, an *enormous dump truck* cannot be changed to a *dump enormous truck.*

dangling modifier   A modifier that is not clearly attached to what it modifies.

data   The plural form of *datum;* it takes plural verb forms.

declarative   A sentence that makes a statement.

dependent clause   See **subordinate clause.**

determiners   Words that initiate noun phrases, including possessive nouns *(Pedro's);* possessive pronouns *(my, your);* demonstrative pronouns *(this, that);* and indefinite pronouns *(all, both, many).*

differ from/differ with   To *differ from* means to "be unlike"; to *differ with* means to "disagree."

different from/different than   Use *different from* where possible.

Dark French roast is different from ordinary coffee.

direct object   A noun, pronoun, or noun clause that names who or what receives the action of a transitive verb.

discreet/discrete   Both are adjectives. *Discreet* means "prudent" or "tactful"; *discrete* means "separate."

disinterested/uninterested   *Disinterested* is often misused to mean *uninterested.* Disinterested means "impartial." A judge can be interested in a case but disinterested in the outcome.

double negative   The incorrect use of two negatives to signal the same negative meaning.

due to the fact that   Avoid this wordy substitute for *because.*

each other/one another   Use *each other* for two; use *one another* for more than two.

effect   See **affect/effect.**

elicit/illicit   The verb *elicit* means to "draw out." The adjective *illicit* means "unlawful."

emigrate from/immigrate to   *Emigrate* means to "leave one's country"; *immigrate* means to "settle in another country."

ensure   See **assure/ensure/insure.**

enthused   Nonstandard in academic and professional writing. Use *enthusiastic* instead.

etc.   Avoid this abbreviation for the Latin *et cetera* in formal writing. Either list all the items or use an English phrase such as *and so forth.*

every body/everybody; every one/everyone   *Everybody* and *everyone* are indefinite pronouns referring to all people under discussion. *Every one* and *every body* are adjective-noun combinations referring to all members of a group.

except   See **accept/except.**

except for the fact that   Avoid this wordy substitute for *except that.*

expletive   The dummy subjects *it* and *there* used to fill a grammatical slot in a sentence. *It is raining outside. There should be a law against it.*

explicit/implicit   Both are adjectives; *explicit* means "stated outright," while *implicit* means just the opposite, "unstated."

farther/further   *Farther* refers to physical distance; *further* refers to time or other abstract concepts.

fewer/less Use *fewer* with what can be counted and *less* with what cannot be counted.

flunk In formal writing, avoid this colloquial substitute for *fail*.

fragment A group of words beginning with a capital letter and ending with a period that looks like a sentence but lacks a subject or a predicate or both.

further See **farther/further.**

gerund An *-ing* form of a verb used as a noun, such as *running, skiing,* or *laughing.*

good/well *Good* is an adjective and is not interchangeable with the adverb *well.* The one exception is health. Both she feels *good* and she feels *well* are correct.

hanged/hung Use *hanged* to refer only to executions; *hung* is used for all other instances.

have/of *Have,* not *of,* follows *should, could, would, may, must,* and *might.*

he/she; s/he Try to avoid language that appears to exclude either gender (unless this is intended, of course) and awkward compromises such as *he/she* or *s/he.* The best solution is to make pronouns plural (the gender-neutral *they*) wherever possible.

helping verb See **auxiliary verb.**

hopefully This adverb is commonly used as a sentence modifier, but many readers object to it.

illusion See **allusion/illusion.**

immigrate See **emigrate from/immigrate to.**

imperative A sentence that expresses a command. Usually the subject is implied rather than stated.

implicit See **explicit/implicit.**

imply/infer *Imply* means to "suggest"; *infer* means to "draw a conclusion."

in regards to Avoid this wordy substitute for *regarding.*

incredible/incredulous *Incredible* means "unbelievable"; *incredulous* means "not believing."

independent clause See **main clause.**

indirect object A noun, pronoun, or noun clause that names who or what is affected by the action of a transitive verb.

infinitive The word *to* plus the base verb form: *to believe, to feel, to act.* See also **split infinitive.**

infinitive phrase A phrase that uses the infinitive form of a verb.

interjection   A word expressing feeling that is grammatically unconnected to a sentence, such as *cool, wow, ouch,* or *yikes.*

interrogative   A sentence that asks a question.

intransitive verb   A verb that does not take an object, such as *sleep, appear,* or *laugh.*

irregardless   Nonstandard for *regardless.*

irregular verb   A verb that does not use either *-d* or *-ed* to form the past tense and past participle.

it is my opinion that   Avoid this wordy substitute for *I believe that.*

its/it's   *Its* is the possessive of *it* and does not take an apostrophe; *it's* is the contraction for *it is.*

-ize/-wise   The suffix *-ize* changes a noun or adjective into a verb *(harmony, harmonize).* The suffix *-wise* changes a noun or adjective into an adverb *(clock, clockwise).* Some writers are tempted to use these suffixes to convert almost any word into an adverb or verb form. Unless the word appears in a dictionary, don't use it.

kind of/sort of/type of   Avoid using these colloquial expressions if you mean *somewhat* or *rather. It's kind of hot* is nonstandard. Each is permissible, however, when it refers to a classification of an object. Be sure that it agrees in number with the object it is modifying.

lay/lie   *Lay* means "place" or "put" and generally takes a direct object (see Section 24c). Its main forms are *lay, laid, laid. Lie* means "recline" or "be positioned" and does not take an object. Its main forms are *lie, lay, lain.*

less   See **fewer.**

lie   See **lay/lie.**

linking verb   A verb that connects the subject to the complement, such as *appear, be, feel, look, seem,* or *taste.*

lots/lots of   Nonstandard in formal writing; use *many* or *much* instead.

main clause   A group of words with a subject and a predicate that can stand alone as a sentence. Also called an *independent clause.*

mankind   This term offends some readers and is outdated. Use *humans, humanity,* or *people* instead.

may/can   See **can/may.**

may be/maybe   *May be* is a verb phrase; *maybe* is an adverb.

media   This is the plural form of the noun *medium* and requires a plural verb.

might of   See **have/of.**

modal   A kind of auxiliary verb that indicates ability, permission, intention, obligation, or probability, such as *can, could, may, might, must, shall, should, will,* or *would.*

modifier A general term for adjectives, adverbs, phrases, and clauses that describe other words.

must of See **have/of.**

noncount noun A noun that names things that cannot be counted, such as *air, energy,* or *water.*

nonrestrictive modifier A modifier that is not essential to the meaning of the word, phrase, or clause it modifies and should be set off by commas or other punctuation.

noun The name of a person, place, thing, concept, or action. See also **common noun** and **proper noun.**

noun clause A subordinate clause that functions as a noun.

number See **amount/number.**

object Receiver of the action within the clause or phrase.

OK, O.K., okay Informal; avoid using in academic and professional writing. Each spelling is accepted in informal usage.

owing to the fact that Avoid this wordy, colloquial substitute for *because.*

parallelism The principle of putting similar elements or ideas in similar grammatical form.

participle A form of a verb that uses *-ing* in the present (*laughing, playing*) and usually *-ed* or *-en* in the past (*laughed, played*). See Section 24a. Participles are either part of the verb phrase (*She had played the game before*) or used as adjectives (*the laughing girl*).

participial phrase A phrase formed either by a present participle (for example, *racing*) or by a past participle (for example, *taken*).

parts of speech The eight classes of words according to their grammatical function: nouns, pronouns, verbs, adjectives, adverbs, prepositions, conjunctions, and interjections.

passive A clause with a transitive verb in which the subject is being acted upon. See also **active.**

people/persons *People* refers to a general group; *persons* refers to a collection of individuals. Use *people* over *persons* except when you're emphasizing the idea of separate persons within the group.

per Try not to use the English equivalent of this Latin word except in technical writing or familiar usages like *miles per gallon.*

phenomena This is the plural form of *phenomenon* ("observable fact" or "unusual event") and takes plural verbs.

phrase A group of words that does not contain both a subject and predicate.

plenty In academic and professional writing, avoid this colloquial substitute for *very.*

plus Do not use *plus* to join clauses or sentences. Use *and, also, moreover, furthermore,* or another conjunctive adverb instead.

precede/proceed   Both are verbs but they have different meanings: *precede* means "come before," and *proceed* means "go ahead" or "continue."

predicate   The part of the clause that expresses the action or tells something about the subject. The predicate includes the verb and all its complements, objects, and modifiers.

prejudice/prejudiced   *Prejudice* is a noun; *prejudiced* is an adjective.

preposition   A class of words that indicate relationships and qualities.

prepositional phrase   A phrase formed by a preposition and its object, including the modifiers of its object.

principal/principle   *Principal* means first in importance (*school principal, principal reason*). *Principle* applies to beliefs or understandings (*It goes against my principles*).

pronoun   A word that stands for other nouns or pronouns. Pronouns have several subclasses, including personal pronouns, possessive pronouns, demonstrative pronouns, indefinite pronouns, relative pronouns, interrogative pronouns, reflexive pronouns, and reciprocal pronouns.

pronoun case   Pronouns that function as the subjects of sentences are in the **subjective** case (*I, you, he, she, it, we, they*). Pronouns that function as direct or indirect objects are in the **objective** case (*me, you, him, her, it, us, them*). Pronouns that indicate ownership are in the **possessive** case (*my, your, his, her, its, our, their*).

proper noun   A noun that names a particular person, place, thing, or group. Proper nouns are capitalized.

question as to whether/question of whether Avoid these wordy substitutes for *whether*.

raise/rise   The verb raise means "lift up" and takes a direct object. Its main forms are *raise, raised, raised*. The verb *rise* means "get up" and does not take a direct object. Its main forms are *rise, rose, risen*.

real/really   Avoid using *real* as if it were an adverb. *Really* is an adverb; *real* is an adjective.

reason is because   Omit either *reason is* or *because* when explaining causality.

reason why   Avoid using this redundant combination.

relative pronoun   A pronoun that initiates clauses, such as *that, which, what, who, whom,* or *whose*.

restrictive modifier   A modifier that is essential to the meaning of the word, phrase, or clause it modifies. Restrictive modifiers are usually not set off by punctuation.

rise/raise   See **raise/rise.**

run-on sentence   Two main clauses fused together without punctuation or a conjunction, appearing as one sentence.

sentence   A grammatically independent group of words that contains at least one main clause.

sentence fragment   See fragment.

set/sit   Set means "put" and takes a direct object; its main forms are *set, set, set.* *Sit* means "be seated" and does not take a direct object; its main forms are *sit, sat, sat. Sit* should not be used as a synonym for *set.*

shall/will   Shall is used most often in first person questions, while *will is* a future tense helping verb for all persons. British English consistently uses *shall with* first person: *I shall, we shall.*

should of   See **have/of.**

sit/set   See **set/sit.**

some time/sometime/sometimes   *Some time* means "a span of time," *sometime* means "at some unspecified time," and *sometimes* means "occasionally."

somebody/some body; someone/some one   *Somebody* and *someone* are indefinite pronouns and have the same meaning. In *some body, body* is a noun modified by *some,* and in *some one, one* is a pronoun or adjective modified by *some.*

sort of   See **kind of/sort of/type of.**

split infinitive   An infinitive with a word or words between *to* and the base verb form, such as *to boldly go, to better appreciate.*

stationary/stationery   *Stationary* means "motionless"; *stationery* means "writing paper."

subject   A noun, pronoun, or noun phrase that identifies what the clause is about and connects with the predicate.

subject-verb agreement   See agreement.

subordinate   A relationship of unequal importance, in terms of either grammar or meaning.

subordinate clause   A clause that cannot stand alone but must be attached to a main clause. Also called a *dependent clause.*

subordinating conjunction   A word that introduces a subordinate clause. Common subordinating conjunctions are *after, although, as, because, before, if, since, that, unless, until, when, where,* and *while.*

sure   A colloquial term used as an adverb to mean "certainly." Avoid using it thisway in formal writing.

sure and/sure to; try and/try to   *Sure to* and *try to* are correct; do not use *and* after *sure* or *try.*

take   See **bring/take.**

that/which   *That* introduces a restrictive or essential clause. Restrictive clauses describe an object that must be that particular object and no other. Though some writers occasionally use *which* with restrictive clauses, it is most often used to introduce nonrestrictive clauses. These are clauses that contain additional nonessential information about the object.

transition   A word or phrase that notes movement from one unit of writing to another.

transitive verb   A verb that takes a direct object.

unique   *Unique* means one of a kind. Things cannot be "very unique" or "more unique." They are either unique or not.

verb   A word that expresses action or characterizes the subject in some way. Verbs can show tense and mood.

verbal   A form of a verb used as an adjective, adverb, or noun. See also **gerund, infinitive, participle.**

well/good   See **good/well.**

which/that   See **that/which.**

who/whom   *Who* and *whom* follow the same rules as other pronouns: *Who* is the subject pronoun; *whom* is the object pronoun.

will/shall   See **shall/will.**

-wise/-ize   See **-ize/-wise.**

would of   See **have/of.**

you   Avoid indefinite uses of *you*. It should only be used to mean "you, the reader."

your/you're   The two are not interchangeable. *Your* is the possessive form of "you"; *you're* is the contraction of "you are."

Index

Credits

Text Credits

Excerpt from *Creating Black Americans: African American History and Its Meanings, 1619 to the Present* by Nell Irvin Painter. Copyright © 2006 by Nell Irvin Painter. Reprinted with permission of Oxford University Press and Charlotte Sheedy Literary Agents, Inc. on behalf of the author.

LexisNexis archive search for "college organic farm". From the LexisNexis Academic website. Copyright 2010 LexisNexis, a division of Reed Elsevier Inc. All Rights Reserved. LexisNexis and the Knowledge Burst logo are registered trademarks of Reed Elsevier Properties Inc. and are used with permission of LexisNexis.

LexisNexis article search. From the LexisNexis Academic website. Copyright 2010 LexisNexis, a division of Reed Elsevier Inc. All Rights Reserved. LexisNexis and the Knowledge Burst logo are registered trademarks of Reed Elsevier Properties Inc. and are used with permission of LexisNexis.

Sample article page from "A Cross-Regional Assessment of the Factors Affecting Ecoliteracy: Implications for Policy and Practice" by Sarah Pilgrim, Jules Pretty, and David Smith, from *Ecological Applications,* 17(6) 2007, p. 1742. Copyright © 2007 by Ecological Society of America. Reproduced with permission of Ecological Society of America via Copyright Clearance Center.

Photo Credits

p. 6 Library of Congress

p. 146 Screen capture of Colby Magazine. Courtesy of Colby College.

p. 184 Screen capture of Environmental Health Perspectives.

Common Error Image: iStockphoto

Unless otherwise noted, all photos © Lester Faigley Photos.

Writing Summary

WHAT IS A SUMMARY?

The best way to demonstrate that you understand the information and the ideas in any piece of writing is to compose an accurate and clearly written summary of that piece. By a *summary* we mean a *brief restatement, in your own words, of the content of a passage* (a group of paragraphs, a chapter, an article, a book). This restatement should focus on the *central idea* of the passage. The briefest of summaries (one or two sentences) will do no more than this. A longer, more complete summary will indicate, in condensed form, the main points in the passage that support or explain the central idea. It will reflect the order in which these points are presented and the emphasis given to them. It may even include some important examples from the passage. But it will not include minor details. It will not repeat points simply for the purpose of emphasis. And it will not contain any of your own opinions or conclusions. A good summary, therefore, has three central qualities: *brevity, completeness,* and *objectivity*.

CAN A SUMMARY BE OBJECTIVE?

Objectivity could be difficult to achieve in a summary. By definition, writing a summary requires you to select some aspects of the original and leave out others. Because deciding what to select and what to leave out calls for your personal judgment, your summary really is a work of interpretation. And, certainly, your interpretation of a passage may differ from another person's.

One factor affecting the nature and quality of your interpretation is your *prior knowledge* of the subject. For example, if you're attempting to summarize an anthropological article and you're a novice in that field, then your summary of the article will likely differ from that of your professor, who has spent twenty years studying this particular area and whose judgment about what is more or less significant is undoubtedly more reliable than your own. By the same token, your personal or professional *frame of reference* may also affect your interpretation. A union representative and a management representative attempting to summarize the latest management offer would probably come up with two very different accounts. Still, we believe that in most cases it's possible to produce a reasonably objective summary of a passage if you make a conscious, good-faith effort to be unbiased and to prevent your own feelings on the subject from coloring your account of the author's text.

USING THE SUMMARY

In some quarters, the summary has a bad reputation—and with reason. Summaries are often provided by writers as substitutes for analyses. As students, many of us have summarized books that we were supposed to *review critically*. All the same, the summary does have a place in respectable college work. First, writing a summary is an excellent way to understand what

WHERE DO WE FIND WRITTEN SUMMARIES?

Here are just a few of the types of writing that involve summary:

Academic Writing

- **Critique papers** summarize material in order to critique it.
- **Synthesis papers** summarize to show relationships between sources.
- **Analysis papers** summarize theoretical perspectives before applying them.
- **Research papers** require summary for note-taking and reporting research.
- **Literature reviews** are overviews of work presented in brief summaries.
- **Argument papers** summarize evidence and opposing arguments.
- **Essay exams** demonstrate understanding of course materials through summary.

Workplace Writing

- **Policy briefs** condense complex public policy.
- **Business plans** summarize costs, relevant environmental impacts, and other important matters.
- **Memos, letters, and reports** summarize procedures, meetings, product assessments, expenditures, and more.
- **Medical charts** record patient data in summarized form.
- **Legal briefs** summarize relevant facts and arguments of cases.

you read. This in itself is an important goal of academic study. If you don't understand your source material, chances are you won't be able to refer to it usefully in a paper. Summaries help you understand what you read because they force you to put the text into your own words. Practice with writing summaries also develops your general writing habits, because a good summary, like any other piece of good writing, is clear, coherent, and accurate.

Second, summaries are useful to your readers. Let's say you're writing a paper about the McCarthy era in the United States, and in part of that paper you want to discuss Arthur Miller's *The Crucible* as a dramatic treatment of the subject. A summary of the plot would be helpful to a reader who hasn't seen or read—or who doesn't remember—the play. Or perhaps you're writing a paper about the politics of recent American military interventions. If your reader isn't likely to be familiar with American actions in Kosovo and Afghanistan, it would be a good idea to summarize these events at some early point in the paper. In many cases (an exam, for instance), you can use a summary to demonstrate your knowledge of what your professor already knows; when writing a paper, you can use a summary to inform your professor about some relatively unfamiliar source.

Third, summaries are required frequently in college-level writing. For example, on a psychology midterm, you may be asked to explain Carl Jung's theory of the collective unconscious and to show how it differs from Sigmund Freud's theory of the personal unconscious. You may have read about Jung's theory in your textbook or in a supplementary article, or your instructor may have outlined it in her lecture. You can best demonstrate your understanding of it by summarizing it. Then you'll proceed to contrast it with Freud's theory—which, of course, you must also summarize.

THE READING PROCESS

It may seem to you that being able to tell (or retell) in summary form exactly what a passage says is a skill that ought to be taken for granted in anyone who can read at high school level. Unfortunately, this is not so: For all kinds of reasons, people don't always read carefully. In fact, it's probably safe to say that usually they don't. Either they read so inattentively that they skip over words, phrases, or even whole sentences, or, if they do see the words in front of them, they see them without registering their significance.

When a reader fails to pick up the meaning and implications of a sentence or two, usually there's no real harm done. (An exception: You could lose credit on an exam or paper because you failed to read or to realize the significance of a crucial direction by your instructor.) But over longer stretches—the paragraph, the section, the article, or the chapter—inattentive or haphazard reading interferes with your goals as a reader: to perceive the shape of the argument, to grasp the central idea, to determine the main points that compose it, to relate the parts of the whole, and to note key examples. This kind of reading takes a lot more energy and determination than casual reading.

CRITICAL READING FOR SUMMARY

- *Examine the context.* Note the credentials, occupation, and publications of the author. Identify the source in which the piece originally appeared. This information helps illuminate the author's perspective on the topic he or she is addressing.
- *Note the title and subtitle.* Some titles are straightforward; the meanings of others become clearer as you read. In either case, titles typically identify the topic being addressed and often reveal the author's attitude toward that topic.
- *Identify the main point.* Whether a piece of writing contains a thesis statement in the first few paragraphs or builds its main point without stating it up front, look at the entire piece to arrive at an understanding of the overall point being made.
- *Identify the subordinate points.* Notice the smaller subpoints that make up the main point, and make sure you understand how they relate to the main point. If a particular subpoint doesn't clearly relate to the main point you've identified, you may need to modify your understanding of the main point.
- *Break the reading into sections.* Notice which paragraphs make up a piece's introduction, body, and conclusion. Break up the body paragraphs into sections that address the writer's various subpoints.
- *Distinguish among points, examples, and counterarguments.* Critical reading requires careful attention to what a writer is *doing* as well as what he or she is *saying*. When a writer quotes someone else, or relays an example of something, ask yourself why this is being done. What point is the example supporting? Is another source being quoted as support for a point or as a counterargument that the writer sets out to address?
- *Watch for transitions within and between paragraphs.* To follow the logic of a piece of writing, as well as to distinguish among points, examples, and counterarguments, pay attention to the transitional words and phrases writers use. Transitions function like road signs, preparing the reader for what's next.
- *Read actively and recursively.* Don't treat reading as a passive, linear progression through a text. Instead, read as though you are engaged in a dialogue with the writer: Ask questions of the text as you read, make notes in the margin, underline key ideas in pencil, and put question or exclamation marks next to passages that confuse or excite you. Go back to earlier points once you finish a reading, stop during your reading to recap what's come so far, and move back and forth through a text.

But in the long run it's an energy-saving method because it enables you to retain the content of the material and to draw upon that content in your own responses. In other words, it allows you to develop an accurate and coherent written discussion that goes beyond summary.

HOW TO WRITE SUMMARIES

Every article you read will present its own challenge as you work to summarize it. As you'll discover, saying in a few words what has taken someone else a great many can be difficult. But like any other skill, the ability to summarize improves with practice. Here are a few pointers to get you started. They represent possible stages, or steps, in the process of writing a summary. These pointers are not meant to be ironclad rules; rather, they are designed to encourage habits of thinking that will allow you to vary your technique as the situation demands.

GUIDELINES FOR WRITING SUMMARIES

- *Read the passage carefully.* Determine its structure. Identify the author's purpose in writing. (This will help you distinguish between more important and less important information.) Make a note in the margin when you get confused or when you think something is important; highlight or underline points sparingly, if at all.
- *Reread.* This time divide the passage into sections or stages of thought. The author's use of paragraphing will often be a useful guide. *Label,* on the passage itself, each section or stage of thought. *Underline* key ideas and terms. Write notes in the margin.
- *Write one-sentence summaries,* on a separate sheet of paper, of each stage of thought.
- *Write a thesis—a one- or two-sentence summary of the entire passage.* The thesis should express the central idea of the passage, as you have determined it from the preceding steps. You may find it useful to follow the approach of most newspaper stories—naming the *what, who, why, where, when,* and *how* of the matter. For persuasive passages, summarize in a sentence the author's conclusion. For descriptive passages, indicate the subject of the description and its key feature(s). Note: In some cases, *a suitable thesis statement may already be in the original passage.* If so, you may want to quote it directly in your summary.
- *Write the first draft of your summary* by (1) combining the thesis with your list of one-sentence summaries or (2) combining the thesis with one-sentence summaries *plus* significant details from the passage. In either case, eliminate repetition and less important information. Disregard minor details or generalize them (e.g., Bill Clinton and George W. Bush might be generalized as "recent presidents"). Use as few words as possible to convey the main ideas.
- *Check your summary against the original passage* and make whatever adjustments are necessary for accuracy and completeness.
- *Revise your summary,* inserting transitional words and phrases where necessary to ensure coherence. Check for style. *Avoid a series of short, choppy sentences.* Combine sentences for a smooth, logical flow of ideas. Check for grammatical correctness, punctuation, and spelling.

Synthesis

WHAT IS A SYNTHESIS?

A *synthesis* is a written discussion that draws on two or more sources. It follows that your ability to write syntheses depends on your ability to infer relationships among sources—essays, articles, fiction, and also nonwritten sources such as lectures, interviews, visual media, and observations. This process is nothing new for you because you infer relationships all the time—say, between something you've read in the newspaper and something you've seen for yourself, or between the teaching styles of your favorite and least favorite instructors. In fact, if you've written research papers, you've already written syntheses. In a *synthesis,* you make explicit the relationships that you have inferred among separate sources.

The skills you've already learned and practiced in the previous chapters will be vital in writing syntheses. Before you're in a position to draw relationships between two or more sources, you must understand what those sources say; you must be able to *summarize* those sources. Readers will frequently benefit from at least partial summaries of sources in your synthesis essays. At the same time, you must go beyond summary to make judgments—judgments based on your *critical reading* of your sources: what conclusions you've drawn about the quality and validity of these sources, whether you agree or disagree with the points made in your sources, and why you agree or disagree.

In a synthesis, you go beyond the critique of individual sources to determine the relationships among them. Is the information in source B, for example, an extended illustration of the generalizations in source A? Would it be useful to compare and contrast source C with source B? Having read and considered sources A, B, and C, can you infer something else—in other words, D (not a source but your own idea)?

Because a synthesis is based on two or more sources, you will need to be selective when choosing information from each. It would be neither possible nor desirable, for instance, to discuss in a ten-page paper on the American Civil War every point that the authors of two books make about their subject. What you as a writer must do is select from each source the ideas and information that best allow you to achieve your purpose.

PURPOSE

Your purpose in reading source materials and then drawing on them to write your own material is often reflected in the wording of an assignment. For instance, consider the following assignments on the Civil War:

> *American History:* Evaluate the author's treatment of the origins of the Civil War.

> *Economics:* Argue the following proposition, in light of your readings: "The Civil War was fought not for reasons of moral principle but for reasons of economic necessity."

WHERE DO WE FIND WRITTEN SYNTHESES?

Here are just a few of the types of writing that involve synthesis:

Academic Writing

- **Analysis papers** synthesize and apply several related theoretical approaches.
- **Research papers** synthesize multiple sources.
- **Argument papers** synthesize different points into a coherent claim or position.
- **Essay exams** demonstrate understanding of course material through comparing and contrasting theories, viewpoints, or approaches in a particular field.

Workplace Writing

- **Newspaper and magazine articles** synthesize primary and secondary sources.
- **Position papers and policy briefs** compare and contrast solutions for solving problems.
- **Business plans** synthesize ideas and proposals into one coherent plan.
- **Memos and letters** synthesize multiple ideas, events, and proposals into concise form.
- **Web sites** synthesize information from various sources to present it in Web pages and related links.

Government: Prepare a report on the effects of the Civil War on Southern politics at the state level between 1870 and 1917.

Mass Communications: Discuss how the use of photography during the Civil War may have affected the perceptions of the war by Northerners living in industrial cities.

Literature: Select two Southern writers of the twentieth century whose work you believe was influenced by the divisive effects of the Civil War. Discuss the ways this influence is apparent in a novel or a group of short stories written by each author. The works should not be *about* the Civil War.

Applied Technology: Compare and contrast the technology of warfare available in the 1860s with the technology available a century earlier.

Each of these assignments creates a particular purpose for writing. Having located sources relevant to your topic, you would select for possible use in a paper only the parts of those sources that helped you in fulfilling this purpose. And how you used those parts—how you related them to other material from other sources—would also depend on your purpose. For instance, if you were working on the government assignment, you might draw on the same source as a student working on the literature assignment by referring to Robert Penn Warren's novel *All the King's Men*, about Louisiana politics in the early part of the twentieth century. But because the purposes of the two assignments are different, you and the other student would make different uses of this source. The parts or aspects of the novel that you find worthy of detailed analysis might be mentioned only in passing—or not at all—by the other student.

USING YOUR SOURCES

Your purpose determines not only what parts of your sources you will use but also how you will relate them to one another. Because the very essence of synthesis is the combining of information and ideas, you must have some basis on which to combine them. *Some relationships among the material in your sources must make them worth synthesizing.* It follows that the better able you are to discover such relationships, the better able you will be to use your sources in writing syntheses. Notice that the mass communications assignment requires you to draw a *cause-and-effect* relationship between photographs of the war and Northerners' perceptions of the war. The applied technology assignment requires you to *compare and contrast* state-of-the-art weapons technology in the eighteenth and nineteenth centuries. The economics assignment requires you to *argue* a proposition. In each case, *your purpose will determine how you relate your source materials to one another.*

Consider some other examples. You may be asked on an exam question or in the instructions for a paper to *describe* two or three approaches to prison reform during the past decade. You may be asked to *compare and contrast* one country's approach to imprisonment with another's. You may be asked to *develop an argument* of your own on this subject, based on your reading. Sometimes (when you are not given a specific assignment) you determine your own purpose: You are interested in exploring a particular subject; you are interested in making a case for one approach or another. In any event, your purpose shapes your essay. Your purpose determines which sources you research, which ones you use, which parts of them you use, at which points in your paper you use them, and in what manner you relate them to one another.

TYPES OF SYNTHESES: EXPLANATORY AND ARGUMENT

In this chapter, we categorize syntheses into two main types: *explanatory* and *argument*. The easiest way to recognize the difference between the two types may be to consider the difference between a news article and an editorial on the same subject. For the most part, we'd say that the main purpose of the news article is to convey *information*, and the main purpose of the editorial is to convey *opinion* or *interpretation*. Of course, this distinction is much too simplified: News articles often convey opinion or bias, sometimes subtly, sometimes openly, and editorials often convey unbiased information along with opinion. But as a practical matter we can generally agree on the distinction between a news article that primarily conveys information and an editorial that primarily conveys opinion. You should be able to observe this distinction in the selections shown here as explanation and argument.

Explanation: News Article from the New York Times

PRIVATE GETS 3 YEARS FOR IRAQ PRISON ABUSE

By David S. Cloud
September 28, 2005

Pfc. Lynndie R. England, a 22-year-old clerk in the Army who was photographed with naked Iraqi detainees at Abu Ghraib prison, was sentenced on Tuesday to three years in prison and a dishonorable discharge for her role in the scandal.

After the sentence was announced, Private England hung her head and cried briefly before hugging her mother, one of the few signs of emotion she showed in the six-day trial.

She had been found guilty on Monday of one count of conspiracy to maltreat prisoners, four counts of maltreatment and one count of committing an indecent act.

She made no comment on Tuesday as she was led out of the courthouse in handcuffs and leg shackles.

5   Earlier in the day, though, she took the stand and apologized for abusing the prisoners, saying her conduct was influenced by Specialist Charles A. Graner Jr., her boyfriend at the time.

She said she was "embarrassed" when photographs showing her posing next to naked detainees became public in 2004.

"I was used by Private Graner," she said. "I didn't realize it at the time."

Specialist Graner was reduced in rank after he was convicted in January as ringleader of the abuse.

Often groping for words and staring downward, Private England directed her apology to the detainees and to any American troops and their families who might have been injured or killed as a result of the insurgency in Iraq gaining strength.

10   Prosecutors argued on Tuesday that the anti-American feeling generated in Arab and Muslim countries by the Abu Ghraib scandal justified sentencing Private England to four to six years in prison and dishonorably discharging her from the Army. The charges the jury found her guilty of on Monday carried a maximum penalty of nine years....

Argument: Editorial from the Boston Globe

MILITARY ABUSE

September 28, 2005

The court-martial conviction Monday of reservist Lynndie England for her role in the abuse of Iraqi prisoners at Abu Ghraib should fool no one that the Pentagon is taking seriously the mistreatment of Iraqis, especially after the release last Friday of a report on torture by members of the 82d Airborne Division stationed near Fallujah....

If the [new] allegations are found credible, they further demolish the contention by officials that the abuse first reported at Abu Ghraib in 2004 was an isolated case of a few bad apples. Pentagon brass also tried to explain away the activities of England's unit as the actions of relatively untrained reservists. It is less easy to dismiss as a fluke such abuse when it occurs at the hands of the 82d Airborne, a thoroughly trained and highly decorated division.

The new charges, along with other accusations of abuse that have emerged since Abu Ghraib, including 28 suspicious detainee deaths, provide strong evidence that both reservist and active duty troops throughout Iraq were confused about their responsibility to treat detainees as prisoners of war under the terms of the Geneva Conventions....Congress should have long since created a special commission, as proposed in a bill by Senator Carl Levin of Michigan, to investigate the issue of prisoner abuse....

A truly independent inquiry, along the lines of the one done by the 9/11 commission, could trace accountability for prisoner abuse through statements and policies by ranking civilian and military officials in the Bush administration. Accountability for the shame of prisoner torture and abuse should not stop with Lynndie England and her cohort.

We'll say, for the sake of convenience, that the news article provides an *explanation* of England's sentence and that the editorial provides an *argument* for investigating responsibility *beyond* England.

As a further example of the distinction between explanation and argument, read the following paragraph:

> Researchers now use recombinant DNA technology to analyze genetic changes. With this technology, they cut and splice DNA from different species, then insert the modified molecules into bacteria or other types of cells that engage in rapid replication and cell division. The cells copy the foreign DNA right along with their own. In short order, huge populations produce useful quantities of recombinant DNA molecules. The new technology also is the basis of genetic engineering, by which genes are isolated, modified, and inserted back into the same organism or into a different one.*

Now read this paragraph:

> Many in the life sciences field would have us believe that the new gene splicing technologies are irrepressible and irreversible and that any attempt to oppose their introduction is both futile and retrogressive. They never stop to even consider the possibility that the new genetic science might be used in a wholly different manner than is currently being proposed. The fact is, the corporate agenda is only one of two potential paths into the Biotech Century. It is possible that the growing number of anti-eugenic activists around the world might be able to ignite a global debate around alternative uses of the new science— approaches that are less invasive, more sustainable and humane and that conserve and protect the genetic rights of future generations.†

Both of these passages deal with the topic of biotechnology, but the two take quite different approaches. The first passage comes from a biology textbook, while the second appears in a magazine article. As we might expect from a textbook on the broad subject of biology, the first passage is explanatory and informative; it defines and explains some of the key concepts of biotechnology without taking a position or providing commentary about

---

*Cecie Starr and Ralph Taggart, "Recombinant DNA and Genetic Engineering," *Biology: The Unity and Diversity of Life* (New York: Wadsworth, 1998).
†Jeremy Rifkin, "The Ultimate Therapy: Commercial Eugenics on the Eve of the Biotech Century," *Tikkun* May–June 1998: 35.

the implications of the technology. Magazine articles often present information in the same ways; however, many magazine articles take specific positions, as we see in the second passage. This passage is argumentative or persuasive: Its primary purpose is to convey a point of view regarding the topic of biotechnology.

While each of these excerpts presents a clear instance of writing that is either explanatory or argumentative, it is important to note that both the textbook chapter and the magazine article contain elements of both explanation and argument. The textbook writers, while they refrain from taking a particular position, do note the controversies surrounding biotechnology and genetic engineering. They might even subtly reveal a certain bias in favor of one side of the issue, through their word choice and tone, and perhaps through devoting more space and attention to one point of view. Explanatory and argumentative writing are not mutually exclusive. The overlap of explanation and argument is also found in the magazine article: In order to make his case against genetic engineering, the writer has to explain certain elements of the issue. Yet even while these categories overlap to a certain extent, the second passage clearly has argument as its primary purpose, and the first passage is primarily explanatory.

We noted that the primary purpose in a piece of writing may be informative, persuasive, or entertaining (or some combination of the three). Some scholars of writing argue that all writing is essentially persuasive, and even without entering into that complex argument, we've just seen how the varying purposes in writing do overlap. In order to persuade others of a particular position, we typically must inform them about it; conversely, a primarily informative piece of writing must also work to persuade the reader that its claims are truthful. Both informative and persuasive writing often include entertaining elements, and writing intended primarily to entertain also typically contains information and persuasion. For practical purposes, however, it is possible—and useful—to identify the *primary* purpose in a piece of writing as informative/explanatory, persuasive/argumentative, or entertaining. Entertainment as a primary purpose is the one least often practiced in purely academic writing—perhaps to your disappointment!—but information and persuasion are ubiquitous. So, while recognizing the overlap that will occur between these categories, we distinguish in this chapter between two types of synthesis writing: explanatory (or informative) and argument (or persuasive). Just as distinguishing the primary purpose in a piece of writing helps you to critically read and evaluate it, distinguishing the primary purpose in your own writing will help you to make the appropriate choices regarding your approach.

HOW TO WRITE SYNTHESES

Although writing syntheses can't be reduced to a lockstep method, it should help you to follow the guidelines listed in the box below.

GUIDELINES FOR WRITING SYNTHESES

- *Consider your purpose in writing.* What are you trying to accomplish in your paper? How will this purpose shape the way you approach your sources?
- *Select and carefully read your sources,* according to your purpose. Then reread the passages, mentally summarizing each. Identify those aspects or parts of your sources that will help you fulfill your purpose. When rereading, *label* or *underline* the sources for main ideas, key terms, and any details you want to use in the synthesis.
- *Take notes on your reading.* In addition to labeling or underlining key points in the readings, you might write brief one- or two-sentence summaries of each source. This will help you in formulating your thesis statement and in choosing and organizing your sources later.
- *Formulate a thesis.* Your thesis is the main idea that you want to present in your synthesis. It should be expressed as a complete sentence. You might do some predrafting about the ideas discussed in the readings in order to help you work out a thesis. If you've written one-sentence summaries of the readings, looking them over will help you to brainstorm connections between readings and to devise a thesis.

   When you write your synthesis drafts, you will need to consider where your thesis fits in your paper. Sometimes the thesis is the first sentence, but more often it is *the final sentence of the first paragraph.* If you are writing an *inductively arranged* synthesis, the thesis sentence may not appear until the final paragraphs.
- *Decide how you will use your source material.* How will the information and the ideas in the passages help you fulfill your purpose?
- *Develop an organizational plan,* according to your thesis. How will you arrange your material? It is not necessary to prepare a formal outline. But you should have some plan that will indicate the order in which you will present your material and that will indicate the relationships among your sources.
- *Draft the topic sentences for the main sections.* This is an optional step, but you may find it a helpful transition from organizational plan to first draft.
- *Write the first draft* of your synthesis, following your organizational plan. Be flexible with your plan, however. Frequently, you will use an outline to get started. As you write, you may discover new ideas and make room for them by adjusting the outline. When this happens, reread your work frequently, making sure that your thesis still accounts for what follows and that what follows still logically supports your thesis.

(continued)

- *Document your sources.* You must do this by crediting sources within the body of the synthesis—citing the author's last name and the page number from which the point was taken—and then providing full citation information in a list of "Works Cited" at the end. Don't open yourself to charges of plagiarism!
- *Revise your synthesis,* inserting transitional words and phrases where necessary. Make sure that the synthesis reads smoothly, logically, and clearly from beginning to end. Check for grammatical correctness, punctuation, and spelling.

Note: The writing of syntheses is a recursive process, and you should accept a certain amount of backtracking and reformulating as inevitable. For instance, in developing an organizational plan (step 6 of the procedure), you may discover a gap in your presentation that will send you scrambling for another source—back to step 2. You may find that formulating a thesis and making inferences among sources occur simultaneously; indeed, inferences are often made before a thesis is formulated. Our recommendations for writing syntheses will give you a structure that will get you started. But be flexible in your approach; expect discontinuity and, if possible, be assured that through backtracking and reformulating you will produce a coherent, well-crafted paper.

Commonly used editing and proofreading symbols are listed here, along with references to the relevant chapters and sections of this handbook.

Words, Sentences, and Paragraphs

abbr	Abbreviation problem: 35c	*num*	Number problem: 35e
adj	Adjective problem: 27a-b	*p*	Punctuation problem: 29-34
adv	Adverb problem: 27a, 27c	*pass*	Passive voice misused: 18a
agr	Agreement problem, either subject-verb or pronoun-antecedent: 23, 25b	*pl*	Plural form misused or needed: 28a
apos	Apostrophe missing or misused: 32	*pron*	Pronoun problem: 25
		ref	Reference of a pronoun unclear: 25d
art	Article is missing or misused: 28b	*run-on*	Run-on sentence problem: 22b
		sexist	Sexist language: 21e
cap	Capitalization is needed: 35a	*sp*	Spelling needs to be checked: 6d
case	Case of a pronoun is incorrect: 25a	*sub*	Subordination is faulty: 20a
coh	Coherence lacking in a paragraph: 5a	*trans*	Transition misused or needed: 6c
cs	Comma splice occurs: 22c	*vb*	Verb problem: 24
dm	Dangling modifier appears: 27e	*w*	Wordy: 19
		ww	Wrong word: 21
frag	Fragment instead of complete sentence: 22a	¶	Paragraph break needed: 5
		no ¶	No paragraph break needed: 5
ital	Italics missing or misused: 35b	//	Parallelism needs to be checked: 20c
lc	Lower case needed: 35a		
mm	Misplaced modifier: 27b-c		

Punctuation and Mechanics

⌄	Comma needed: 29	( )	Parentheses needed: 31
⌄	Apostrophe needed: 32	[ ]	Brackets needed: 34d
⌄ ⌄	Quotation marks needed: 33	#	Add a space
⊙	Period needed: 34a	⌒	Close up a space
?	Question mark needed: 34b	⌒	Delete this
!	Exclamation point needed: 34c	∧	Insert something
—	Dash needed: 31	∼	Transpose (switch the order)
. . .	Ellipses needed: 34e		

·Contents

PART 1
Composing

PART 2
Analyzing, Reflecting,
Informing, Arguing

PART 3
Planning Research and
Finding Sources